Remember the Feeling

A History of the Southeast Unitarian Universalist Summer Institute

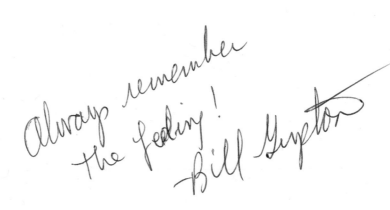

always remember
the feeling!
Bill Gupton

Remember the Feeling

A History of the Southeast
Unitarian Universalist
Summer Institute

by Bill Gupton

ISBN 978-1-57074-076-3

Printed in the United States of America

Printed by:
Greyden Press, LLC
2251 Arbor Blvd.
Dayton, Ohio 45439
www.greydenpress.com

Table of Contents

Foreword

You hold in your hands a labor of love.

Like many who can still recall, in vivid detail, their very first day at SUUSI, I remember well that beautiful summer Sunday afternoon when I first experienced the Southeast Unitarian Universalist Summer Institute. It was July 25, 1982, and I had come to Radford to spend a week with my niece and nephew, Jen and Win Lucas. My intention was to get away from it all for a much-needed summer vacation in the mountains. What I got instead was a changed life. What I found was a lifelong community.

Twenty-nine SUUSIs later, inspired by Director Jerry King's 2010 theme, "Beyond Tomorrow," I made a public commitment to that community that I would write a history of the Southeast Unitarian Universalist Summer Institute. Once again, I got more than I bargained for.

I had in mind a small history that would recount the highlights and signature events of an institution that had survived for six decades and had touched the lives of tens of thousands of people. Silly me. No small volume could possibly capture the heart and soul – the *feeling* – that is SUUSI. It is my hope that this somewhat larger volume might at least begin to do justice to a rare and beautiful example of true human community – one that is, when all is said and done, beyond words.

Through nearly three years of interviews, research, phone calls and emails – as I flipped through files of yellowed old papers or read brightly pixilated Facebook posts – there have been many times when I've simply had to stop and have a good cry. You can gauge how much something means to you by how easily it can bring you to tears. SUUSI has that effect on me with regularity. That is the *real* reason I have written this book.

I can now say that I have attended half the SUUSIs that have ever taken place. As I complete this particular labor of love, I find myself wondering where all those years have gone. It seems like only yesterday that my son, now about to bridge out of the Teen Dorm, was a little boy at SUUSI, carrying his baseball bat and watching a balloon slip out of his fingers and soar skyward.

Such is SUUSI. Beautiful and colorful, but fleeting.

It has been a great gift first to gather and then to pour through more than six decades of SUUSI records and memorabilia. You never know what gems you will find, hidden in the minutes of a meeting or the pages of a newsletter. One of the most insightful comments I've ever heard about SUUSI was tucked away in an article (sadly unattributed, because I'd love to give the author credit) in a 1998 copy of the SUUSI NUUS: "One of the greatest things about SUUSI is that everyone says 'Hello.' We don't avert our eyes as we pass, or ignore each other." This person's simple observation, I realized, is not only *true*, but it summarizes the very essence of the SUUSI experience, and of what can make the SUUSI week so different from the other 51 weeks of our year. To be so reverently, deeply engaged, with others and with life is, to me, the true meaning of SUUSI.

I am profoundly aware that this book is the fruition of the dreams of many of my predecessors. The first SUUSI mugbook, in 1980, included a one-page history of the Summer Institute. In 1988 Al Swanson – father of future SUUSI Director Reid Swanson – led a workshop on the history of SUUSI, hoping to "compile the reminiscences into a published collection." At the Ingathering Ceremony in 2000, a brief history of SUUSI was distributed in the printed program. In 2004 (when the SUUSI theme was "Reunions") Roger Comstock, Kathee Williams, Nancy Heath, Alexis Jones and Bob Irwin – some of whom had not been together at a SUUSI in many years – shared a narrative history with the community. Roger concluded that presentation by saying, "Memories are sketchy. Lots of folks can tell lots of stories, but few of us know the whole history. There are many other stories that need to be told... Maybe someone will be inspired to try to pull all of it together in a written history."

Roger, it has taken quite a while – but here is that history.

Finally, a word about the title of this book. Trudy Atkin (now Trudy Moneyhan), SUUSI's Youth Director for most of the 1980s, was responsible for bringing me into the circle of leadership at SUUSI (and thus, at least in part, for setting me on a path that eventually led to the Unitarian Universalist ministry). At the end of every SUUSI week, and throughout the year as she signed the many cards and letters she would write us, Trudy would say simply, "Remember the Feeling!" It is something I have always sought to do.

May this book help *you* remember the feeling.

Bill Gupton
April 25, 2013

Acknowledgements

Since the very inception of this project, I have been blessed with an abundance of assistance, guidance and support from both individuals and institutions. Let me begin by expressing my love and gratitude to my family, Jennifer and Patrick Sanders, for their encouragement and patience throughout this process. As plastic bins of SUUSI records gradually took over our basement, and as I spent more and more hours in front of my computer, they remained steadfast in their support of me, and of what I was doing. So, too, my congregation – Heritage Universalist Unitarian Church in Cincinnati, Ohio – which has graciously granted me periods of study leave to help complete the project.

I want to thank my editor, Lindsay Bennett-Jacobs, who read my manuscript with a sharp eye and a gentle touch, teaching this old dog of a former journalist some new tricks along the way, while finding enough errant commas to fill a filing cabinet. She was ably assisted by proofreaders Jennifer Sanders and Jen Lucas. The finished product owes more to them than you can ever imagine.

Many thanks as well go to: The SUUSI Board of Trustees, who provided both funding and moral support; Fran O'Donnell, Curator of Manuscripts and Archives at the Andover-Harvard Theological Library of the Harvard Divinity School in Cambridge, Mass.; Ginger Littrell of the Lake Waccamaw Depot Museum in Lake Waccamaw, N.C.; Robb Cross, Columbus County historian, Lake Waccamaw, N.C.; Nancy DuPuy Beaver of Black Mountain, N.C.; Erin Ratliff and Joshua Domin at the YMCA Blue Ridge Assembly in Black Mountain, N.C.; Ann Wilkinson at the Brevard Music Center in Brevard, N.C.; Annie Armour at The University of the South in Sewanee, Tenn.; Michael McGlone,

Rachel Walden and Joshua Craft at the Unitarian Universalist Association in Boston, Mass.; Kay Montgomery, Executive Vice President of the Unitarian Universalist Association in Boston, Mass.; Tom Kersen, historian and Assistant Professor of Sociology at Jackson State University in Jackson, Miss.; David Braughler and Samantha Goyings at Greyden Press in Dayton, Ohio; Zivan Mendez at Cord Camera in Cincinnati, Ohio; SUUSI photographers Rick Hallmark, Doug Throp and Uncle Flip; Alexis Jones; Dana Taylor; Trudy Atkin; and SUUSI Teens of every era – you are always our future, and our brightest light.

This book is dedicated to founders Alfred Hobart and Richard Henry, to the memory of Wink Lucas, and – most of all – to Jennifer and Patrick.

Chapter 1:
In the Beginning

O n the afternoon of Wednesday, August 30, 1950, about
two dozen Unitarians arrived at a remote state park near
the North Carolina coast to begin an experiment in church
growth and leadership that would one day blossom into a
week-long, intentional community numbering more than a
thousand participants annually: SUUSI, the Southeast Unitarian
Universalist Summer Institute.

In the months leading up to that auspicious day at Lake
Waccamaw, N.C., two visionary Unitarians – ministers Alfred
Hobart and Richard Henry – had been in regular contact,
carefully planning a five-day leadership training retreat and
working vacation for the handful of Unitarian clergy, lay leaders
and their families who were just beginning to plant the seeds of
liberal religion in the Jim Crow South. Hobart was the brand-
new minister of the historic Unitarian Church in Charleston,
S.C. Henry, who was Hobart's junior by a generation, was serving
as the first minister of the recently formed Tennessee Valley
Unitarian Church in Knoxville.

Prior to arriving in Charleston that summer, Hobart had been
the minister of the First Unitarian Church in New Orleans, a
member congregation of the *Southwest* Unitarian Conference.
Each year since 1940, churches in the Southwest had held a
"Summer Institute" at Lake Murray State Park near Ardmore,
Oklahoma. In the late 1940's, Hobart had attended that Institute,
and he sought to replicate the Southwest experience in his new
locale. Hobart found an eager ally in the young Henry, who now

Alfred Hobart

Richard Henry

says "I felt as strongly as Al that there really *ought* to be such a thing in our own region. The original motivation we had was to create a regular, ongoing summer session for Unitarians in the South."

The two ministers communicated throughout the spring and summer of 1950. They ultimately chose to reserve accommodations for their experiment at Lake Waccamaw State Park, located along the southern edge of an unusually large, naturally occurring freshwater lake in eastern North Carolina. Among other claims to fame, Lake Waccamaw boasted being home to several marine species found nowhere else on earth. Conveniently located on a major north-south train line, and an hour's drive inland from Wilmington and the Atlantic Ocean, Waccamaw was a popular tourist destination in the first half of the 20th century, offering outdoor pursuits such as camping, fishing and hiking.

Early that summer, Hobart and Henry crafted an announcement that went out to each of the ten Unitarian congregations that then existed in Virginia, the Carolinas and Tennessee:

The Southern Unitarian Institute will convene at Lake Waccamaw, North Carolina, with headquarters at the Goldston Hotel, on August 30 at 4:00 P.M. At the hotel there will be a desk for the Institute, and there all necessary information can be secured. Mrs. Faye Efird will have charge of room assignments for delegates.

At 5:00 P.M., all delegates will gather at an announced place, and introduction of leaders and delegations will take place. Announcements concerning the program and activities will be made.

Dinner will be at 6:30 P.M. At 7:45 P.M., there will be a religious service. At 8:30 P.M., the first session of the course given under the direction of the Rev. Dale DeWitt on "The Organization and Principles of the Unitarian Movement" will be held.

Thus, on an otherwise ordinary late-summer afternoon in 1950, delegates from nine of the ten regional Unitarian congregations found their way to the Goldston Hotel, hopeful perhaps of learning something about the "Unitarian Movement," or of building congregational connections and making new friendships. They were surely unaware of the scope of what they were about to create – or of the thousands of people it would eventually reach. Over the course of the next several decades, this nascent Summer Institute would evolve into SUUSI, growing to become the second largest gathering of UUs in the world, and representing – for countless open-hearted, free-spirited souls from the Southeast and beyond – nothing less than a sacred annual pilgrimage.

The Goldston Hotel, site of the first Southern Unitarian Institute in 1950

Lake Waccamaw (1950)

The registration list for the 1950 Southern Unitarian Institute included 28 full-time delegates, 16 weekend-only delegates, and three denominational staff members sent by the American Unitarian Association. Represented were churches in Charlottesville, Norfolk, Lynchburg and Arlington in Virginia; Charlotte and Monroe in North Carolina; Charleston in South Carolina; and Knoxville and Oak Ridge in Tennessee. There were half a dozen ministers among those in attendance –

Hobart and Henry, of course, along with Paul Bliss from Oak Ridge, John Morgan from Charlotte, Malcolm Sutherland from Charlottesville, and Dale DeWitt, who at the time was serving as the Regional Director of the Middle Atlantic States Council of the AUA (there was not yet a denominational organization in the South). At least three of these men led "religious services" during the week. In his sermon titled "Where Thy Treasure Is," Hobart concluded the inaugural Southern Institute by preaching, "Let us be numbered among those who believe and work [so] that there shall be a better chance for manhood and womanhood – a grander openness, fearlessness and serenity, a fuller personal initiative – that there may be more love and laughter and fine spontaneous humanity."

As not only the group's elder statesman, but also its most local clergy delegate (Charleston being a mere 150 miles from Lake Waccamaw), Hobart was seen as the unofficial host that hot, dry summer. Unlike his other colleagues, Hobart also brought his family – wife Mary Aymar Hobart, son Jimmie and daughter Barbara. Jimmie, now the Rev. James Hobart, recalls, "Even then [at age 15], I knew this was something more than just a family vacation. I had the sense that it was a very important gathering."

It was important enough for the two Tennessee groups to drive more than 400 miles, over treacherous mountain roads in an era before interstate highways, to participate. It was important enough for the AUA to provide leading denominational speakers and educators to facilitate workshops. It was important enough for the All Souls Chapel in Monroe, N.C., to send the largest delegation (a dozen participants, fully one fourth of all the attendees, including most of the Institute's lay leadership). The very first "Chairman," Ray Shute, was from the Monroe fellowship (he also happened to be the *mayor* of the town of Monroe). The first registrar, Faye Efird, and the first children's program director, Lucee Helms, were also from the Monroe group.

While the Lake Waccamaw gathering had all the trappings of a typical mid-century church leadership training retreat – worship services, meetings, and workshops with titles like "What Makes a Good Church School" and "The Making of a Unitarian Church" – it also included many aspects of the kind of community that to this day remain indispensible parts of the SUUSI experience: music and dancing, children's activities, late-night conversations, theme talks and nature outings.

In fact, what could be considered the very first "nature trip" grew out of a serendipitous occurrence early that first year at Lake Waccamaw. Frances Wood, who worked in the AUA's Division of Education, had been brought down from Boston to train those participants who would become Sunday School teachers and Religious Education Directors in the upcoming church year. As the group of educators gathered around Wood that first full day of programming, a loud rumbling noise arose from a nearby pier, startling both Wood and her audience. Soon a pontoon plane was flying overhead, its engines roaring so loudly that the training session was quickly abandoned while excited adults and curious children raced from the workshop and the hotel to watch the low-flying plane. It seems the pilot, one Cotton Cutrell, had been seeking to get the group's attention and offer his services for hire.

By the next day, Institute participants were lining up to take plane rides over the lake. As the Institute went on, other spontaneous outdoor activities arose. There was the opportunity to enjoy swimming off a massive 600-foot pier, or enjoy some evening dancing at The Pavilion dance hall, or have fun at Weaver's nightspot, or simply take relaxing walks along the lovely boardwalk. That weekend, some parents even loaded all the children into a couple of cars and drove them to Wrightsville Beach for the day – marking the only time in SUUSI history that a nature outing culminated with a swim in the ocean.

Meals that week were likely taken either at Weaver's, at the Lakeview Inn, or at the quaint Jones Tourist Grille, which was the headquarters for Cotton Cutrell's seaplane adventures.

By Monday (which was Labor Day) the Southern Unitarian Institute was deemed "a glorious success" by the contingent from

The Jones Tourist Hotel and Grill at Lake Waccamaw. In the center, to the right of the pier on the lake, Cotton Cutrell's seaplane is visible.

Monroe, and as the participants said their goodbyes following lunch that day, plans were already being laid for an encore the following summer. There was only one caveat: Everyone agreed that a more central location – and a cooler climate – were imperative for the next Institute.

Planting Institutional Roots (Blue Ridge 1951)

During a meeting held at the Monroe Fellowship the weekend of April 27-28, 1951, arrangements were finalized to gather the second annual Southern Unitarian Institute at the YMCA Blue Ridge Assembly just outside Black Mountain, N.C. "The location was simply ideal," recalls Richard Henry. "It was a matter of propinquity for the congregations in the region, and we were delighted to find that Blue Ridge was open-minded enough to take us in." Blue Ridge Assembly included comfortable housing, a family-style dining hall, and a meeting space – College Hall – that housed not only a large auditorium for worship, general assembly and speakers, but also more than a dozen smaller meeting rooms.

Both Henry and Hobart now saw the Institute as an ideal vehicle to harness and build on the momentum of the rapidly growing Unitarian movement in the Southeast, and they believed Blue Ridge was the perfect place to make it happen. The number of congregations represented at the 1951 springtime planning meeting in Monroe was already double that which had attended the first Summer Institute at Lake Waccamaw. Participants expressed a strong desire to create an ongoing organization that would link the churches of the South and promote their outreach. Hobart contacted Boston, proposed a new "Southern Region" of the American Unitarian Association, and indicated that an organizational meeting would take place at the 1951 Summer Institute.

The following announcement, the result of the Monroe meeting, was then sent to congregations throughout the South:

> Let's talk about the 1951 Southern Unitarian Institute! The date: August 23-27, beginning at noon with lunch, and ending with breakfast on the 27th. To save you consulting your calendars, the time is from Thursday to Monday.
>
> The place: Blue Ridge Assembly, Blue Ridge, N.C. Blue Ridge is located 15 miles east of Asheville, N.C., on US Route 70, and three miles from Black Mountain (which is the railway, bus, express and telegraph address). The Southern Railroad and the Queen City Trailway offer easy access.
>
> Registration is $2.50 for adults, $1.50 for children 12 years and under. Room rates are $19.44 for the conference period, per person, for room without a bath; $24.44 for room with bath.

Daily rates for those attending less than full time:
$5.11 for room without bath; $6.41 for room with
bath, meals included. Children 10 years and under
are one-half these rates.

The Blue Ridge Assembly is magnificently
equipped. There are facilities for practically all
forms of sport and recreation, including a fully
equipped playground for children.

Please promote the Institute in your group. We
want at least 100 people present. There will be an
excellent program. The surroundings are ideal.

And indeed they were. As those who had answered the call
walked up the steps of stately Robert E. Lee Hall and gathered
in its reception area on August 23, there was a sense of history in
the making. Some people were renewing old friendships, created
the previous summer at Lake Waccamaw. Many were curious to
see how other Unitarians in the South were "doing church" in
their congregations, while others were looking for nothing more
than a few leisurely days away from the heat and monotony of late
summer. There were more children and youth in attendance than
the year before, and considerably more religious educators, church
board members and the like. In the end, folks came from places as
far flung as Lafayette, La. and Louisville, Ky.

The emphasis that year was squarely on denominational
business. After three days of debates and discussion, workshops and
worship, on the last full day of the Institute – Sunday afternoon –
congregational delegates voted unanimously to secede, as it were,
from the Middle Atlantic States Unitarian Council, and to create
their own denominational entity. Bylaws for the new Thomas
Jefferson Conference of Unitarians were adopted, and Henry was
elected Chair of the new Board of Trustees. Hobart was named
Executive Secretary and Regional Director. Other officers elected
to that first Board were Walter Adams of Asheville (who at the
time was the editor of the Asheville *Citizen-Times* newspaper) as

vice-president; Mrs. Paul Bliss, wife of the minister in Oak Ridge, as secretary; and Ralph Conner of Charlotte, as treasurer.

It was determined that all Southern states east of the Mississippi would be included in the new region. The Baltimore church, along with All Souls Church in Washington, D.C., were admitted as "associate member congregations" of the T.J. Conference. A notice was forwarded to the national headquarters of the American Unitarian Association, along with a request for funding and extension support. The events were recorded in an article printed in the November 1951 edition of the *Christian Register*, the newspaper that was the Unitarian precursor of the *UU World* magazine.

The 1951 Institute offered its 110 participants more than simply institutional business, of course. Memories were created that helped begin to form the lore of the Institute. Among the speakers that first year at Blue Ridge was the renowned Unitarian religious educator Sophia Lyon Fahs. Paul Hennigar, Youth Director for the AUA, also attended, helping to organize a program for the teenagers. Harlow Shapley, head of the Astronomy Department at Harvard University, served as a "resource leader" and conducted well-attended workshops.

Richard Henry relates the following story about the energetic Shapley's presence at the Institute:

> He was a big-name draw. Somehow we had persuaded him to come – we gave him an honorarium, of course – and he took folks out under the stars at night, with a telescope. We were far away from any city lights. I remember him pointing at a place where we couldn't see anything, and calling it a "black hole" in space.
>
> He told us we were receiving a kind of radio signal from outer space, all the time. "Wouldn't it be fascinating if another civilization was out there?" he asked. He really made people think.

Then – and I'll never forget it – the next morning I came across him, down on the ground, on his hands and knees. He was intensely studying an ant hill! He was absolutely fascinated by it. He called eagerly out to me, and invited me to get down on the ground and join him. "Just look at this *institution* these little guys have built!" he exclaimed.

Harlow Shapley's ant hill was a perfect metaphor for the institution that Henry and Hobart were building. Participants from 1951 recall a palpable sense of synergy – the feeling that people were engaged in building something important.

The Institute closed that year with what would become its first official tradition: the group portrait. Young and old alike donned their best outfits to pose for a formal picture on the steps of Lee

The 1951 group portrait, the oldest known photograph of Summer Institute participants. In the very center, second row, is Richard Henry. To the left of Henry is Alfred Hobart.

Hall, looking out over the Blue Ridge Mountains. Ed DuPuy, a local professional photographer, had been enlisted to chronicle the group and record for posterity the smiling faces of those who had attended. Thereafter, the annual group portrait was a significant part of each Institute at Blue Ridge, providing an important memento for those in attendance. James Hobart and Gordon Gibson, both of whom were teenagers at the time, still own their treasured copies of those glossy, black-and-white group portraits from Blue Ridge in the 1950s. Many of the young people in them, including Hobart, Gibson and Dick Weston, went on to become Unitarian Universalist ministers, or otherwise to serve in denominational leadership.

Aided by the Southern Institute, Unitarianism in the South was about to take off.

Chapter 2:
Nothin' Could Be Finer

Blue Ridge, with its idyllic mountain location, brilliant nighttime sky, cool evening breezes and a vista that stretched as far as the eye could see, was a tailor-made setting that quickly became the "home of the heart" for those who were committed to the project of growing a liberal religion in the South.

The entrance to Blue Ridge Assembly

"Once that first week at Blue Ridge happened," Henry says, "we knew we had found a home. And we knew this Institute would be the center of [our] Unitarian life." Indeed, over the course of the next decade and a half, "Blue Ridge" was synonymous with Unitarianism in the South – and with summer fun and spirituality, recreation and renewal. Unitarians from all over the region uttered the words "Blue Ridge" with a wistful reverence. Those who were there (and there are still a few around who were) remember the feeling with passion.

The Early Fifties

One Blue Ridge tradition that began early on was the morning wakeup ritual. Participants remember peacefully sleeping after a full day (and evening) of activities shared with friends both new and old, the window over their bed open to the fresh mountain air – when suddenly, shortly after sunrise over loudspeakers strategically placed to reach every corner of the campus, came the blaring bugle call of "reveille." As they stretched and yawned, a scratchy recording of Mitch Miller singing "Carolina in the Morning" would resound through the same loudspeakers:

> Nothin' could be finer than to be in Carolina in the
> morning.
> No one could be sweeter than my sweetie when I
> meet her in the morning.
> Where the morning glories, twine around the door,
> Whispering pretty stories, I long to hear once more.
> Strolling with my girlie where the dew is pearly early
> in the morning,
> Butterflies all flutter up and kiss each little buttercup
> at dawning.
> If I had Aladdin's lamp for only a day,
> I'd make a wish and here's what I'd say:
> Nothing could be finer than to be in Carolina in the
> morning.   *(lyrics in public domain)*

Summer Institute participants from the 1950s recall with fondness this morning ritual, and the way folks would cheerfully sing or whistle the tune throughout the day or – whenever they needed to remember the feeling of the good times at Blue Ridge – throughout the rest of the year.

Morning wakeup was followed by breakfast in the dining hall. Guests at Blue Ridge were served each meal family style, on large platters at heavy wooden tables, by a wait staff comprised of summer employees, most of them young people from the surrounding towns. Southern-style grits were on the breakfast menu each and every morning, a particular surprise (and in some cases, delight) to visiting Unitarians from the Boston area.

Though the cost of meals was included in the room-and-board fee charged to each participant, it was expected that a generous tip should be left on the table for the servers. Apparently, this was a source of some ongoing concern for the leaders of the new Institute, as there were repeated admonitions in the newsletters of the day to "remember to leave an appropriate gratuity" after each meal.

The morning serenade and family-style Southern cooking, something new for the many Unitarians who were transplants from the North, were just two aspects of life at Blue Ridge that endeared the place to SUUSI's ancestors. Relaxing in large rocking chairs on the veranda of the antebellum style Lee Hall was a popular pursuit. With the vast panorama of mountains in the distance, cool evenings were spent rocking, chatting with friends and drinking iced tea, or listening to "Sunset Talks" on the steps, given by speakers from the denomination and the wider world. (Though no records exist to prove the claim, it has been said that a young Jesse Jackson once spoke to the Unitarians at Blue Ridge).

Those who were children at Blue Ridge fondly remember the annual tradition of damming up a nearby stream in order to create a more user-friendly swimming hole and play area. There was also the annual "race up the mountain" – on foot – to the peak of High Top Mountain. This became a nearly day-long event for the teenagers, with only two rules: "You must be accompanied by an [athletically inclined, we presume] adult chaperone, and you must

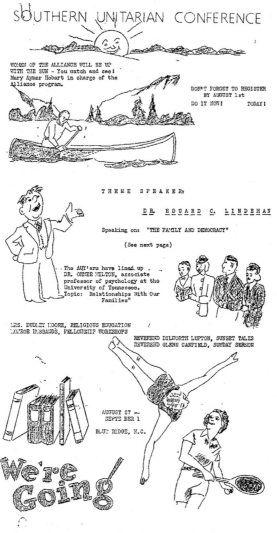

Flyer announcing the 1952 Institute

return in time for a hearty dinner!"

Of course, the delegates also had the seemingly ubiquitous denominational business to attend to. Thanks to the AUA's Fellowship Movement – an intentional effort to start new, lay-led Unitarian congregations in strategically located cities and towns where no liberal religious presence previously existed – the post-War period proved to be a booming time for Unitarian churches, especially in the South. At the 1952 Institute the national leader of the Unitarian Fellowship Movement, Monroe Husbands, offered workshops "on ways and means of increasing fellowship membership and improving programs."

Buoyed by a startling growth in the number of churches in the Thomas Jefferson Conference, attendance at the Institute continued to increase each year. By the mid 1950s, more than 200 people were coming, and by the end of the decade there were nearly 600 people making the annual pilgrimage to Blue Ridge.

"This attendance [is] significant as a reflection of the growth of the Unitarian movement in the South, where churches of the future are now being started," wrote Jeannette Hopkins in the *Christian Register*. Indeed, many of the churches from which SUUSI now draws a significant portion of its participants were formed – and began their tradition of Summer Institute attendance – during those early years. Congregations in Jacksonville (organized in 1950), Clearwater (1951), Gainesville and Sarasota (1952) in Florida; Roanoke (1954), Fairfax (1955), Blacksburg and Fredericksburg (1956) in Virginia; Asheville (1950) and Greensboro (1951) in North Carolina; Columbia and Greenville (1950) as well as Spartanburg (1954) in South Carolina; Nashville (1950) and Chattanooga (1951) in Tennessee; Athens and Atlanta (1954) in Georgia; and Birmingham in Alabama (organized in 1952 with Alfred Hobart as its first minister) – all were formed within five years of the initial Lake Waccamaw gathering. Unitarianism was spreading across the South like kudzu, and the Southern Unitarian Institute was one of the main reasons.

It is no wonder, then, that early Institutes emphasized what was at the time known as "churchmanship" – the development of effective church leaders and congregational systems. The stated purpose of the 1952 Institute, which opened on Aug. 27 and concluded on Labor Day, was

To provide leadership training for youth, religious education workers, and church and fellowship group members to bring together Unitarians of the South so that they may become better acquainted; to encourage the exchange of ideas for the mutual enrichment of individual and congregational life; to encourage and practice serious thought and study about religious problems; and to provide meaningful experience of worship in fellowship with people from our own and other congregations.

The featured speaker that year was George Mitchell of Atlanta, a member of the American Unitarian Association staff. Participants also heard from Dilworth Lupton, minister in Richmond, and Glenn Canfield, the AUA's Minister-at-Large for the South. At the time, Canfield was in the process of resurrecting a Unitarian congregation in Atlanta. Religious educator Tillie Moore from the UUA came to address the gathering as well.

Even then, what we might today think of as "quality control" was on the minds of those in charge of the Institute, as evidenced by a small article that appeared in the January 1953 issue of the *Register*, under the heading "Conference Standards Examined." According to the article, "Standards of programs and facilities of Unitarian conferences are being examined under the Denominational Planning Council. Equipment, location, health and welfare, relation of management to employees and guests – all these will come under the committee's eye." Though no further report from the committee was forthcoming, it is safe to assume that our fledgling Summer Institute, and the YMCA Blue Ridge Assembly, passed the test, given what developed into the Institute's longest uninterrupted tenure at any location – 16 consecutive summers meeting at Blue Ridge.

It was not long before folks from the new congregations in Florida went "all in" on the action. During the final week of August

1953, Eugene Pickett, who was then the Assistant Minister of the First Unitarian Church of Miami (he later became President of the Unitarian Universalist Association) made the arduous 775-mile pilgrimage from south Florida to Blue Ridge with several equally curious congregation members. Pickett was eager to see the summer conference he had heard so much about from colleagues. He found that "extension, excitement and enthusiasm characterized the mood" of the Institute, and – along with an ever-growing contingent from Miami – Pickett continued to return. In 1982, after several years away, he came back to SUUSI to serve as theme speaker and share memories of his first "SUI" experience, nearly three decades earlier.

Planners chose a very cerebral theme in 1953, seeking to balance participants' passion and enthusiasm with intellectual stimulation. According to the *Register*, Dr. Howard Odum, considered the "dean of Southern sociologists," was invited to be the theme speaker that August, on the topic "The Challenge of Morality in Any Age of Science."

By the following summer, it seems Unitarians nationwide had embraced wholeheartedly the idea of camps and conferences. The 1954 Unitarian Year Book lists a total of 19 different summer gatherings, many of them with words like "family," "youth" or "religious education" in their names. Nonetheless, perhaps reflecting our earliest roots as a training ground for church leaders, our own Institute was one of just two to include the word "leadership" in its name; the 1954 gathering was officially called the Southern Unitarian Leadership Institute.

In those days, the cost of leadership, for both lay and ordained leaders who chose to attend, could hardly have been more reasonable. Room and board, with bath, for the week of Aug. 24-29, 1954, was $30 ($15 for children). If one chose to share a bath, fees were $25 for adults and $12.50 for children. There were 144 total registrants.

Among them was the largest group of teenagers to date. Earlier that summer, the Unitarian and Universalist national youth organizations had merged (leading the way for the denominations themselves, which would soon follow), creating Liberal Religious Youth Inc., or LRY. The LRY culture was one of youth autonomy and independent leadership, so it is not surprising that the teenagers brought their own distinctive energy to the Summer Institute community. LRY'ers were housed in Asheville Hall, well away from the adults in Lee Hall. Boys and girls lived on separate floors, and the teenagers arranged for all of their own registration and programming, inviting adult chaperones (often religious education directors) and speakers and workshop leaders (often ministers) to live and work with them in Asheville Hall.

Each night the LRY gathered around a campfire, singing and reading poetry. They held youth worship under the stars. And apparently, they enjoyed giving one another backrubs; at one point in the week, probably right before or after a meal, they convened en masse in front of the fireplace in Lee Hall, underneath a large portrait of Jesus, and began massaging one another's shoulders and

The portrait of Jesus over the fireplace in Lee Hall

necks. The Blue Ridge staff quickly brought this "inappropriate behavior" to the attention of the Unitarian leaders, and Alfred Hobart had to be called in to negotiate a resolution with YMCA officials.

In addition to the presence of so many LRY'ers, and perhaps adding to the Blue Ridge staff's anxiety level, in 1954 the Institute shared the Blue Ridge campus with another group for the first time. The Southern Labor Conference of the Congress of Industrial Workers (which just a year later was to join forces with the American Federation of Labor to form the AFL-CIO), was meeting concurrently with the Unitarians. Gordon Gibson,

Arriving at Blue Ridge

an LRY'er from Louisville who was at Blue Ridge that year, remembers being awestruck at sharing meals and facilities with "real-life labor organizers," and reports that the LRY joyously "adopted some of their most militant union songs to add to our campfire repertoire."

From then on, both teenagers and social activism would be

important threads in the distinctive fabric that is now SUUSI.

Perhaps not coincidentally, the theme the next year was "Religion in Action." At the 1955 Summer Institute, groups from different churches were responsible for leading workshops on various aspects of social action. The Oak Ridge church offered "Community Health and Welfare," while the Atlanta congregation spoke on "Implementing Racial Integration." Those from Richmond tackled "Relations of the Church with Local Government," and Charlottesville focused on "Relations Between Churches and Schools."

Meanwhile, in the wake of the recent merger of the Unitarian and Universalist youth organizations, momentum was beginning to build among national leaders to combine the two denominations. A letter written by 1955 Chairman Thomas L. Carroll to frequent Summer Institute religious education consultant Frances Wood of Boston, dated Feb. 4, 1955, read in part:

> In the past we have had a few Universalists register for our conference, and we are extremely hopeful that in the future we will attract a good many more.
>
> Participation is by no means restricted to Unitarians. I have not heard of any formal plans for regional [inter-denominational] cooperation this summer, but I am sure we would be glad to have a delegation of Universalists attend to observe our plans and procedures, looking toward such possible cooperation in the future.

It should be noted that Southern Universalists already had a summer gathering of their own, held each year at Camp Hill, Alabama.

Carroll and the Blue Ridge Planning Committee came under some pressure, later in the spring, to consider changing the meeting dates for the 1955 Institute (which were Aug. 23-28).

That particular week – long since contracted with Blue Ridge Assembly, of course – directly conflicted with an important Joint Conference between the American Unitarian Association and the Universalist Church of America, set for Aug. 25-29 in Detroit, at which denominational merger was to be explored. This scheduling conflict cost the Summer Institute the kind of Universalist participation Carroll had been hoping for (it would come later). But more importantly, at least in the short term, it resulted in a noticeable absence of the kind of top-tier, national Unitarian workshop leaders and theme speakers to which Institute attendees had grown accustomed. The large scale national meeting in Detroit (which resulted in a recommendation that the Unitarians and the Universalists merge) took precedence that summer.

Yet the denominational dustup didn't seem to hurt overall turnout at Blue Ridge that year. In fact, registration actually *doubled* from the previous summer, to an all-time high of 282. This necessitated a change in meeting time for the following year, since Blue Ridge Assembly could no longer accommodate both the Unitarians and the Southern labor leaders on campus the same week.

The Late Fifties

In 1956, the Southern Unitarian Institute shifted to July (where, with the exception of the "Nomad Years" described in Chapter 3, it has remained ever since). That summer proved to be transitional in more ways than one, marking a clear shift in the emphasis of the now rapidly growing community. While the early Institutes had been largely that – *institutes*, focused primarily on "churchmanship," church growth and administration, and denominational outreach – the 1956 Planning Committee, led by Chairman Owen D. Lewis of Winston-Salem, had a very different vision for what the annual summer gathering could become. Lewis wanted to be responsive not only to feedback received from the previous year's record number of attendees, but also to the cultural changes taking place within Unitarianism and in society at large.

"Toward Creative Religion" was the theme he chose. Though denominational business remained on the schedule, the emphasis of the Institute clearly shifted to enhancing the *individual* experience – through large-group events and new and different workshops about personal growth. The 1956 Southern Unitarian Institute was well ahead of its time.

In a letter declining the offer of a workshop by Monroe Husbands, Fellowship Director of the UUA, dated March 27, 1956, Lewis explained what he had in mind:

> Dear Monroe...
>
> As much as we would like to avail ourselves of the comprehensive program you have mapped out for Blue Ridge, we are sorry to report that time considerations just will not permit it. We only have three and a half days this year, instead of the usual... [and] we have even more activities to put into the shorter time than ever before...
>
> Although Fellowship and Religious Education activities are extremely important, they do not appeal to the entire Institute attendance. Our theme, "Toward Creative Religion," is a radically different approach from that followed in previous conferences, and the [Planning] Committee is convinced of its significance for the entire Institute...
>
> Cordially,
> Owen D. Lewis

A total of 337 people, 52 of whom hailed from North Carolina, attended what wound up being the shortest Summer Institute ever. The long weekend began, interestingly enough, on Friday the 13th and concluded with a festive "Picnic in the Dell" lunch on Tuesday, July 17, 1956. Particularly memorable for participants was a "sacred dance" worship service led by Erika Thimey, director of The Dance Theatre in Washington, D.C. One reviewer wrote in the "Blue Ridge Bugle," the Institute's newsletter, that Thimey "made such an impact on the enrapt audience... [that] through the movement of the dance, she gave us a feeling for our wholeness as persons."

In a provocative concluding sermon on Tuesday morning, Vincent Silliman of Chicago (who had been editor of the new denominational hymnal *We Sing of Life*) left attendees buzzing throughout the closing picnic – and likely throughout the year. Titled "Toward Creative Religion Through Worship," Silliman's talk questioned, and then sought to reframe, traditional religious language such as "prayer," "God" and "worship." Mirroring developments within Unitarianism itself, what was considered a "religious service" at the Summer Institute had changed drastically in the six short years since Lake Waccamaw.

Yet the most popular way of experiencing the spiritual among Blue Ridge participants had never changed. Though the number of people doing so, at any one time, had dramatically increased, most would aver that there was still nothing finer than simply sitting in a rocking chair on the veranda at Lee Hall, contemplating the stunning view that unfolded for as far as the eye could see. Thus, it was only a matter of time before someone came up with the idea of an *organized* rocking event. One of the many creative innovations instituted in 1956 was the first annual Rocking Chair Competition.

This competition was judged (anonymously) over the course of the entire weekend, so that one never knew when or if their "style" was being observed by a judge. There were three categories for individual recognition: "Sittin' Loose," "Getting the Feet Higher Than the Head" and "Quality of Serenity." Dan Welch, the minister in nearby Asheville – perhaps benefitting from a home-field advantage – was deemed the overall winner, and a new Blue

*Dan Welch (pointing), the perennial winner of the
"Rocking Chair Competition"*

Ridge tradition was born.

The following year, with scheduling issues ironed out, the Institute returned to its regular week-long format, meeting from July 8-14 and concluding with a Sunday morning worship service in College Hall. The theme in 1957 continued the emphasis on the individual: "Person to Person – A Workshop for Life."

By this time, a custom had developed of rotating the responsibility of organizing the Southern Unitarian Institute among the different states and geographic regions in the T.J. Conference. Whatever group was responsible for the *next* year's Institute began meeting and planning in late spring, giving them 14 or 15 months to create the program and put into place the volunteers that were necessary to successfully handle an increasingly complex Institute. This practice also allowed the following year's leaders to "shadow" the group that was in charge any given July. During these years, professional staff support also was provided by the Regional Director, who was an employee of the American Unitarian Association. Early on, this had been Alfred Hobart, but the role was now held by Clif Hoffman, who was based in Atlanta.

Even with Hoffman's help, the bulk of the responsibility for putting on the Institute rested with the laity – as it does to this day – and it was becoming clear that someone with particularly strong organizational skills, including the ability to coordinate a large and diverse group of volunteers, was now needed to run the show.

In 1958, Major Mary C. Lane, a no-nonsense military woman from Norfolk, Va., took the reins as the first female "Chairman" of the Institute. "Major Lane," as everyone called her, led the Virginia Unitarian Conference – numbering by now a dozen congregations – in the meticulous planning and organization of the Institute that year, setting a model that would be used for the next five years. Her Planning Committee held regular meetings during the year leading up to the Institute, kept detailed minutes and notes, and – at the end of the Institute – produced an impressive (and very useful, to the next Planning Committee) 31-page typed report. Perhaps it is not

Lee Hall's front porch, the hub of activity at Summer Institute

27

surprising that it took a military veteran to devise the detailed "annual report" system, but there is no question the process Major Lane introduced paid huge dividends in the quality and organization of succeeding Institutes.

During the 12 months leading up to the 1958 Institute, Lane also put in place an extensive network of "Blue Ridge Boosters" – at least one in every Unitarian congregation in the region – to publicize and promote the Institute. The result was a record attendance of 418 participants. Through the Boosters, she distributed a remarkable 5,000 copies of a six-part, blue tri-fold brochure that was the most thorough Summer Institute publicity document to date. This is how that brochure described the upcoming Institute:

> In one of America's great vacationlands, the heart of the Appalachian Mountains, the Southern Unitarian Institute offers Unitarian families in one all-too-short week an ideal family vacation, a stimulating atmosphere for mental, spiritual and physical development, and a priceless opportunity to cultivate friendships with like-minded people from the southeastern quarter of the United States.
>
> The program is designed to provide a balanced diet for the heart, the mind and the body, with a free choice to partake of that which appeals to you most. Here you have an opportunity to learn techniques and skills to take back to your local church and fellowship or community.
>
> ...Who should come? Everybody! That is, everyone who is a member of, or affiliated with, or interested in a Unitarian church or fellowship in the Thomas Jefferson Conference. The Institute is for lay members just as much as for church administrators, church school teachers, superintendents or ministers.

Children? Yes! Institute arrangements provide programs for children of all ages. Not only will they be well cared for, but they will also have a glorious time.

LRY'ers? Yes! The Dixie Federation of the LRY meets at Blue Ridge each summer as part of the Southern Unitarian Institute.

Indeed, the Liberal Religious Youth program at Blue Ridge had become so large by 1958 that one full page of the six-page tri-fold brochure was devoted to LRY information and registration procedures. Young people entering ninth grade through college were considered "Senior LRY," whose program was described as one in which "fun and fellowship prevail in the dining room, in Asheville Hall and all over Blue Ridge." The Senior LRY theme in 1958 was a defiant "We're Liberals. So What?"

Meanwhile, those entering seventh and eighth grades were offered a "Junior LRY" experience, which included a "program especially designed to help junior highers form their own philosophy of religion and life." Both LRY groups were housed in Asheville Hall, with the younger youth on the third floor, chaperoned by five adult program leaders and facing a posted lights-out curfew of 10:15 p.m. Evidently, even those safeguards were not enough to allay adult concerns about behavior and maturity, because the feedback in the post-Institute report recommended for the following year "the complete separation in theory as well as in fact of the two groups [Junior and Senior LRY] ... so that the junior high program can be set up as a part of the religious education program."

The typical program day for adults in 1958 was divided into a morning "Study-Discussion Series" from 9 a.m. until noon, with a choice of four tracks: "The Ways of Mankind," "Ways to Justice," "Jefferson and Our Times" or "Discovering Modern Poetry." After lunch, seminars and workshops (1:30-3:00 p.m.) offered the following options: "Dynamics of American Religion,"

"Leading Group Discussions," "Science as a New Force in Our Society," "Fellowship," "Social Action," "Dramatic Arts" and "General [Women's] Alliance." Programming was provided by the University of Virginia Extension Division.

Throughout the 1950s and into the early 1960s, the Southern Unitarian Institute became nationally recognized for its "Laboratory School" (later called the "Demonstration School").

Religious educators listen attentively to a lecture at Blue Ridge.

Each morning and afternoon, Tuesday through Saturday, top professional religious educators from the AUA and the region would offer sample Sunday School programming to the children. Local directors of religious education and R.E. volunteers were invited to observe, learn classroom techniques and obtain curriculum to take back home for use during the year. The Unitarian and later Unitarian Universalist religious education teacher-training offered at Blue Ridge had a far-reaching and long-lasting impact on a generation of Southern Unitarian Universalists, and was perhaps one of the greatest legacies of the early Institute. Parents were expected to attend "Parents' Seminars" each afternoon in which, for 1958, leading denominational figures explained "the role of the parent in religious education, and [addressed] special problems such as God, worship, prayer, and the relation of the liberal parent and child to the community."

Evening programs (at 8 p.m.) that year began with an orientation on Monday night, followed by a worship service led by the LRY. On Tuesday, Prof. Thomas T. Hammond of the University of Virginia offered an illustrated lecture on "Russia Today," while on Wednesday Prof. Edward J. Jurji of Princeton spoke on "Comparative Religion." Thursday's lecture was titled "The Education of Our Ministers," by Dr. Sidney E. Mead, president of Meadville Theological School. Friday night was reserved for the annual meeting of the Thomas Jefferson Unitarian Conference (in which delegates voted to change the organization's name to the Thomas Jefferson Unitarian *Council*, and created five geographic sub-groups – the Virginias, the Carolinas, East/Middle Tennessee, Florida, and Georgia-Alabama-Mississippi). Denominational complexity was clearly evolving.

On the final night, Saturday, the Asheville congregation offered an "Original Musical Revue" before the evening concluded with an outdoor candlelight worship service, again provided by the LRY. Sunday morning's worship service was an abbreviated version of "Inherit the Wind," followed by lunch and heartfelt goodbyes until the following year.

Also gleaned from Major Lane's extensive notes regarding 1958:

- Evening babysitting was offered by Blue Ridge staff at a rate of $1 per hour.
- In addition to leading two evening worship services for the entire Institute, the Senior LRY continued to publish "The Bugle," the Institute's daily newsletter.
- Due to an increase in the "service fee" Blue

Ridge was charging per attendee (to $1.50 for all participants over 9 years of age), adult registration fees were raised to $7.50, with LRY'ers paying $6.50 and children $3.75.

- Room and board was still $30 for adults without a bath. It was raised to $42 with a private bath. The brochure clearly states that room assignments were to "be made in the order of registration. The number of rooms with private bath is limited, so if you desire these accommodations, early registration is advisable."
- Recreation included swimming in a private lake (lifeguard on duty), tennis ("furnish your own racquet"), golf at a nearby nine-hole course, hiking, badminton, horseshoes, shuffleboard, roller skating, ping pong and basketball in the gymnasium.
- The Institute opened at 2 p.m. on Monday, and closed at 1 p.m. on Sunday. The Planning Committee expected 325 attendees; in the end, 418 persons came.
- For the first time, Florida tied (with Virginia) for the highest number of participants, at 73.
- The total budget in 1958 was $2,585. Of that, honoraria for speakers ranged from $30 to $149. Teachers of R.E., and adult workshop leaders, were each paid $30 (not coincidentally, the exact cost for basic room and board). Insurance for the Institute cost $68.75.
- A slide show featuring 40 slides from the week was produced to provide publicity for the following year.

The overwhelming success of the 1958 Institute – both in terms of attendance and organization – created word-of-mouth buzz

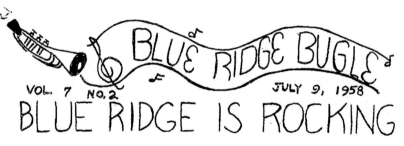

BLUE RIDGE BUGLE

VOL. 7 NO. 2   **JULY 9, 1958**

BLUE RIDGE IS ROCKING

ANNOUNCEMENTS

For those interested there will be on Thursday afternoon , July 10, at three o'clock, an informal discussion interpreting the Council of Liberal Churches and its program. The discussion will be led by Miss Frances Wood assisted by Miss Alice Harrison and Mr. Royal Cloyd, CLC Staff members. The discussion will be held in Room 5, Lee Hall basement area.

Anyone wishing to play bridge can contact Mrs. Eoline Vockroth of Richmond, Virginia. They need players.

The Beacon Press Book Shop, set up by Mr. Clinton Balmer, Beacon Press representative, will be open in the Hall lobby from 9:30 'til 5:30 every day. All samples will be half price at the end of the week.

LRY-ers are invited to participate in the Dramatic Arts workshop with the voice choir. The voice choir will take part in the Sunday Morning worship service.

PLEASE: Do not walk on the gymnasium floor in street shoes. It has just been refinished.

The Blue Ridge Assembly store is run on the honor policy, so please don't forget to pay your bill as you go out the door.

CORRECTION: The adult recreation hike at 3 p.m. today is to Hi-Top colony rather than to Hi-Top mountain. This is a more graduated hike and will appeal to those of us who are faint-hearted

ROCKING CHAIR CONTEST

Mr. Andy Anderson, Adult recreation chairman, has announced the second annual Rocking Chair Contest at Blue Ridge. Contestants will be judged on "sittin' loose" (relaxed posture), getting the feet higher than the head, and the quality of serenity they demonstrate through their meditations while rocking. Rev. Dan Welch, one of the winners last year, opined that during his year as rocking chair champion he has worn his voctory laurels with amazing grace and humility. The judges prefer to remain anonymous, but — They may BE WATCHING YOU!

ADDITIONAL ANNOUNCEMENTS

Duty hours for the nurse of the Blue Ridge Assembly are:

7:30 - 11:00 a.m.
5:30 - 7:00 p.m.

It is requested that the nurse be contacted outside these hours only in case of real emergency. If an emergency arises outside these hours please contact the main desk of the Assembly in Lee Hall lobby, and the person on duty will summon the nurse. Your cooperation in this matter will be greatly appreciated.

Training sessions for Church Budget Canvass Directors will be meeting in Abbott Hall lobby mornings from 9:00 to 12:00 Wednesday through Saturday. Ten churches were represented in the opening sessions today. David A. Bergmark, Continental Campaign Director of the United Unitarian appeal is leading the training discussions.

throughout the Southeast, and the following year, aided by a huge surge in registration from Floridians, Blue Ridge participation soared to 584, "raising concern that the Blue Ridge Assembly facilities ... may prove inadequate in future sessions."

Clif Hoffman (center) holding court on the porch of Lee Hall

Thomas Jefferson Council Executive Director Clif Hoffman worried that if the popularity of Blue Ridge continued to grow, "We shall be faced with the necessity of splitting our Institute, or finding a new place." No such drastic measures were necessary, however, as the decidedly cramped, near capacity experience campers endured at the end of the 1950s – along, perhaps, with the challenges of denominational consolidation with the Universalists – led to a 20 percent drop in attendance by the start of the next decade.

Interestingly (and for reasons that are now unclear), the name of the Institute in 1959 was changed to the "Thomas Jefferson Unitarian Institute." (It remained that in 1960 as well). Florida was becoming the dominant force, at least in terms of attendance, with 170 of the 584 verified participants in 1959 coming from that southernmost state. There were 80 Senior LRY'ers on campus that year, 45 Junior LRY'ers and 143 children below junior high age – prompting Liese Steinhaus, Director of the 1959 Religious

Education Demonstration School, to recommend capping the following year's children's program at 130. Even the kindergarten class had to be divided into Senior Kindergarten and Junior Kindergarten groups.

There also appear to have been issues developing with what Institute leaders had come to call "freeloaders" (those who participated at the Institute but avoided paying registration fees). Since room and board costs were paid directly to Blue Ridge Assembly by each participant, "freeloading" was not only possible, but apparently increasingly common. This caused concurrent challenges regarding housing assignments, which were only exacerbated by the far greater demand for, than supply of, rooms with baths. Complaints were lodged about what was seen as preferential housing treatment given to those in charge of the Institute. These tensions were sufficient to compel those who were responsible for planning in 1959 – the Deep South congregations of Alabama, Georgia and Mississippi, under the co-chairmanship of Dr. and Mrs. Francis Binkley – to state in their final report that "the problem has gone beyond the stage in which it can be handled by a fully volunteer and temporary group [which rotates from year to year among different states]... The appointment of a *permanent registrar* to apply equitable and uniform methods" of assigning housing was the recommendation of the Binkleys.

The theme for 1959, "The Anatomy of Prejudice," offered a preview of the issue that would consume the thoughts – and actions – of Unitarians throughout the South during the next decade. Speakers from Duke University and Gammon Theological Seminary in Atlanta were among those to offer their thoughts and lead discussions as Institute participants began to examine what it was like for both black and white, Christian and Jew, to live in the South during the Civil Rights era. Especially popular were small-group discussions in which about two dozen people reviewed their reactions to each morning's presentation. In these conversations, group participants shared openly about prejudice and bigotry not only in the communities where they lived, but in their own hearts.

Analysis of the success of this small-group discussion format varied. Although Dr. Abner Golden remarked that "the omnipresence of segregation in Southern life hampered a basic discussion of the problem of prejudice," Mrs. Francis Binkley, Institute co-chair, contended in the final report of the Planning Committee that "certainly, all who attended carried away with them a better understanding, and effective means of dealing with, theirs and others' prejudices."

Leon Hopper, then Executive Director of the national Liberal Religious Youth, was among the speakers in 1959. He noted that "a constant theme of race relations dominated the atmosphere. But back then, we tended to look at the issue more intellectually than we did in later years. The youth in LRY were very concerned with the topic in their own programming, and it affected them deeply. It was a very generative time." Differing somewhat from the reports of their elders, post-conference notes from the LRY group called the 1959 Institute program "the best ever."

The Southern Institute, the South, and America itself were now at a crossroads. The innocence of the 1950s was about to give way to the experimentation and dislocation of the 1960s.

The Early Sixties

As the decade began, the comfortable status quo of the 1950s was starting to erode. In the broader culture, a charismatic young Catholic named Kennedy was running for President. An even more charismatic young singer named Presley had returned from military service and was changing the face of rock and roll. Liberal religion, too, was in transition. The American Unitarian Association and the Universalist Church of America held concurrent meetings in Boston in May of 1960, putting in place the final pieces of the plan to merge the two denominations. The merger – technically a "consolidation" – would be finalized and implemented over the next 12 months.

Lee Hall as seen from the Blue Ridge Assembly parking lot

The Thomas Jefferson Unitarian Institute of 1960 began with patriotic pomp and circumstance at an ingathering worship service on Monday evening, the Fourth of July. The Institute theme, "A Look at Ourselves," captured the spirit of self-examination and re-invention that was going on within the wider contexts of country and church. William B. Rice, chair of the Joint Merger Commission that had been formed in May in Boston, flew in to address the Institute on Tuesday night, speaking on the subject of "Our New Unitarian-Universalist Association" (note the hyphen, which was later dropped). Eugene Pickett, by then the minister in Richmond, led an animated discussion on the same topic, and Alfred Hobart, then of Birmingham, explored the topic "Regions in Our Denomination." Reflecting the changes that were in the air, a new workshop section was instituted at the request of the influential General Alliance women's group, titled "The Place of Women in the Church."

By Saturday morning, at the annual meeting of the Thomas

Jefferson Unitarian Council, delegates had a good sense of what was on the horizon – and how it might impact their beloved Blue Ridge gathering. There was considerable consternation about the sharp drop in attendance from 1959. After the high water mark of 584 the previous year, the 1960 registration total of 468 was troubling to say the least. Henry McKown of Oak Ridge, the Director in 1960, wrote, "This total attendance was considerably less than the 690 that [we] estimated." Yet when all was said and done, the 1960 Institute did manage to end up in the black – by $2.

Having anticipated continuing growth prior to 1960, however, the leadership had begun looking into possible alternative locations for the Summer Institute. But for various reasons, each site they examined "proved to be unsatisfactory, and [was also] found to be booked up several years in advance," McKown reported. Instead, he advocated preparedness in case there was ever a need to move – a warning that, though it largely fell on deaf ears, proved to be prophetic.

There appears to have been another reason for the disappointing attendance in 1960. The final publicity brochure was not completed and mailed out until mid-June, a mere three weeks before the Institute. Jack Lynes and Robert Palmer of Nashville, who were co-chairs of publicity that year, wrote in the final report that "with this experience of a failure of responsibility to deliver on schedule [evidently by members of their church, who had volunteered to produce the brochure], we recommend that contracts for publicity material be negotiated on a strictly professional basis [in the future], even though the job can be done more cheaply by members or friends of the church."

However, the last-minute arrival of publicity and registration materials does not appear to have dampened the enthusiasm, or the commitment, of the Institute's farthest-flung members. Participants from Florida seem to have included Blue Ridge in their summer plans from the beginning; of the 468 people in attendance, 131 were from the Sunshine State, once again accounting for more than a fourth of the overall population.

The 1960 edition of the Summer Institute officially ended with breakfast on Sunday morning (there was no closing worship service), but the week had really culminated the night before with "an original play" performed by the LRY. This play, perhaps something of a precursor to modern-day Teen Way Off Broadway, had been shifted from its originally scheduled Friday night position in the schedule, in order to accommodate expanded business sessions related to the denominational consolidation. When the schedule change was first proposed, the teenagers expressed concern that having their performance on the last night of the Institute would negatively impact their own now-traditional semi-formal dance. Yet those worries were forgotten amid the enormously positive response the play received from the adults.

Perhaps the play's success could be attributed at least partially to the tight ship being run in Asheville Hall in those days. The "LRY Blue Ridge Guideposts" from 1960 were:

1. To bed at 11:15 – lights out – Quiet
2. Late hours for special group activities
3. Smoking only in Social Rooms – not in bedrooms
4. No electrical appliances in resident halls except radios, lamps, and electric razors
5. The use of alcoholic beverages is to be omitted
6. No couples to take hikes alone after dark
7. All hikes and climbs must be approved
8. Cars are not to be used off the assembly grounds
9. Everyone is expected to participate in all scheduled activities
10. Those who do not fit into the spirit, or who fail to follow the above rules, will be asked by the [LRY] Institute Chairman, Mr. Fuller, to return home on vote of the Camp Affairs Committee, or to change residence halls

A group meets on the lawn in front of Lee Hall

In wrapping up the 1960 Institute, the Planning Committee used the occasion of the Institute's tenth anniversary – and its theme, "A Look at Ourselves" – to conduct a participant feedback survey. One question, "Give a numerical rating in order of importance to your reasons for attending the T.J. Institute at Blue

Ridge," offered a particularly interesting snapshot of the Institute a full decade after its founding.

With four points being given to the most important reason for attendance, and one point to the least important, participants overwhelmingly cited "the program (subject matter, churchmanship, religious Demonstration School, etc.)" as the primary reason they came to Blue Ridge. A distant second was "vacation (change of pace and activities)." "Other reasons (fellowship, etc.)" came in third, and last was "business meetings."

Another question, "Check common-interest groups you would like to join," again provided some intriguing results. In order, the top choices were psychology/philosophy, drama, art, nature and painting. Considerably less popular were tennis, music, creative writing, interpretive dance and ballet.

Armed with this feedback from the 1960 participants, those planning the following year's program soon mailed a different questionnaire to all Unitarian Universalist church members in the region who had not attended the 1960 Institute. Asked their reason for not attending, half of the respondents indicated that the program did not interest them. Other answers gave contradictory impressions; in one case, a slight plurality preferred more recreational opportunities than program offerings, while at the same time a strong majority in another question did *not* want a "conference that is primarily recreational/social." But there was near unanimity – an "overwhelming no," as it was reported – in response to the question "Would you like the meeting to be at a different time and place?" Thus, formal inquiries about other possible locations came to an end, and planners renewed their efforts to offer a "balanced" program at Blue Ridge in 1961.

The next Summer Institute convened less than two months after the ceremony that officially gave birth to the Unitarian Universalist Association. Nonetheless, the name of that 1961 gathering inexplicably reverted to being the "Southern Unitarian Institute." Attendance was back up, though not quite yet to the level of 1959. Among the 44 "Blue Ridge Boosters" spread across the Southeast whose job it was to drum up attendance that year was Janet A. Haas of Butner, a tiny town in northeast North Carolina. An active member of the Church of the Larger Fellowship, a "mailbox" congregation composed primarily of Unitarian Universalists who lived long distances from any UU church, Haas wrote a lovely letter to her CLF compatriots, dated January 25, 1961:

Dear Fellow Member of UCLF,

As I read over the list of those "lonely liberals" in the Southeast, in the area of the Thomas Jefferson Unitarian Conference, I am struck not only by our numbers, but by the speculation that we live within easy meeting distance of each other in many cases, and [yet we] don't even know there is another kindred spirit nearby.

Now many of us remain aloof by choice, preferring the relative disengagement of semi-monthly transfusions from Boston. But many [others] are lonely by default, unaware that we can be vital parts of an ever-growing whole. Did you know, for example, that each summer the Thomas Jefferson Unitarian Conference sponsors a week-long Institute for all Unitarians in this area (us, too!), at Blue Ridge Assembly, Blue Ridge, N.C.? This year it will be held from July 10 to July 16, and all are eligible.

When I first attended in 1958, I encountered 450 fellow Unitarians, all highly individual and yet imbued with a common hospitality toward one another's thinking. I have never felt less lonely. The week involved lectures, seminars and workshops – on topics of Unitarian concern ranging from ... prejudice to modern poetry. There is much opportunity for recreation and socializing – a <u>real</u> vacation, all in all.

This year the Carolinas Unitarian Conference – a subdivision of the Thomas Jefferson Unitarian Conference, including North and South Carolina and part of Georgia – will be responsible for planning our Blue Ridge program. Dale Blosser, President of the Carolinas Conference, has asked me to contact each of you and write you all to come to Blue Ridge, to share in the revitalizing experience of being together – [part] of a group where you won't feel peculiar, a non-participant, as so often happens to us here in the South. It seems to me we need this reinforcement now, more than ever, in these storm-tossed times…

Several CLF members answered the call and met Haas – who taught a creative dance workshop – at Blue Ridge.

Changes in the registration process in 1961 resulted in "the smoothest registration yet." An onsite visit to Blue Ridge in the spring by registrar William Sapp of Columbia, S.C., included a meeting with one Mr. McNary from Blue Ridge Assembly. In that meeting, it was agreed that forms for all pre-registrants should be filled out ahead of time, "thereby easing the confusion between our registration table and the B.R.A. desk." Sapp also came up with the idea of using building floor plans to facilitate the making of room assignments. Following his year as registrar (which he described as a "full-time job"), at the conclusion of the week, Sapp recommended that "a permanent Registrar-Treasurer be selected for the Institute, at an annual salary of not more than $300, plus one week and one day minimum room and board at the Institute."

The recommendation was implemented the following year, albeit with a salary of $150. By this point in the Institute's history all important leadership positions – what would now be considered "Core Staff" – as well as theme speakers and honored guests, received a "salary." Most were $50 – just about enough to cover the cost of room and board.

Volunteer organizations began to proliferate in 1961. Options offered that year included the Layman's League, the General (Women's) Alliance, the Unitarian Fellowship for Social Justice, the Unitarian Service Committee, the Church of the Larger Fellowship, the T.J. Minister's Association, the United Unitarian Appeal and the Unitarian Development Fund.

Finances continued to be a concern – so much, in fact, that a contribution box was placed in the lobby of Lee Hall on Friday for donations. The Sunday morning collection plate was also diverted to the Institute (apparently, it often went to other causes). Each collection brought in more than $100, and assured the Institute's solvency for another year.

Heavy and consistent rain was a major issue in 1961, forcing attendees to spend far more time indoors than they would have liked and causing the cancellation of several workshops and trips. The teens' "campfire" had to be held indoors, around the fireplace. Another popular indoor venue was the gymnasium, which

The Blue Ridge vista as seen from an upper floor Lee Hall window, including Abbott Hall

participants packed on Friday afternoon for the highly anticipated Adults vs. LRY basketball game. All week long, each side had been taunting the other in daily announcements. One of the adults was quoted as saying, "It's our duty to show this unfortunately not-so-silent generation a thing or two" on the basketball court. In the end, however, youth prevailed, with the LRY squeaking out a 40-37 victory. That the margin was not larger was attributed by one boasting teen only to "the fact that most of [us] stayed up all night and climbed to High Top to see the sunrise." So much for curfew!

Innovations in 1961 included a "souvenir booklet" which contained a list of registrants (names and addresses only) along with "daily bulletins and key lectures" from the week. The "Daily Bugle" – which had come to be known, whether affectionately or derisively, as "The Daily Bungle" – was no more, and had been replaced by a printed broadside, now produced by adult volunteers, called simply a "daily bulletin." Here are a few tidbits from the 1961 bulletin:

"Our contract with Blue Ridge Assembly specifically and emphatically states that dogs are not allowed in the lobby."

"The roster lists Jim Lee as the 'Rev. Jim Lee.' Please correct – Jim is not a Reverend, he is a Republican."

"The Senior LRY is presenting a meller drammer [sic] Friday evening in College Hall Auditorium at 8:15 P.M. ... The play will last 40 minutes, give or take a couple (as Bill Sapp says), so the adults will not be too late for their discussion groups."

The final number of registrants in 1961 was 542; once again Florida led the way with 183, of which 66 were from Orlando (more than came from the entire states of either Virginia or Tennessee).

Attendance jumped once more the following year, when an

unprecedented 628 participants arrived at Blue Ridge in July 1962. The new name of the gathering was the "Southern Unitarian Universalist Institute," marking the first time (and strangely, the only time for several years to come) that Universalists were included in the Institute's name. This first official fully "UU" Summer Institute was planned by the Florida churches, and co-chaired by Rev. Bob and Mrs. Pat Sonen, though the couple spent part of the planning year on sabbatical in Washington. The gathering now lasted a *full week*, beginning on Sunday afternoon and ending the following Sunday morning. This particular practice was continued through 1967. The extra day added a dollar to the registration fee for adults (now up to $11), and 50 cents for Senior LRY (now up to $8).

No one grumbled, of course; "one more day in paradise" could hardly be cause for complaint. In fact, many parents were apparently also willing to shell out $7 more for nursery staffing (the nursery was fully open and staffed from 9 a.m. to 8 p.m.). Most of the families were housed during that jam-packed year, by request, in Abbott Hall. Abbott was sufficiently removed from the hubbub of Lee Hall and the youthful energy of Asheville Hall to provide ample quiet time for sleeping children (and their tired parents).

"Camper's insurance," which had been provided as part of the registration fee for several years now – covering Institute attendees from 48 hours prior to the beginning of camp to 48 hours after its end – was actually utilized for the first time in 1962 when a Junior LRY participant was bitten by a poisonous snake and the child's family incurred $365.05 in hospital and medical expenses. Thankfully, the child recovered.

Kay Hoffman of Atlanta, who had long been active in the children's program and who carried considerable influence at the Institute, offered comments in the 1962 final report that would have an important effect on the following year's program decisions. She wrote:

Those of us concerned with Religious Education throughout the region have felt for some time that it is unfortunate when we are forced to conduct the Demonstration School during the same hours set aside for the adult education program at Blue Ridge. We felt this way even more strongly this year, when we found the Demonstration School competing with the popular appeal packed by Bill Hollister's program. A good number of people who had originally planned to share in the R.E. program finally could not resist the pull of Bill's topic ["Human Relations"] and his personal appeal...

We realize that overlapping of program is often unavoidable. We do feel, however, that people who come to learn new ideas and techniques of R.E. as seen and discussed at Blue Ridge should not be faced with such a complete overlap of program as occurred this year.

It is true that there was a lot going on at Blue Ridge in 1962. Recreational activities included square dancing and a hayride. A new offsite road trip, to see the historical pageant "Unto These Hills" in nearby Cherokee, N.C., was offered. Apparently, theme talk "talkbacks" (the overall theme that year was "Bridges of Understanding") were particularly lively, beginning each night at 10 p.m. and often lasting "into the small hours of the morning."

The outside world had even begun to take notice of the Institute. There was coverage, including voice interviews with participants, on a local Black Mountain radio station, and an article also appeared in the Asheville newspaper. Internally, information was disseminated in a revived newsletter, produced by Frances Sacks of Tampa (who was given one of the $50 stipends for her efforts).

Bob Sonen, never one to think small, had that year invited several big-name national personalities, including Martin Luther

King Jr., Hubert Humphrey, Adlai Stevenson and Supreme Court Justice William O. Douglas (at least the latter two were Unitarians!) to address the Institute. All declined the kind offer – it is suspected that their speaking fee may have been considerably more than the egalitarian $50 going rate at Blue Ridge – but, as Sonen put it, "The nicest thing, by far, about being involved in planning a program for Blue Ridge is the autographs you collect" on the rejection letters.

With typical dry humor, Sonen also provided these "Unsolicited Comments and Observations" in the final report on the 1962 Institute:

> Every year there are those who say that too much has been planned. That the programs are too full. It is our humble opinion that with this many people involved, it is no go to say 'At this hour, this program and this program only, will be offered,' or even to say 'At this hour, nothing at all is planned; everybody start playing or resting.' A full program, with a variety of offerings, will give mature Unitarian Universalists the opportunity to decide for themselves what they want to do out of several possibilities at any given hour. We are no longer running a one-room schoolhouse!
>
> ...We [also] eliminated all use of the public address system in the dining room during meals. No grace. No announcements. No political speeches. No brief summaries of world news. No reading of devotional material. There was nothing democratic about this. We never even voted on it. We just never turned the voice machine on. And not a single voice was raised to say 'I missed it'!

But for all his flair, Sonen could not have dreamed of the departures from tradition that lay ahead in 1963.

1963: A Year of Change
(And Trouble on the Horizon)

In 1963 the responsibility for planning the Institute rotated back to the Virginia delegation. Bob Conklin of Richmond was the chair. Conklin worked closely with Emerson Schwenk, minister of the Richmond church, to envision a radically different kind of program for what was called that year simply "Blue Ridge '63." The theme was "The Forward Edge of Concern."

The 16-page, stapled booklet brochure, far and away the most elaborate yet, included a center spread consisting of a planning grid for the week – indicative of the "do-it-yourself" approach in 1963. A careful look through the publicity material indicated that change – significant change – was afoot. For one thing, there would be *no* Demonstration School (an institution unto itself, that had effectively trained countless religious education directors and volunteers throughout the Southeast and one that had long been a flagship program at Blue Ridge, at least in the eyes of Boston). Furthermore, there would be no theme talks, in the traditional sense. There would be no evening worship services.

The goal was to create a powerfully, provocatively *experiential* (some would say "experimental") Blue Ridge Institute built around the organizing theme of "The Forward Edge of Concern."

Following the previous year's unprecedented attendance of 628, Conklin and Schwenk expected UUs to flock to Blue Ridge in 1963 – and come they did, roughly 700 of them, a record not challenged again for more than a dozen years. Participants had to be shoehorned into every nook and cranny of the Blue Ridge campus "with the help of ... cottages [and] a motel down the road, and cots and cribs two-deep in most of the rooms," according to the newsletter. The LRY slept "three to a bed in Asheville Hall" (segregated by gender, of course). In all, when the week began, there were 698 Unitarian Universalists on campus with "a number of late arrivals expected" to join in for the final weekend.

For perspective, the housing capacity of Lee Hall was 300,

while Asheville and Abbott supposedly held a hundred each. The overflow was accommodated primarily in nearby cabins, which were described by one participant as "essentially two-story, four-bedroom homes. All our meals were still taken in the Dining Hall with everyone else," she said, "and we actually loved the cabin and the other couples we got to know better by living there with them."

But the experience most Blue Ridgers had that week did not generate universally positive reviews. Some loved it. Some hated it. Many argued about it. In the end, the 1963 Institute was perhaps the most divisive ever held. By choosing to "emphasize the do-it-yourself quality that is the essence of our religion," as he put it, Conklin, for better or worse, broke the very popular mold that had been Blue Ridge.

Right before lunch on Monday, Conklin spoke to the experiential/experimental nature of the week's plans, asking the assembled participants:

> Will you do something with me right now? Will you overcome your intellectual self-consciousness enough to pause, and take a look at the people around you?... Can you overcome your inhibitions long enough to feel the love that's present?... Can you look at me and feel my embarrassed but genuine sensation that I love you too? I suspect that you can receive this love only if your transmitter is tuned to the same frequency. Tune to that frequency this week. Go to your workshops, and come to this afternoon's program, with open hearts – and the frequently clenched fists that love involves. My hope, and believe me, it is a deep and terrifying hope, is that nothing less than *our religion* will happen.

Thus, following lunch, hundreds of curious participants

College Hall, scene of the "experiential"
1963 programming experiment

(including those who would have, previously, been involved in the now-eliminated Demonstration School) convened in College Hall to find not the customary nationally recognized theme speaker, or an illustrious panel prepared to discuss the week's theme – but rather what could only be described as *chaos.* Many felt they had been hoodwinked, or were guinea pigs in some kind of giant social experiment.

Here is how Conklin later described the scene:

> The large group was asked to decide for themselves, individually, how they might best achieve [their assignment, which was to, as Schwenk had put it, "reach out for each other by examining our deepest concerns"]. About 45 minutes were spent in developing alternatives. Approximately half the group wanted to form small groups of eight or ten to explore the 'concerns letters' [which the first 80 Institute pre-registrants, 40 men and 40 women, had been asked

to write, ahead of time, responding to the question, "What concerns you most deeply?"]. It was done. These were the people who started and stayed in high gear.

Simultaneously, another group of about 30 to 35 took possession of an adjoining room and sent a spokesman back... insisting that they be provided with a minister-leader... Gene Pickett answered their call.

Meanwhile ... at Room 3, the remaining people seemed to fall into two groups. First, there was a quiet, small group who either wanted to see what the final alternatives were before choosing, or were too fascinated by the confusion to leave. The second of the remaining groups sang a medley of needs and demands. Certainly some of them were very hostile, having come to Blue Ridge with an apparent expectation of being led, of being taught or lectured, or to be given a task-oriented discussion [like] examining something safely intellectual, or witnessing a formal panel. Some wanted the ministers, jointly, to take the letters of concern, one by one, and examine them all. Others wanted the ministers each assigned to a room where people could gather to the leader of their choice. Others wanted the panel [of ministers] to operate as a panel, period. Still others made it clear they wanted nothing to do with making the choice.

Parliamentary rules started being invoked, although the few motions to get to the floor were defeated or ignored. Many in this group found ... self-direction anarchic, disgusting or terrifying. Notebooks and pencils started taking on the look of weapons.

In explanation, it should be said here that the ministers had no intention of manipulating or frustrating anyone. There was a prior recognition that frustration would play a part in the early organizational stage [of the week's program, and] that this frustration had to find its voice before it was resolved. If we could have neatly dished out to each individual what we hoped each person could achieve for himself, it would have only been more words. Try more words as you will – and we tried our best – experiencing can only be *experienced*.

What is impossible to say, we were shortly able to demonstrate. Starting from the low gear of Tuesday [when the various groups' different processes began to be implemented], an acceleration began which continued throughout the week and ended, we thought, with some steam. For instance, some of the independent smaller groups enthusiastically scheduled themselves into extra sessions as the conference approached its close. Many of the dropouts returned. Although a kind of sourness remained in a few people, a solid value was found in the *doing* that could not have been achieved in the *telling*.

Following Monday afternoon's chaotic beginning, the whole campus was abuzz. Vigorous and animated discussions, pro and con, of the new experiential "do-it-yourself" program kept participants up late that night. Letters to the editor of the "Morning Blast" (each year now, the newsletter seemed to have a different name) debated what was happening at the Institute. Barbara Baum wrote, "My concern previous to Monday afternoon's gathering was over the loss of individual freedom through over-organization. It occurs to me now that little or no organization also gives one the fear that his freedom as an individual is threatened." John Bregger, on the other hand, wrote under the heading "Report from a Small Theme Group" that "in the words of one long-time participant at Blue Ridge, the small-group method of discussion adopted in part by the Theme Workshop on Concerns 'was a complete success.' Members of the group, 12 to 16 in size, provided ... a wealth of personal experience from a wide area of geographical, educational, nationality, family and religious backgrounds."

Another significant and much-debated change to Blue Ridge tradition that year was the introduction of a film festival. Participants had come to expect evening theme reflections by big-name speakers, and evening worship services led by the region's top ministers. All that was replaced in 1963 by a nightly Foreign Film Festival. Serious, thought-provoking films by Japanese, French and Italian directors (including Fellini) were shown each night beginning at 9:00 p.m., following two hours of evening "free time." Only one film was in English; the rest had subtitles.

Friday morning's workshops were cancelled so that as many adult delegates as possible could be present for preliminary discussion and debate that would culminate on Saturday with the dissolution of the Thomas Jefferson UU Conference – the interim, umbrella organization for the new Unitarian Universalist Association in the Southeast. By the end of Saturday, the regional T.J. Conference had been replaced by three "districts" (Florida, Mid-South and Thomas Jefferson), all of which were to be coordinated by an Inter-District Office in Atlanta.

WELCOME *to* BLUE RIDGE

This is ROBERT E. LEE HALL

Part of a Christian Conference Center Owned by the YMCA's of the South.

CAPACITY 600 GUESTS

We Hope You Enjoy The View From Our Porch and Will Visit Us Again

BLUE RIDGE ASSEMBLY, INC.

With so many changes taking place, when participants left Blue Ridge on Sunday, July 14, 1963, many felt that their beloved Summer Institute (and the traditions they had come to cherish) would never be the same.

There were also other signals that trouble was on the horizon. Relations with the YMCA staff at Blue Ridge Assembly were growing strained – to the point that, early the following spring, it was discovered that the Unitarian Universalists had been dropped from the Blue Ridge summer schedule. This was quickly rectified, but the damage had been done – and though there was no direct indication as to why such an oversight might have occurred, there is little question that by the summer of 1963, the increasingly liberal (and often very vocally so) UUs were beginning to get on the nerves of the more conservative Blue Ridge staff.

Indeed, a notice went out to all Institute participants prior to 1964 which read:

> Blue Ridge Assembly is owned and operated by the YMCA of the Southeast, as a training center for Christian leadership, as envisioned in traditional Christian terms. The young people who staff the institute as waitresses, chambermaids, bell boys and desk clerks are college students who have felt a call to dedicate themselves to the work of the Christian religious program.
>
> We Unitarian Universalists also represent a religious tradition and dedication, although of a different character, but one nonetheless concerned with tolerance and the inherent dignity of the individual. We naturally, therefore, will want to respect the dedication of these young people, respect them as individuals, and treat them at all times with courtesy and consideration.

That such an admonishment was deemed necessary by Institute leaders speaks volumes.

Serving to further widen the rift between participants and their Blue Ridge hosts was the parsimonious nature of many Institute attendees, which was now a major sore spot among the young staff of students (many of whom worked eight-hour days and attended classes at night, while their UU guests were out making merry). The servers relied on tip income to pay their college tuition. While the average tip per participant among other visiting groups was reported to range from $7 to $10 for the week for adults, and

$5 for the week per child (in other words, roughly 15% of the room and board charges, a figure that was widely disseminated in Blue Ridge literature in a not-so-subtle attempt to offer guests a tipping guideline) – it seems the average Unitarian Universalist tip for the week was an appalling *one dollar* per person.

Other issues had also begun to arise. While there had been no mention either of alcohol or alcohol consumption in any of the literature or reports during the first decade of the Institute – aside from the annual, perfunctory statement that "alcoholic beverages are not permitted at Blue Ridge" – reading between the lines, it is clear that by 1963, alcohol was becoming an important part of the Institute. One welcome packet joked of the importance of giving more than "lip service" to the Blue Ridge alcohol policy. The number of offsite trips to local restaurants and entertainment establishments (dinner theatres, movies, museums and the like) increased, and a nearby watering hole called Ada's became a very popular destination, even inspiring this limerick ode in a 1965 newsletter:

> Cried a veteran U.U. in his sleep,
> "This ubiquitous talk's a bit steep.
> Now they're out on the porch,
> Still waving the torch.
> I'll slide down to Ada's and weep!"

In fact Ada's was, one 1963 attendee recalls, "the second favorite activity at Blue Ridge, just behind sitting on the front porch of Lee Hall in the rocking chairs. The tavern was located at the bottom of the mountain, and was actually within walking distance, though most drove." One aspect of nightlife at Ada's (and back at the top of the mountain as well) was "dancing the Alley Cat," a dance craze that year.

On a more serious note, Southern Unitarian Universalists were beginning to openly explore and discuss race relations and the impact of the civil rights movement. A resolution was introduced and adopted at the 1963 Institute to "establish a [UU] program on race relations in the South." The annual summer gathering was indeed changing – in ways that were proving uncomfortable both for the group's Blue Ridge hosts, and for many original and long-time Blue Ridge participants. Attendance the next summer plummeted by more than 250.

The Mid-Sixties

In the wake of the discovery that the Institute was not on the Blue Ridge calendar for the summer of 1964, the Inter-District Office in Atlanta hastily formed a "Blue Ridge Liaison Committee," which managed to salvage "Blue Ridge '64." Its charge was to "re-establish communication between various parts of our program and the representatives of the Blue Ridge YMCA Assembly" – communication which had, by all indications, completely fallen apart. The committee was composed of representatives from all three districts (including some LRY representation) and other persons deemed particularly capable of resolving "tensions destructive to the spirit and purpose of the Institute, [even] to the extent of requesting departure of participants who refuse ... to cooperate ... in honoring the rules and regulations of the Blue Ridge Assembly."

Again, the fact that such language was used is indicative of the wide gap that had arisen in the behavioral expectations of the Unitarian Universalists of the mid-1960s and those of the YMCA conference center administrators. Even with those differences, the Blue Ridge Liaison Committee was able to reach an agreement that allowed the Institute to convene on July 5, 1964, at Blue Ridge.

In response to the strong negative feedback about the radical changes of the previous year, Blue Ridge '64 steered back toward the traditions of earlier Institutes. The theme talk panel was reinstituted. Each day, a different minister and two lay persons made early-afternoon presentations on the year's theme,

"Science and Human Purpose." Then, later in the afternoon, small group breakout sessions were encouraged to respond and react to the presentation. Workshops – fewer in number but also much more traditional in nature – included the tried and true "Churchmanship," along with "Unitarian Universalist History and Philosophy." Religious education workshops remained morning-only affairs, allowing their participants and leaders to partake in the adult theme talks in the afternoon. In Asheville Hall, as they had always done, the LRY'ers explored their own theme: "A Universal World – Fact or Fantasy?"

A family friendly hootenanny was held on Monday night. On

Don Male at Blue Ridge

Thursday night, in what would become a tradition spanning three decades, Don Male led an evening of stargazing. In the "Liberal Light" newsletter that day, Male invited participants to join him later for a look at the stars, writing simply, "Naked Eye Sky Event... No scientific terms. Y'all come!" Another notice in the "Liberal Light" invited "All ministers' wives ... to tea, at the cottage of Mrs. Limbert. Meet on the dining room steps before 4 o'clock, or go directly to Rhododendron Cottage." Clearly more wholesome activities, and a return to the leisurely and orderly norms of previous years, predominated Blue Ridge '64.

Though it was agreed that the Blue Ridge Liaison Committee "did a superior job" in 1964, keeping the Institute afloat and smoothing over relations with their YMCA hosts, attendance fell from 698 the previous year to an alarming 450. Long-time participant Ewald "Wally" Vockroth of Richmond was moved to write to the UUA on Sept. 1, 1964, asking that someone "investigate acquiring sites [to be] denominationally owned in regions or districts where summer conferences are now *renting* such locations." There was also talk of the LRY Dixie Federation holding its annual summer conference elsewhere in the future, away and separate from the adult Summer Institute.

Further complicating what had once been a very smooth, year-to-year flow for the Institute, the Mid-South group, which had planned and put on the 1964 gathering, failed to produce a final written report – much to the chagrin of the Floridians, who were next in the rotation for 1965.

Nonetheless, following a relatively drama-free 1964, attendance shot back up for "Blue Ridge '65," which began on Sunday, July 4th. A total of 541 people participated that year – including the LRY, which did not, in the end, break away.

The theme for the adults was "The Contemporary Revolution." Each day of the week, Monday through Friday, speakers addressed a different aspect of the theme – exploring, in order, the contemporary revolution in drama, in literature, in politics, in religion, and in "opportunity." One memorable evening movie, *The Hangman*, offered a disturbing commentary on humanity's penchant for scapegoating and prejudice.

Special guest speakers in 1965 included a Republican Congressman from Kansas, Robert F. Ellworth, and the Rev. C.T. Vivian of the Southern Christian Leadership Conference. Vivian had been one of the first "Freedom Riders," and was part of the fateful civil rights march in Selma, Ala., earlier that spring. Unitarian Universalist minister James Reeb and layperson Viola Liuzzo had been killed by white supremacists after participating in the Selma march, forging a deep bond between African-American activists, particularly those involved in the SCLC, and Unitarian Universalists, particularly those in the South. Martin Luther King, Jr., had delivered the eulogy at Reeb's funeral.

Thus, that July, a high-ranking representative of the SCLC

was sent to address the Southern UU Institute, which was itself becoming ever more vocal and visible in its civil rights activism – a fact not lost on the YMCA Blue Ridge leadership. As Nancy Grimm (now Kellman), co-director in 1965, remembers, "We were beginning to grow much too liberal for the YMCA Assembly."

Serving in many ways as the conscience of their adult counterparts (and of the Institute itself), the LRY was particularly impatient for collective Unitarian Universalist engagement in the activism and politics of the "contemporary revolution" – though as always they chose to put their own spin on the year's official theme. The LRY theme in 1965 was "The Shattering of Liberal Orthodoxy, or Slaughterhouse for Unitarian Universalist Sacred Cows." In their publicity literature for that year's program, the teens incisively wrote, "We pride ourselves on substituting rationality for emotion. In the gradual process of growing up feeling that we are, ourselves, facing the world realistically, we see our brethren and sistren still groping around in the bog of superstitions and fables. We compare our intelligent, reasonable attitude of searching for truth to others' stupid stubbornness to see life in a clear light. At this point, we become intolerant. And is it not at this point, that we turn against our own religion?"

For all their radical idealism, however, the teenagers of the 1965 Institute were still concerned with attempting to maintain appropriate decorum, as evidenced by their self-imposed community expectations. Note the many similarities (and some differences) between the LRY "Rules for Southern Liberal Religious Youth While at Blue Ridge 1965" and the version from five years earlier:

1. No climbing on fire escapes
2. All Blue Ridge swimming rules shall be observed
3. No firecrackers, alcoholic beverages, or gambling
4. No smoking in bed or in restricted areas
5. All electrical appliances shall be OK'd with registrar
6. All cars shall be grounded during the week

7. No hiking in the woods without a YMCA guide
8. No boys in girls' rooms and no girls in boys' rooms
9. Lights out at 12:00
10. Singing only during lunch and dessert at dinner
11. Violators of these rules will come before the Camp Affairs Committee with their sponsor. They may be subject to dismissal from the conference.
Note: Other rules may be adopted at the 7:00 evening meeting, and these may be discussed.

The mention of singing in the LRY rules is noteworthy. One of the most cherished (and long-standing) Blue Ridge traditions was frequent outbursts of loud, enthusiastic LRY singing during meals. Whether it was "This *liberal* light of mine, I'm gonna let it shine," union songs learned from the labor leaders in the previous decade, or the current decade's civil rights protest songs, the Blue Ridge dining hall would frequently reverberate with song. Many years the teens mimeographed a multi-page "Blue Ridge Songbook," which was distributed to adults and children alike, for singing during meals or around the campfire and at LRY-led worship services.

Also in 1965, the Planning Committee put in place a strange practice that was apparently meant to encourage all younger participants to get to bed on time. Serving as the "omega" to the traditional morning wakeup reveille's "alpha," each evening (at 8:15 for young children in Abbott Hall; 11:00 p.m. in Asheville Hall for the teens) "Taps" was played over the loudspeakers to indicate the beginning of "quiet time." By midweek, letters to the editor began to appear in the newsletter (which was known that year as "The Morning Warning"), expressing frustration with "Taps." Parents, teens and children alike soon were taking part in a "contemporary revolution" of their own against the offensive interruption.

Perhaps part of the motivation for "Taps" was a growing desire among many adult participants to get the children off to bed in order to take part in the increasing number of late-night, offsite social events. That year there was a trip to see "The Glass Menagerie," performed by the Brandywine Players, and another excursion to see "A Thousand Clowns" at the Thomas Wolfe Playhouse in Asheville. For those who weren't responsible for small children, and thus could leave campus earlier, dinner out was becoming a more popular option as well. Organized outings in 1965 included a gathering at the Pisgah Ranch, and a well-attended dinner at the Sunset Buffet. And of course, there was always Ada's. The Unitarian Universalists were growing restless – politically *and* socially. Our time at Blue Ridge was drawing to a close.

One Last Year at Blue Ridge (1966)

On February 7, 1966, the Southern Unitarian Universalist Institute signed its 16th and final conference contract with the YMCA Blue Ridge Assembly. The contract included – as it long had – exclusive use of the Blue Ridge facilities throughout the week of the Institute. But on March 25, Blue Ridge Assembly abruptly "announced that they intended to sign a contract with the Atlanta Falcons," and on April 10 the YMCA officially notified the Southern Regional Office of the UUA that the 1966 Summer Institute, which was contracted for July 3-10, would be sharing space with the brand-new National Football League expansion team. The Falcons would be holding their summer training camp at Blue Ridge, which had recently upgraded its facilities – making improvements to the old indoor gymnasium and adding a new, "covered outdoor gymnasium" called Ware Pavilion. There was also a brand new Olympic-size swimming pool.

Minutes from a Blue Ridge Planning Committee meeting held in Knoxville on April 19 indicate the anxiety this announcement created, noting that although "both Dr. Limpert, the Executive Secretary [of the Blue Ridge Assembly], and R.F. Jaenicke, the Business Manager, were apologetic ... the details of any substitute housing [caused by the addition of the Atlanta Falcons to the July schedule] have *not* been forthcoming." Meeting again four weeks later to try to get a handle on the situation, the Planning Committee expressed its frustration with Blue Ridge Assembly: "The contract with The Blue Ridge Assembly Incorporated... specified all facilities, all meeting rooms and accommodations... It must be stated in these minutes," wrote Institute Co-Chairmen John and Reina Cleland of Knoxville, "that the original intent of the contract with the Blue Ridge Assembly, honored during the past 16 years," had been violated.

In fact, come July, basement rooms in the older Blue Ridge gymnasium, which formerly were home to Institute activities such as the Craft Shop and children's art programs, had been converted into shower and locker room facilities to accommodate the football team. The kindergarten classroom and the nursery both had to be moved, and three adult meeting rooms were also lost. Most troubling, however, was the displacement of the LRY from its long-time physical and spiritual home in Asheville Hall. After some tense negotiations with Blue Ridge – and even more internal discussion and debate within the Planning Committee (which included exploring the possibility of moving the LRY to an alternative location at the Christmont Retreat Center, located a few miles away) – it was decided that the teens would be housed at Blue Ridge, in Abbott Hall. "This was a difficult decision for the Planning Committee," said Reina Cleland, "since it was recognized that Abbott Hall contained most of the rooms with private baths. The alternative of housing the LRY in a section of Lee Hall was [also] thoroughly discussed; however, it was decided that this would not be a satisfactory arrangement."

Blue Ridge Assembly agreed to charge the Institute at the lower Asheville Hall rate for housing the LRY in Abbott. With those and other last-minute accommodation snafus finally overcome, slightly less than 500 Unitarian Universalists made their way to "Blue Ridge '66," not yet knowing it would be their last pilgrimage to the much-beloved mountain.

It is perhaps appropriate that during the planning for the final Institute at Blue Ridge, the first known use of the acronym "SUUSI" appears in the records. The minutes of a Jan. 12, 1966, Planning Committee meeting, also held in Knoxville, describe the appointment of another liaison committee to coordinate with the Blue Ridge Assembly (which turned out to be a prescient move on the part of that year's planners, given what was about to unfold with the Atlanta Falcons). One of the responsibilities of the new committee was described as helping smooth the "administration of the Southern [still not 'Southeastern'] Unitarian Universalist Summer Institute (Blue Ridge)." Elsewhere in the minutes, it was noted that "the committee [shall] also function ... at the time of the SUUSI."

With space tight due to the loss of Asheville Hall, cabins proved to be even more popular housing alternatives in 1966. Lee Hall was once again filled with an awkward mix of families with small children, and adults who were not so eager to share their space, particularly in the evenings, with little ones. Feelings were raw, and Robbie Walsh, editor of the newsletter (that year called "The Blue Ridge Runner)" wrote:

> A Caution: The editor should not consider the prime purpose of the conference newsletter to be the encouraging of the free expression of opinion. The newsletter is a house organ, and its proper role is furthering the ends of the conference – one of which was enunciated by the House Chairman as seeing that everything "runs smoothly." This editor, early in the week, earnestly solicited letters to the editor. About the middle of the week, we got one that we could not, with prudence, publish. The lesson we learned was this: Unitarians can calmly and dispassionately discuss nuclear war, extramarital sex and Black Power, but some of them can be expected to fly into a blind rage on the subject of the proper discipline of their neighbor's children!"

Nonetheless, by week's end that same House Manager, Dr. Morton Gaines, wrote, "All factors considered ... the cooperation of all did allow for a smooth operation." And the Clelands wrote in the last newsletter ever printed at Blue Ridge, "We want to take this opportunity to express our appreciation for the excellent cooperation we have received from so many wonderful people. It is not possible to acknowledge in detail or individually the many fine programs and persons that have been an integral part of the Conference, [but] we are extremely grateful to the Blue Ridge YMCA staff and the entire program staff of the Uni-Uni Family Institute."

Unitarian Universalist Association President Dana Greeley visited that final Blue Ridge Institute, delivering a theme talk titled "Are We a Secular Culture?" to a packed house of adults and teens in College Hall Auditorium. He later delighted the children who, according to Peggy Palmer, chair of the R.E. Program that year, "were *very* impressed at the importance of having the President at Blue Ridge ... [to] tell them about Unitarians and Universalists all over the world."

Unitarian Universalist Association President Dana Greeley at Blue Ridge in 1966

Also of note from the 1966 editions of "The Blue Ridge Runner":

- "Special Notice: Furniture must not be dismantled or moved out into the hallway under any circumstances."

- "There will be a give and take session with Dr. Hylan Lewis this afternoon in College Hill Auditorium. For this session, all questions will come from the floor in their customary random, desultory fashion. Hopefully some semblance of order will be maintained by our capable moderator."

- "That Noisy Dining Room: The Chairman of the LRY has announced that the LRY is voluntarily giving up their mealtime stamping and table-pounding."

- "Most Unkind Cut?: A certain member of the Blue Ridge staff dropped in at the Conference Office and asked whether the Unitarians would accept a special contribution. Our faces must have shown evidence of skepticism. 'I'm serious,' he continued. 'I'd like to donate $15 for haircuts.'"

- By the end of the week, after a daily dose of one-upmanship among several congregations, it was announced that the Orlando church had retained its title as the most well-represented congregation, with 47 registrants, roughly 10 percent of the entire Institute.

Many curious participants spent their afternoons that year watching the Falcons' practices. The three-generation Vockroth family was among those watching the scrimmages, which were open to the public for an hour and a half each day. George Vockroth, son of Wally and Eoline Vockroth, had grown up at the Summer Institute. "We were at Blue Ridge every time they opened the doors," he jokes. "It was very sad when we had to leave there." But before the UUs left, George got a great memento: One afternoon at the Falcons' practice, a hulking lineman posed in a crouching stance for a photo with George's 5-year-old son Graham.

There was more than football on the minds of the Institute participants in 1966. The war in Vietnam was fodder for discussion groups, at least one workshop and even a documentary film. The Vockroths' minister in Richmond, Bill Gold, brought the film and led the discussion. Civil rights, too, remained a hot-button issue. At the end of the week, the drama workshop put on a play in the College Hill Auditorium titled "The White Sheep of the Family."

At what would be the last worship service at Blue Ridge – on Saturday, July 9, 1966 – a newly formed group that had been rehearsing together all week, the self-proclaimed "Blue Ridge Uni-Uni Choir," sang under the direction of Reed Walsh. Helen Pickett (whose children had grown to love Blue Ridge so much that they later became summer students there, serving tables in the Dining Hall) accompanied on piano. Nashville minister Robert Palmer delivered the sermon, titled "Morality for the Age of Man."

Room rates in 1966, for most participants, ranged from $8.50 per day for a single room without bath, to $18 a day for a double room with bath. LRY rates had been negotiated down to $7.50 per day per person, with most rooms including bath. Registration fees were $13 for adults, $9 for LRY, $8 for Junior High, and $3.50 for children. Babysitting in the nursery in Coker Hall remained a bargain at $7 for the week.

Some financial disputes with Blue Ridge arose when the books were closed in the fall, after it had become known that the Institute was parting ways with its long-time home. Treasurer John C. Voorhees of Knoxville wrote to Blue Ridge on Oct. 18, 1966:

Gentlemen:

Enclosed is our check No. 64 for $1346.00, the amount of your billings of Sept. 26... This is payment in full of all balances owed Blue Ridge Assembly, Inc., by Unitarian Universalist Summer Institute.

Your billings presented us with several concerns which we mention here only in the interest of accuracy and for the record.

1. Room and meals for "Jack Hann." We had no such person. His handwriting no doubt was not clear; his name is Homer Jack.

2. Program fees. Your billing [was for] 417 adults ... our estimate [is] 375 adults (270 in Lee Hall and 105 in Abbott Hall). Your billing [was for] 117 children ... our estimate [is] 80 children (in Lee Hall). [This resulted in an estimated overcharge of $113.] These figures do not include our Senior LRY group.

We understood that there was not supposed to be a program fee for cabin registrations. Also that "adults" are those 10 years of age and over.

3. The unidentified billing item of $100.00 we assume is for certain damages to rooms in Lee Hall.

In all, it was not the most pleasant way to end a 16-year relationship with Blue Ridge, which for literally every 1966 registrant except Alfred Hobart was the only Summer Institute home they had ever known. But those Blue Ridge participants who are alive today remember not the difficulties, but *the feeling*– and still speak wistfully of those long, lazy summer weeks spent with hundreds of fun-loving, like-minded companions. The rocking chairs on the porch of Lee Hall, the strains of "nothin' could be finer than to be in Carolina in the morning" resounding in the mountain air, the enthusiastic singing of the LRY'ers and the bugle call of reveille – these have since become the stuff of SUUSI legend. And absence, certainly, makes the heart grow fonder.

Chapter 3:
The Nomad Years

For eight summers, from 1967 through 1974, those Southern Unitarian Universalists for whom an annual reunion in the mountains with beloved friends and colleagues had become a way of life struggled simply to keep the tradition alive. In that short period, their Institute migrated to four different locations, and even missed convening one year altogether. It was of little consolation that their difficulties were reflective of the times: They were living through one of the most tumultuous periods in the country's history, with society seemingly coming unraveled at the seams in a traumatic era of war and assassination, cultural upheaval and civil unrest. Within the Unitarian Universalist Association itself, any institutional stability that had begun to take shape as a result of the merger of the two small denominations was rocked by crises of both funding and identity. UUA districts were restructured, and regional staff was reorganized – over and over again. All this upheaval could not have come at a worse time for the Institute, which was facing its own organizational and institutional challenges.

It is a wonder that the Southern Unitarian Institute survived at all. But survive it did, though by the end of the "Nomad Years," it was a very different institution than the one that had parted ways with Blue Ridge in 1966.

Brevard Music Center (1967-1968)

L ess than two weeks after his final letter and payment to the Blue Ridge Assembly, treasurer John C. Voorhees deposited, on Oct. 31, 1966, all of the Institute's remaining financial assets – $725.27 – into a new savings account at the Park National Bank in Knoxville, under the name "Southern Unitarian Universalist Summer Institute." The next day, on Nov. 1, Manuel Holland, a native of Franklin, N.C., but most recently the minister in Framingham, Mass., was hired as the Executive Secretary of the Thomas Jefferson District. The newly independent T.J. District was to be co-sponsor of the 1967 Institute, before taking over sole responsibility for maintaining the Summer Institute in the future.

Two thousand dollars were added to the SUUSI bank account from the Southern UU Inter-District Committee's budget, in order to provide startup costs for the 1967 Institute (even though a site had not yet been located). Meanwhile, the T.J. District Board – which included Voorhees and District President Florence Cargill, both of whom were long-time, active Blue Ridgers – was working feverishly with Holland to find a new home for "the SUUSI." In January 1967, they announced that the Summer Institute would be held June 25-July 2 at the Brevard Music Center ("the Summer Cultural Center of the South") in Brevard, N.C.:

> We are very fortunate in obtaining a beautiful new location for our Summer Institute '67 – the Brevard Music Center...The Center covers 116 acres of scenic beauty. The lodge and cabins are located on a wooded hillside area overlooking a peaceful mountain lake on the edge of Pisgah National Forest, with its scenic drives, waterfalls, picnic and camping areas.

The T.J. District office was located on the outskirts of Charlotte, just over a hundred miles from Brevard. With full-time secretarial support for Holland, the office provided localized asssistance for volunteers from south Florida, whose turn it was to help plan the 1967 programming. Luke and Ellen Dohner were the Institute co-chairmen. The theme was "The Individual on Trial." Registration fees were intentionally unchanged from the prior year at Blue Ridge, and the cost of most accommodations remained in line with what it had been previously. Participants could now choose between living in a dormitory room, small four-person cabins or their own camper or trailer.

A month before "the SUUSI" – which was to be the earliest summer week the Institute had ever gathered – all pre-registrants received notice of several changes to the accustomed routine, in the form of a "Poop Sheet for Registrants, Southern Unitarian Universalist Summer Institute." (Note in item #3 that the pronunciation of the acronym had not yet been settled):

1. Please bring your own linens, towels, sheets, pillowcases and your own pillows and your own blankets or your own sleeping bag.

2. The first meal of the Institute will be Sunday evening, at 6:00 p.m., for LRY and Junior Highs; at 6:30 p.m. for children and adults.

3. Speaking of sleeping bags – for old timers, a word to the wise. It will be cooler at night slightly, and warmer during the day, than at Blue Ridge. In addition, the buildings where programs will be held at night are open on all sides. For new friends of our SUUSI (pronounced Suzi?), bring an extra sweater; it's mountain country, about 2,750 elevation.

4. For campers – you may camp at Pisgah National Forest. It's only three miles distant. Write to the District Ranger's Office, U.S. Forest Services, Pisgah Forest, North Carolina. Meals at Brevard will be $25.00 for the week, or pay at the cafeteria door for each meal. There is also a use fee of $5.00 and, of

course, the Institute registration.

You may elect to park your camper (no tents), for sleeping only, in a regular parking space adjacent to the cabin of a friend who will share his toilet facilities with you, rather than go to live in a dormitory. The fee for meals and parking for the week [is] the same as [the] dormitory, i.e., $55.00.

5. And now about the little people – if you need a crib, please let the registrars know immediately, so rentals can be arranged.

Each weekday of the Institute, after lunch, a different theme speaker addressed the adults on an aspect of "The Individual on Trial." On Tuesday, the speaker was celebrated poet John Beecher, whose radical, activist poetry focusing on racism, civil rights and labor rights shone a harsh light on societal ills in the 20th century American South. Beecher, a descendant of *Uncle Tom's Cabin* author (and Unitarian) Harriet Beecher Stowe, had been among the artists blacklisted during the McCarthy era, and so was a riveting figure for the Unitarian Universalist audience at Brevard. Beecher spoke about "The Individual on Trial by Society." On Thursday, Julian Bond, then a member of the Georgia House of Representatives, spoke on "The Individual on Trial by the Future."

Programming for children and LRY took place outdoors, in picnic shelters and covered pavilions. Unlike the family-style, all-you-could-eat dining hall service at Blue Ridge, meals at Brevard were cafeteria-style. There would no longer be an ongoing controversy about poor tipping; in fact, the information distributed by the Institute happily proclaimed, "No tipping!"

Given the significant logistical challenges involved in moving such a large community, along with all its programming and infrastructure – not to mention intangibles like its traditions and "feeling"– to a new location on short notice, the first year at Brevard came off remarkably well. A total of 266 people participated, a little more than half the number that had attended Blue Ridge the

LRY'ers wait for dinner outside the dining hall at Brevard in 1968

year before. But the Institute had been successfully perpetuated. SUUSI survived the move.

The following year was to be the last summer at Brevard, however. Manuel Holland issued a word of warning to congregations in the T.J. District late in 1967, writing that the "Summer Institute is in trouble – maybe," because no volunteer lay leaders could be found for the Planning Committee. As the months passed, Holland, in his capacity as the Thomas Jefferson District Executive Secretary, gradually took on the responsibility for coordinating the planning of the 1968 Institute. Mrs. Hans Schmettau of Spartanburg eventually volunteered to be the registrar. Sandi Whidden would be chair of the LRY. Pete and Mary Leta Tolleson of Charleston were brought in to lead the junior high group. Mrs. Jesse Riley of Charlotte was in charge of the pre-school program, while Mrs. John Ralston of Savannah led the children's program.

The Institute began on Sunday, June 23, 1968, but ended on Saturday for the first time in several years. Publicity materials noted that the cost would therefore "be less than last year, and linens will be supplied as well."

When participants gathered for their second and final year at Brevard Music Center, it was less than three weeks after the assassination of Robert F. Kennedy, and just two and a half months after the assassination of Martin Luther King, Jr. Against this traumatic backdrop, an unspecified number of registrants (presumably, attendance was still dwindling) dealt with two different themes – "Developing an Awareness of Group Process" and "Affecting the Future of Liberal Religion." The latter conversations were led by Philip Giles.

One of the attendees in 1968 was a young girl named Lynn Thompson, who many years later, as Lynn Wheal, would become SUUSI Youth Director. Conveniently for Thompson, her grandparents lived in Brevard. Accompanied by her mother, Margaret Thompson (now Baucus), Lynn spent the last week of June that summer visiting SUUSI by day, and staying at her grandparents' home at night. "I was going to a very conservative junior high school in Raleigh at the time," she says. "I had never seen so much tie-dye in my life! It was a real eye-opener. It was certainly a stretch for me – but a good stretch."

Margaret recalls how daughter Lynn had changed by the time they got home to Raleigh. "The girls in Lynn's school, the social group, were all very concerned about appearances – who had the nicest clothes, who was wearing the right dress," she says. "After Brevard, Lynn only wanted to wear jeans. Her values had taken a 180-degree turn."

Lynn remembers being struck by the fact that "the teens were giving each other massages, taking trust walks. Everyone hung out together. It was wonderful."

Though he was not a UU, Lynn's grandfather, Charles Davis, led some hikes for participants in the Pisgah National Forest. He came home one night saying, "Those Unitarians are crazy. They don't even know what to wear on a hike – most of them had on flip flops and shorts!"

Families enjoying the lake at Brevard Music Center

Manuel Holland's wife Olive has a different kind of memory of Brevard 1968. "Summer Institute was our honeymoon that year," she says. "Gene Pickett had performed our wedding in Atlanta just before the Institute. Then I had to go back to Florida, where I was living at the time, before going to meet Manuel at Brevard. I got there in the middle of the week."

The Hollands came away from that Institute with a new member of the family – a puppy, which they named "Ti." The cabins at Brevard Music Center had the names of musical notes, and the one in which the Hollands were staying was called Cabin Ti. "One person who was there – I can't recall who – had brought a pregnant dog," says Olive. "She had puppies during the week there. So we adopted this very happy, cute little puppy and named her 'Ti.' Ti would leap up in the air, and her ears would fly out like wings. She was a spaniel/beagle mix, so we called her our 'Flying Spiegel.' Ti was like a wedding gift to us. She stayed with us for years. In fact, she died on our 14th wedding anniversary."

The Hollands were among many Institute attendees who

would wander into downtown Brevard in the evenings for the town's nightly outdoor square dancing. Unfortunately, it was some interaction with the local residents that led to the Institute being asked not to return to the Music Center the following year. It seems that some couples – both adult couples and teenage couples – within the Institute community were interracial, and when locals saw those couples holding hands and being affectionate in public, a minor scandal erupted.

Suddenly, once again, SUUSI was looking for a new home.

Sewanee (1969)

If the Institute had been "in trouble," in Manuel Holland's words, before 1968, it was really in danger of collapsing now. Enter Don Male, an energetic UU volunteer (he would later become a minister) from middle Tennessee. Male worked at the University of the South in Sewanee, Tenn., and was able to find accommodations for the Institute at the college in the summer of '69. The theme of the Institute that year was "The Tetrology of the Disaffected."

"Who are the disaffected?" asked the publicity material before answering its own question: "The blacks, the poor, the youth, the forgotten." Ironic, then, that for the first time ever, the 1969 Institute met without the Liberal Religious Youth, who had become such an integral part of the community and its traditions. Whether due to scheduling or space conflicts, or simply the LRY's desire to set out on their own, the adult and family camp in 1969 was held early in the summer – June 15-21 – while LRY held its conference at the end of the summer, Aug. 3-9 (also at Sewanee). Thus, while adult UUs were discussing how "youth" were among the "disaffected" in society, the youth were not around to participate, save for a handful of teenagers who accompanied their parents. (Though it was known that LRY would be meeting later in the summer, at least teenagers were *invited* to the main conference; a line in the publicity material reads "Senior High Program: For those Senior

Highers who wish to come, there will be a special study of liberal religion, the role of the local church, and the development of a personal philosophy of life.") Understandably, most teens opted to attend instead in August, to be with their peers.

Among them was Lynn Thompson. "Sewanee was a gorgeous campus," she recalls. "It's on a plateau, and the views were simply amazing. I remember going to a teen worship service in this beautiful old, ornate chapel. As a UU kid, I had never been in such an impressive worship space – the stained glass, the high, arching ceiling..."

The historic All Saints Chapel provided quite a contrast to the lodging the teens were assigned. "We were staying in some old, derelict dorms," Thompson says. "It was like a barracks. There

All Saints Chapel in Sewanee

were old-timey sinks hanging on the walls. It was a dump."

The LRY's adult leader, Alan Downing, also happened to be Thompson's Raleigh youth group advisor. He would soon become chairman of the reunited Summer Institute, when it relocated to Appalachian State two years hence.

Olive Holland remembers a culinary challenge the adult Institute faced at Sewanee. Evidently, Sewanee's cook was off duty the week the Unitarian Universalists came. "What I remember was boiling lots and lots of pots of water. I think all we ate was spaghetti," she says. "Someone had to feed the hungry masses! It sure wasn't very good, but at least everyone survived."

There was also controversy at Sewanee, in the form of racial tension provoked by one of the adult theme speakers, an African-American representative of the Southern Christian Leadership Conference. In the hot summer of 1969, just a year after the assassinations of MLK and RFK and only

Flyer advertising the 1969 Summer Institute at the University of the South in Sewanee, Tenn.

a month before the first moon landing, the SCLC speaker, who had been invited to expound upon the subject of "disaffected blacks," lit into the self-satisfied (and almost exclusively white) Unitarian Universalists, dismissing the denomination's efforts at promoting racial justice as merely an exercise in "liberal guilt." This was a far cry from the tone of solidarity shared by the SCLC's representative in 1965 in the wake of the murders of James Reeb and Viola Liuzzo. Institute participants were hurt and upset.

Singer/songwriters Pete and Mary Leta Tolleson, who were at Sewanee again as volunteers working with the junior high youth group, were deeply troubled by the talk. In an effort to heal both themselves and the community, they wrote a song, "Domiabra," which they performed at the talent night near the end of the week at Sewanee.

"The speaker – I wish I could remember his name, but I can't – had used the story of an African, actually Ghanan, tradition," says Pete. " '*Domiabra*' means 'Come join me if you love me.' He told us that, when the time comes to start a new village in Ghana, a young man goes out to scout for its location. When he finds the right place, after creating a clearing around which to build the new village, he returns and sings out 'Domiabra.' Those villagers who want to be part of starting a new community – those who 'love him' – go together to build a new village."

The Tollesons' song was a poignant, prophetic call for reconciliation:

Domiabra, oh my brother, in the jungle that is life.
Domiabra, oh my sister, we can clear away the strife.
Come and join me if you love me, come and join me if you can.
Domiabra, domiabra! Come and join me, man to man.

Domiabra, all you people, open doors and windows wide.
Domiabra, all truth seekers, clear away the fear inside.
Come and join me if you love me, come and join me if you can.
Domiabra, domiabra! Come and join me, man to man.

Domiabra, everybody, learn to love and learn to give.
Domiabra, all my brothers, clear the mind and learn to live.
Come and join me if you love me, come and join me if you can.
Domiabra, domiabra! Come and join me, man to man.

(lyrics by Mary C.B. Tolleson © 1970, reprinted by permission)

As Pete put it in his introduction to the song, "This song is a call to community of a far broader kind, in a jungle far more dense and threatening. [It is] a call to community in a true human brotherhood on this little spaceship we call Earth."

With that call, the Institute's one and only year at Sewanee came to an end.

1970?

Informal, oral history has always held that the Southeast Summer Institute has met annually, in an unbroken line, all the way back to that first summer at Lake Waccamaw. Yet there is no evidence that this is true. In fact, extensive research has indicated that apparently there was *no* Summer Institute in 1970. There is no record of such a gathering either in the SUUSI archives, or in the records of the Unitarian Universalist Association or the Thomas Jefferson District – the latter organization having been, at the time, in complete disarray. In fact the *only* mention of 1970 comes in the form of a terse, handwritten note signed by Don Male, sent to the UUA in Boston, probably in early 1970 in reply to the UUA's annual request for summer camp updates. The note says simply that "Our summer institute plans have sadly fallen through a crack in the denominational floor."

What Male was referring to was a financial crisis that threatened, quite literally, the continued viability of the Unitarian Universalist Association itself. When newly elected UUA President Bob West took office in the summer of 1969, the UUA was operating at a $1 million annual deficit, had spent all of its unrestricted funds, and had borrowed nearly half a million dollars – a bank note that was imminently due. (An interesting account of this period in UUA history can be found in West's 2007 memoir *Crisis and Change: My Years as President of the Unitarian Universalist Association*.)

Obviously, drastic budget cuts were in order, and so in mid-November, 1969, half of all UUA staff, including all district personnel, were terminated. Manuel Holland and his support staff at the Thomas Jefferson District office found themselves without jobs, and the T.J. District Board – whose president was Don Male – was left scrambling, with no funds and no staff.

"The District was falling apart," says Holland. "What to do about the Summer Institute was just one of its many problems."

Given these facts, and the complete lack of any records or information regarding a Summer Institute in 1970, it must be concluded that there was no Institute that year. Male's widow, Sue Male, offers confirmation, saying, "I remember that there was one year we did not have SUUSI, and I think it was 1970."

Appalachian State (1971-1973)

B ut Don Male, along with another very active member of the Thomas Jefferson District Board, Rosemary Morris (later Burns), refused to let the Summer Institute die. With a winning combination of passion and perseverance, they convinced the T.J. Board that the Institute was worth saving, and together they eventually found yet another host location. On Aug. 23, 1971 (a Monday), the Southeast Unitarian Universalist Summer Institute reconvened for the first time in fully 26 months, on the campus of Appalachian State University in Boone, N.C. "App State," as many who attended the Institute in the early 1970s still call it, had recently evolved from a small teachers college into a full-service university, and was entering a period of growth and transformation under the leadership of Chancellor Herbert Wey.

The reunion at Appalachian State was marked not only by joyous reconnection, but also by the addition of many new, younger faces to the community. There were people who had never been to Blue Ridge, but whose ideas and needs were about to create new traditions and leave an indelible mark on the culture of the Summer Institute.

The first thing people noticed about the new location was the type of accommodations it offered (and did not offer). Several brand-new, high-rise dormitories reflected the transformation of the ASU campus. All SUUSI participants (it is not known how many actually attended in 1971) were housed in one of these dorms. Long waits for the elevator made for very grumpy campers, as did the ubiquitous presence of loud earth-moving machines just outside the dormitory, where a new football field was being built.

Each floor of the dorm had its own self-contained kitchenette and dining area, so instead of eating together in a common dining hall or cafeteria, for most meals attendees prepared their own food and then ate together as a floor. Other participants chose to dine out at local restaurants. Thus mealtime, which at Blue Ridge and even at Brevard and Sewanee had served to create a sense of community, is remembered at Boone as one of the main factors that contributed to a sense of isolation and frustration.

Furthermore, though the timing of breakfast and lunch was somewhat coordinated (given daytime programming that included children's activities, and speakers and workshops for the adults), by the late afternoon and into the evening, folks were left to follow their own, widely varying, personal interests and schedules. Different groups migrated hither and yon in search of food (and drink). "The feel of the whole thing was pretty fractured," recalls Jill Menadier, who was a newcomer and teenager at Boone. "It definitely did not feel like a community."

One Boone restaurant became popular with SUUSI-goers because of the entertaining antics of its wait staff. It seems the servers at this establishment – the name has been lost to history – were theater and music majors at the university, and throughout the evening (often, even *while* they were serving their tables) would sing songs, or engage one another in lively banter across the room. They even performed short skits or scenes from plays that they were rehearsing as entertainment for their customers – who that week were primarily SUUSI attendees.

In addition to the dining dilemma, Institute planners had to deal with the fact that there was either no appropriate, or no affordable, on-campus space available for the children's program.

Youth Staff made do with rented space at a nearby Presbyterian church. Parents (and children) recall walking up and down the steep, rugged hills of Boone, multiple times a day, to get to and from activities. But while they complained about the walk, and especially the hills, there were no complaints about the children's programming.

Led by the capable and charismatic Pam Cline, who had been pressed into duty as Youth Director as soon as she arrived at her first Summer Institute in 1971, the Youth Staff included just Andy and Pam Wasilewski, along with a couple of teenage helpers. Though small in number, they helped create a lifetime of wonderful memories for the SUUSI children who were present at Boone. Offsite adventures, often on chartered buses, included hikes along the Blue Ridge Parkway or swimming and outdoor play at Seven Devils (better known in the winters as a ski resort). In 1972, there was actually even ice skating at SUUSI, at an ice rink located along the main drag in Boone. A young Karyn Machler – who would become SUUSI Director in 2003 – cut her lip wide open falling onto another child's skate blade on that particular outing.

Other Institute volunteers were instrumental in fostering a wide array of enjoyable intergenerational activities. Arts and crafts workshops appealed to young and old alike. Machler remembers an all-ages macrame workshop led by Jimmie Benedict. Participants also enjoyed athletics, including football and basketball games organized by Vince "Boomslang" Meade, pitting one dormitory floor against another. In 1972, Meade had been recruited by some of the long-time, dedicated Institute participants at his church in Fort Lauderdale to, as he puts it, "go explore the mountains of North Carolina – oh, and while you're at it, be the Athletic Director."

Meade proceeded to tap into the rivalries that were developing between the various dormitory floors, turning them into friendly competition. In the process, he developed something of a rapport with the newly hired ASU basketball coach, Press Maravich, who he says "thought it was very ironic that the Unitarians had their own Athletic Director."

In the early 1970s, the Unitarian Universalist Association published "About Your Sexuality," a controversial human sexuality curriculum for adolescents. SUUSI became one of the first training sites where adult AYS teachers could learn about the curriculum and receive the official training and certification that was required to teach AYS back home in their local congregations. Both at Boone and at later SUUSI locations, William Benedict – an adult LRY advisor from the Knoxville church – was in charge of training AYS teachers from all over the Southeast. "It was very time consuming," he says. "It took up most of my week, but it was well worth it – very rewarding. I felt we really had a positive impact on promoting healthy sexuality education in our churches."

However, not all conversations about human sexuality at SUUSI during the "Nomad Years" were as appropriately expressed. An uproar occurred when a male participant posted flyers around campus, seeking female sexual partners. Community meetings were held, strong feelings on both sides were aired, and – eventually – cooler heads prevailed. Another issue arose when Summer Institute T-shirts were introduced that prominently featured the letters "UU" in a way that tended to accentuate the breasts of female participants.

But by far the biggest controversy centered around notorious UU minister Billy Joe Nichols, who was asked to give a theme talk at Appalachian State in 1973. Nichols had gained national attention for having an "exotic dancer" perform a striptease in one of his Sunday services back home in Richardson, Texas. The flamboyant minister raised eyebrows by arriving at SUUSI piloting his own private plane, accompanied by an extremely young girlfriend. As a clergy colleague who was at Boone that year put it, "It was simply jaw-dropping that the Institute would invite someone who had publicly embarrassed the denomination to be one of its theme speakers."

The highly anticipated theme talk began as an explication of the Humanist Manifesto II – Nichols was one of the signers of that document – but quickly became what one observer described as "vulgar." Nichols' talk culminated with the minister from Texas leading the attendees in singing the chorus of Jimmy Buffett's recently released underground hit, "Why Don't We Get Drunk (and Screw)."

"I felt like I had to wash my hands when it was all over," another person reported. "It was *that* crude." Yet other participants found Nichols, and his sexuality-laced, anti-establishment message "liberating." This much is clear: Incidents such as Nichols' theme talk reflected a radical liberalization that was taking place within the SUUSI community – one that paralleled trends which were beginning to shape not only Unitarian Universalism, but society itself.

A case in point: The two most heavily subscribed workshops at SUUSI in 1973 were called "Open Marriage" and "Nude Massage." Many long-time Institute participants – those who recalled the good old days at Blue Ridge – were appalled by such changes, and found themselves "longing for the years when we were a week-long leadership training institute that provided wholesome training and education," as one Summer Institute veteran put it. A minister who was at Boone was more blunt: "The behavior had become downright appalling." SUUSI was changing rapidly, and tensions within the community began to mount.

If the years in Boone were characterized by outrageous behavior, none was more dangerous than the practices that were developing around a new tradition called Serendipity. Appalachian State was located in a "dry" county (though many an empty or half-consumed wine bottle or beer can was said to be seen on the various floors in the SUUSI high-rise dorm). The response of the SUUSI community to meeting in a dry county was, literally, to take to the road. As *some* had done at Blue Ridge, now *most* adults moved their nightlife activity off campus. Participants would dress up for Serendipity, with men wearing suits or even tuxedos and women in formal evening dresses, then drive to the nightly dance at a fraternal lodge in the ski village of Blowing Rock – in a neighboring county.

The merriment frequently lasted into the wee hours of the night. Staff members – including 1973 Co-Chair Dave Link and youth staffer Andy Wasilewski – provided shuttle service to and from Serendipity in VW buses owned by various SUUSI-ites. Yet each night, many participants chose to do their own driving, setting out over the curving, two-lane mountain roads. Thankfully, there were no reports of accidents or injuries – but drinking (and the need to accommodate it) had become a major problem for SUUSI.

Upon the move to Boone in 1971, the LRY (still an independent, teen-run organization) had rejoined the Summer Institute community. As in previous years, they were housed separately from the other participants – though at Appalachian State, this meant only that they were given the top floor of the same high-rise dorm that accommodated everyone else. This arrangement presented several issues, not the least of which was the fact that there was only one, co-ed, bathroom for the teens, all of whom shared both toilet and shower facilities. (One teenager from that era remembers that co-ed bathrooms "were no big deal to us.")

The real problem the unsupervised teenagers presented, however, was their seemingly insatiable desire to throw everything from water balloons to watermelons off the top of the building. SUUSI lore has it that one such projectile landed smack in the back seat of an open convertible owned by the Appalachian State chancellor. Whether or not this story is apocryphal, one thing is sure: LRY was banned for what would be SUUSI's last year at Boone in 1973. Teens who did choose to come that year were housed in rooms with their parents, and no age-specific programming was provided.

Although one teenager at the time, Lynn Thompson, says that "from my standpoint, it was the adults who were most out of control back then, not the teens," it would be nearly a decade before a structured program for teens returned to SUUSI. When it did, it was Lynn Wheal – formerly Lynn Thompson – who made it happen, in her new role as Youth Director.

By that third and final summer at Appalachian State – even with the banning of LRY – Institute attendance had rebounded to the point that SUUSI required two adjoining high-rise dorms. While there was very little outdoor activity, and though nightlife opportunities were still limited to Serendipity (now under the direction of June Preston), workshop offerings were increasing, and participants were eagerly signing up. One memorable workshop was a popular "fishbowl" discussion in which members of different demographic groups shared what it was like to be a certain gender or age. An effort was made to bring the community together one evening with a "Talent Night," emceed by Fred Thompson.

It was also during the Appalachian State years that the Summer Institute gave birth to its first – though not its last – spinoff conference. Several members of the Miami church, including Bob Sax (who was SUUSI treasurer) and Bud Evans put together what today would be called a "Decompression Party" (a gathering of SUUSI friends some weeks or months after SUUSI, to reconnect and reminisce). They called their party "Is There Life After Boone?" – and the answer, apparently, was a resounding "Yes!" The group then decided to plan a weekend-long campout at the Miami church, which they proclaimed to be "Life After Boone!" Thus, the Southeast Winter Institute in Miami (SWIM) was born; it still continues, now four decades later.

Despite all its troubles at Boone, the vast majority of participants loved the "reinvented" Summer Institute, if not the campus where it was being held. Bob Irwin of Jacksonville describes how he was "dragged to Boone in 1973 by a friend from the Jacksonville church. I had only joined a couple of months earlier. I was simply blown away by the SUUSI experience; I loved it so much that I came back for the next 37 consecutive years!"

That same year, John (now Alexis) Jones had an experience that served to cement his connection to SUUSI music for decades to come. "I was wandering around one day and I happened to enter an auditorium in which Phyllis Hiller was practicing "Love Is a Circle" (her creation) with a group of children. My recollection of that experience still brings tears. It was my peak experience of the week. I was touched by Phyllis and the children, and the camaraderie generated there." Years later, Jones preserved some of the music from that period in SUUSI's history by producing a cassette tape called "Sounds of SUUSI."

Morris Hudgins, whose first SUUSI was 1973, had only been a Unitarian Universalist for a few months when he became the new minister in Boca Raton, Florida, and discovered that 16 members of his congregation were about to make a pilgrimage to North Carolina for a much-beloved summer camp – and that they wanted him to go with them. "I didn't have any idea what to expect," he says, "but I was immediately enamored with the whole experience. Even then, SUUSI was a remarkable place."

Unfortunately, Appalachian State University was not nearly as enamored with the Unitarian Universalists. The Billy Joe Nichols controversy, the tossing of objects both messy and dangerous out of windows, the excessive drinking (in a dry county), damages to furniture and property that ultimately included a small fire (the drapes in one building caught fire, whether by accident or act of vandalism) – all had a cumulative effect, and ASU officials made it clear that SUUSI would not be welcome back at Boone in 1974. The Summer Institute was left, once again, without a home.

Fontana Village (1974)

William Benedict – the architect, LRY advisor and AYS instructor from Knoxville – was to be the Institute Chairman in 1974. He remembers being "very involved in the effort to find somewhere for us to go. We knew we weren't going to be coming back to Appalachian State, so a group was quickly put in place to find another location. As it happened, I had worked for the TVA [the Tennessee Valley Authority] and was familiar with Fontana Village."

The Village was a network of cabins, recreational facilities and meeting areas connected by a dining hall. It had accommodated the engineers and workers who built Fontana Dam in the 1940s. Located well off the beaten path, in a remote area just inside the North Carolina border, Fontana Lake had been created by the TVA with the damming of the Little Tennessee River. At 480 feet in height, Fontana Dam is still the largest dam east of the Mississippi, and the combination of an imposing monument to human engineering prowess with the area's stunning natural beauty had turned Fontana Village into a popular tourist destination after the construction crews departed. The lights of the village and the dam could be seen for miles in the heavy North Carolina forest.

As the summer of 1974 approached, however, America was living through an energy crisis, and the proprietors of Fontana Village were concerned about simply keeping those lights on. Gasoline shortages and rationing made for gloomy predictions of a poor tourist season. Thus, when approached by a desperate William Benedict about the possibility of renting out space to several hundred Unitarian Universalists for an entire week, Fontana eagerly accepted his proposal. The Institute was saved again.

On Sunday, July 21, 1974, an unknown number of UUs drove all the way to the dead end of a twisting, nine-mile long road deep in the mountains of North Carolina – and walked right into what has gone down as the most torturous check-in process in the history of SUUSI. A line quickly developed in front of the lone registration table; soon the line stretched out the door and well beyond, continuing to grow throughout the afternoon and evening. Those who were there tell of waiting three or four hours simply to register.

A combination of factors – including the last-minute nature of the arrangements with Fontana, poor program planning, a decided dearth of pre-publicity, the absence of professional district staff support for the pre-registration process and, according to one witness, the "very heavy consumption of vodka" at the registration table itself – made for a perfect storm. Participants had not selected their workshops in advance, or even been assigned housing. People were scrambling to sign up for the more popular workshops, while less well-known offerings went completely unsubscribed. Men and women who were not partners were in some cases randomly assigned to room together. Words like "disaster" and "dysfunction" were used to describe the scene. One person called it "an outright zoo."

Yet despite this rocky start – and unusually hot and muggy weather – SUUSI's only week at Fontana Village provided many fond memories while helping to create several important SUUSI traditions. It was at Fontana that an organized Nature Program began. Chuck Harty, who had been leading groups on outdoor adventures for years as a member of the Miami UU Congregation, was recruited by Bud Evans to do the same thing at SUUSI. "Bud asked if I would go with him to the mountains and do what I loved to do anyway," Harty recalls. "All I had to do was lead one outdoor activity per day, for five days. How could I resist?"

Among the programs Harty offered that week were horseback riding, hiking and river rafting. One hike on the Appalachian Trail proved to be so popular that Harty had to enlist his teenage sons to help lead the oversized group. But it was the rafting trip that Poncho Heavener and his daughter Tasha remember best. "It was such a rush – the thrill of the experience. It really turned me on to whitewater rafting," says Poncho. "After that, I went on rafting trips every year at Radford."

Appropriate, then, that the theme for the 1974 Summer Institute at Fontana was "Other Rushes and Other Highs." Certainly, the nascent Nature Program – which Harty continued to lead, at Radford, through 1978 – enjoyed a very auspicious beginning, and over the next few years grew beyond Harty's, or anyone else's, wildest expectations.

Ted and Janice Machler also made their mark on SUUSI that summer at Fontana by starting what they called a "Middle Program" for early adolescents and teens. It was designed to fill a glaring gap in Institute programming that dated back even before LRY had been banned at Boone. Pam Cline was still providing wonderful activities for the younger children at Fontana (she would continue to do so into the Radford years), but transitional and older youth had been longing for the kind of community they had heard their older LRY siblings talk about. The Machlers resolved to provide just that – in a safe and supportive atmosphere.

There was swimming in the lake. Late-night group discussions encouraged the youth to talk about matters both serious and silly. One new innovation, a "Love Feast," was so popular that it became a Teen Program staple for decades to come. Allen Bergal has very vivid memories of that first teen Love Feast. "It was so neat to be fed, and to feed someone else. A walnut, a piece of celery, a grape, an orange slice, an apple slice, a Triscuit cracker, a cherry tomato – I can still remember each item," he says. "And you fed each other very slowly and deliberately. The whole thing probably lasted an hour and a half. It was very focused – and it was very cool."

Many Fontana attendees remember that the cabins were very spread out; often folks had to walk quite a distance to visit with friends who lived in a different cabin. This, of course, was a dramatic change from the compact, high-rise dormitories of Appalachian State. But like Boone, Fontana was very hilly. One hill, in particular, would alter youth programming for a generation of SUUSI children to come, leading to the cherished childhood rite of passage known as "Dirty Day."

The un-air-conditioned (as they all were) Fontana cabin occupied by the Machler family – Ted and Janice, as well as their daughters Meredith and Karyn and sons Kurtis and Teddy – was a particularly remote cabin located at the bottom of a small hill. A small, *muddy* hill. According to eyewitness Karyn (who swears she didn't participate, saying she feared getting in "big trouble"), one rainy afternoon some children began sliding down the hill. "It was hilarious," she says. "At Fontana, all the cabins had these chenille sheets. The kids slid down this hill, and instead of running right back up the hill, they decided to crawl in through my parents' bedroom window, stumble across the bed, and run out the door. Then they'd head back up the hill and slide back down, getting as muddy as possible in the process. They'd climb back through the window, and do it all over again."

Among the participants in that proto-Dirty Day was Pam Cline's daughter Rene. Others alleged to have taken part are Shane and Peter Benedict, along with Kurtis and Meredith Machler. Instead of getting in trouble, however, the sliding children eventually drew a crowd of bemused adults, who cheered them on. Dirty Day was born, and the next year at Radford, it became an official, SUUSI-sanctioned youth activity.

One impromptu adult workshop also became a hit that year at Fontana. In response to the registration debacle at the beginning of the week – which resulted in a large number of attendees not getting into the workshops they wanted – Toby Barksdale created a "drop-in workshop" which he held each afternoon on the porch of his cabin. It was known as "Conversations with Toby."

For those participants who were lucky enough to get a space in their desired workshop, many lasting memories were created. Morris Hudgins facilitated a workshop called "Power Play," in which registrants worked through an intense exploration of group and individual power dynamics that quite literally, according to more than one participant, changed people's lives. Hudgins led 25 people – divided into five groups of five – as they interacted with other groups, negotiating for "power."

"All week you could hear and see people scheming and strategizing," he recalls. "It was fascinating to watch. They were very engaged, and it brought out some powerful insights about personalities and the dynamics of power." The workshop got such rave reviews that it was offered again and again, well into the Radford years.

Another popular workshop was titled simply "The Cave." It offered participants the opportunity to role-play a doomsday scenario and examine the impact of individual and community values on decision-making. The goal was to re-create human society following a hypothetical nuclear war. "That workshop was a deeply bonding experience," says Elle Long, who attended her first SUUSI at Fontana that year and has not missed a year since (even after she moved to California in 1990). Long speaks for many SUUSI regulars when she says, "After my first week, I made an important decision: SUUSI would be a permanent part of my life."

Also heavily subscribed at Fontana was a workshop called "Alternative Lifestyles," co-led by Poncho Heavener and Miami minister Lee Strassman. Appealing to the mood of personal exploration and experimentation so prevalent at the time, the workshop included sessions of "primal scream therapy" in the Fontana woods. According to the story, several recently divorced or separated women, in particular, took to the screaming part of the workshop with great enthusiasm. Perhaps he was inspired by the sounds emanating from the woods (which could be heard all over the Village), or perhaps he also had been a participant in the "Alternative Lifestyles" workshop – but Ted Machler that week took the Middle Program teens out into the woods for some late-night screaming of their own, causing a good deal of alarm among locals and SUUSI-goers alike.

But it is safe to say there was no activity more notorious than the 1974 edition of the "Nude Massage" workshop. Having been wildly popular the previous summer at Boone, it was once again filled to capacity. Described carefully as "sensuality, not sexuality," the workshop was scheduled in a multi-purpose room at the Lodge, where high screen partitions were placed to provide privacy for the participants. Unfortunately, however, several children were able to peek in and see the adults – who were in various states of undress – massaging one another. According to one story, the kids peeked in through a strategically located window. By another account, they climbed a ladder and looked *over* the partition. Regardless of their method, the fact that children had witnessed the massaging – and were whispering about it – created quite a stir. This single incident is often cited as the reason the Summer

Institute never returned to Fontana Village.

But although it makes for a good story – as does the fact that participants literally had to go to the next *state* (Tennessee) to purchase alcohol – it turns out that the clothing-optional massage sessions were not responsible for SUUSI's next move. In fact, the folks at Fontana were sufficiently happy with the Unitarian Universalists' business that they invited the Institute back for the following summer. However, with the end of the gasoline crisis tourism was rebounding, and the only dates available were either in June or late August.

Having experienced both those options at other locations, and now very content to be meeting in mid-July, the leadership of the Institute declined the offer, and made the momentous decision to strike out on their own once again. For the first time since 1950, rather than being asked to leave their Summer Institute home, Southern Unitarian Universalists took control of their own destiny, and initiated a search for a new location that would provide room for growth, accommodate the expansion of nature programming, and be conducive to fostering a close-knit community that wanted nothing more than to eat, sleep and play together for a full week in July, somewhere in the Appalachian Mountains.

Chapter 4:
Virginia Is for SUUSI

The decision not to return to Fontana Village left SUUSI with, in the words of 1973 Co-Chair Marge Link, an opportunity "to reinvent ourselves." How the Institute would take advantage of that opportunity, and what the re-invented community would look like, fell to Brad Brown, an employee of DuPont and a visionary church lay leader from Nashville. Having been appointed as the upcoming Summer Institute Chairman by the Thomas Jefferson District Board, Brown spent the entire week at Fontana observing what was working – and what wasn't. By the end of the week, he had recruited a strong team of key staff members for 1975, including Larry and Mo Wheeler as adult program and workshop coordinators, Roger Comstock as treasurer, and Sue Leonard as the incoming "Director" (she refused to be called "Chairman"). Leonard was also asked to run something new called an "Information Office," which would serve as an organizational hub during the week of the Institute. And – in a move designed to eliminate the kind of check-in debacle that had happened at Fontana – Brown asked Bill and Julia Slebos of Hillsboro, N.C., to serve as registrars and insisted that, for the first time in several years, participants *preregister* for both housing and workshops.

As soon as he learned that Fontana Village was asking SUUSI to move its week to the beginning or end of the summer the following year, Brown went to work looking for a new location. He made contact with a small college located in Radford, Va., which until two years earlier had been a women's college. But with the admission of male students in 1972, Radford College was embarking on a new era, under the leadership of President Donald Dedmon. Dedmon's Vice-President of Business, Charlie Belt, had been charged with bringing in business during the summer months. Brown and Belt quickly signed a contract for the Southeast UU Summer Institute to be the first major summer conference ever held at the college. As Radford's Director of Auxiliary Services, Phelps Dillon was in charge of residence halls, food service and the like, and served as the school's primary liaison with Brown and his staff.

SUUSI was moving into the modern era. In a few short months, Brown had transformed the Institute, both organizationally and geographically, positioning it to become the institution it is today. "It is impossible to overstate the importance of Brad Brown," says John Buehrens, then the minister at the church in Knoxville, and later President of the UUA. "What Brad did was truly significant for the development of the Summer Institute, and for the development of Unitarian Universalism."

Larry Wheeler agrees: "He brought a new level of organization, of solid leadership, through proper delegation," he says. "Brad had expectations of responsibility in all his staff, and those expectations then went throughout the organization."

Frony Ward, who was serving on the T.J. District Board and happened to be a graduate student at Virginia Tech in nearby Blacksburg, was recruited as a "local site coordinator" for the move to Radford. She describes the winter planning meeting Brown convened in Atlanta: "Brad was absolutely outstanding. This was the first time I had met all these players – Brad, the Wheelers, the Comstocks, Kay Montgomery. Brad brought incredible group leadership skills to the table, and in the process, he turned us into a *team*."

At that meeting, plans were put in place for the first SUUSI ever held at Radford, to begin July 20, 1975.

*1975 "Chairman" Brad Brown shows off his license plate
upon arriving for the first SUUSI at Radford*

Welcome to Paradise (Radford 1975)

Right from the start, SUUSI and Radford seemed to be a match made in heaven. One long-time participant from Florida made note of the fact that Radford College, though a bit further away than previous North Carolina locations, was located *right off the interstate*, easily accessible to all. Another Floridian described the campus as "simply idyllic." William Benedict, who had been Co-Chairman the previous year at Fontana Village, called Radford "the perfect location."

The fact that the entirety of the Summer Institute community – which that first year at Radford numbered just a few hundred –

An afternoon in the Governors Quad in 1975

could be housed in four small dormitories, arranged in a rectangle around a lovely, grass quadrangle, made for instant community. The "Governors Quad," composed of four three-story brick dorms (Peery, Floyd, Stuart and Trinkle – each named after a former Virginia governor), drew rave reviews from participants, comparing more than favorably with the high-rises at Appalachian State or the far-flung cabins at Fontana Village. For one thing, each dorm included a patio that faced the quad, facilitating easy community interaction and encouraging outdoor activities. A lounge and kitchen adjoined the patios, and each dorm also had a basement that included laundry facilities, as well as spaces for programming or meetings. Another bonus at Radford: Alcohol was allowed on campus.

Buses for field trips and nature outings could park on Adams Street right in front of Peery and Trinkle. A professionally staffed nursery and children's playground was provided at McGuffey Hall, immediately next to Trinkle. Adjacent to the Governors Quad in the other direction, Heth Hall, a brand new, state-of-the-art student center for Radford College, became another focal point of SUUSI activity, with registration, many workshops and theme talks, and Serendipity taking place there. Nearby, Tyler Memorial Chapel offered a lovely (if stuffy, on summer evenings) worship space with stained-glass windows and plenty of ambience; the availability of Tyler allowed SUUSI planners to reintroduce worship services, after an absence of several years. Meals were eaten together at Walker Cafeteria, also just a short walk from the quad.

In short, the Radford campus was like heaven on earth for long-suffering Summer Institute veterans and newcomers alike.

In addition to falling in love with Radford, participants in 1975 gushed about the improvements in the Institute itself. Brad Brown's SUUSI was all about "better customer service." Registrants were delighted at check-in when they were quickly and easily directed to their rooms; workshop leaders were thrilled to learn exactly who, and how many, would be in their programs. The hours-long line of the previous year was no more. Those who had argued that "Unitarians will never accept having to choose their workshops ahead of time" had been proven wrong, and feedback about the new check-in process was almost unanimously positive.

Children's programming didn't miss a beat in the new location. Pam Cline was retained in the role of Youth Director, and most of her staff continued with her. At Radford, Dirty Day became an official Youth Program activity. Cline instructed Andy Wasilewski to locate an off-campus venue where all the children ages 10-12 – not just the ones who had gotten mud all over the Machler cabin the year before – could go on a field trip and get as dirty as they wanted. Wasilewski found some old property outside Pulaski that was owned by the Boy Scouts, and arranged for his group of "church children" to come play there one day.

The site was perfect. There was a long, steep dirt hill, with a creek at the bottom. The children would first get wet in the creek, then climb the hill and roll back down it, growing ever more muddy with each successive trip. At the end of the day, the Youth Staff chose a "Dirty Dozen" – the 12 kids who had gotten the muddiest of all – then everyone rinsed off further upstream (turning the water a deep, dark brown). For many years thereafter, earning and wearing a Dirty Dozen T-shirt was the ultimate achievement for a SUUSI Youth.

Elizabeth Thompson tells of being crushed, in 1975, to learn that the minimum age for that first Dirty Day at Radford was 10 (she was 9 at the time). By the following year – when Dirty Day had been elevated to almost mythical status among the Youth – Thompson was again devastated to find that she had forgotten to bring any jeans to SUUSI (jeans were a requirement, in order to keep the kids from skinning their knees and legs). But Pam Cline's daughter Joy came to the rescue, "borrowing" her brother's jeans and loaning them to Elizabeth. "Joy's brother was 15 and dreamy," Elizabeth remembers. "Joy handed his jeans to me and told me to wear them to Dirty Day and bring them back to her – that she'd wash them for me, and her brother would never know the difference."

Like Dirty Day, there were popular adult workshops that held over from Fontana. Morris Hudgins' "Power Play" filled up during 1975 pre-registration. "Conversations with Toby" Barksdale continued, this time in the quad. Dancing workshops were offered, all the better to prepare participants for Serendipity. And "Nude Massage" continued. During an on-site planning visit, SUUSI staffers asked for a "private space" in which to hold a workshop, studiously not describing the workshop to the Radford representative. They were shown to a band room in the basement of one of the buildings on campus, and declared it ideal.

What they didn't know at the time (but later learned) was that Radford was well aware of SUUSI's "Nude Massage" workshop; its reputation had preceded SUUSI's arrival. The powers that be at Radford, according to 1976 Director Sue Leonard, "thought it was a hoot." In fact, a couple of years later, during the inevitable building renovations that commonly displace workshops and other programs from their accustomed space, a Radford employee matter-of-factly remarked to Larry Wheeler, then the Co-Director, "We'll have to move your nude massage program to a different room."

The biggest hit at Radford, however, was the new Nature Program. Building on the once-a-day outdoor activities he had offered in 1974 at Fontana, Chuck Harty became SUUSI's first official Nature Director. He put together a wide array of options for participants of all ages and abilities with help from Frony Ward, the Blacksburg resident whom Brad Brown had asked to be the "local site coordinator" prior to that first summer at Radford. Ward suggested several nature trips that remain annual favorites to this day – including scenic Cascades, a beautiful 70-foot waterfall in the Jefferson National Forest. The Cascades trip included a gentle-to-moderate hike along the Little Stony Creek, and the option of taking an invigoratingly cold swim in the pool that is formed at the base of the falls – or even standing in the waterfall itself.

Walt Pirie, a nature staffer that first year at Radford, was a single parent who worked as a professor at Virginia Tech. He taught a summer class at Tech in the mornings, then went home for a quick lunch. Shortly after lunch, a bus full of SUUSI folks would show up at his house, collect Pirie and his kids, and head off for a hike or caving trip – which Pirie would lead. At night, Pirie says, he would often go to Serendipity while others looked after his children, before grabbing a lift home for a few hours' shut-eye – only to do it all over again the next day. "After that first year, I knew I was missing out on so much of SUUSI," he recalls, "that I made sure never to be teaching again during SUUSI week. I wanted to be able to stay in the dorm and get the full SUUSI experience."

Others on the Nature Staff in 1975 included Chuck Harty, Frony Ward and Nancy Heath, each of whom led hikes. Heath also took a group out tubing on the New River (which, despite its name, happens to be the third oldest river in the world). But by far the most popular nature trip that first year at Radford was also the longest: a bus ride to Thurmond, W.Va., where participants enjoyed a day of whitewater rafting on the New River. Leaving campus before dawn, and riding through the mountains for more than two hours, was a small price to pay for the thrill of the whitewater experience, the camaraderie of swimming and cooking out together and diving off tall rocks into the river, and the culture shock of going so far into backwater West Virginia that "sometimes it looked like a scene straight out of *Deliverance*," says Ward. "But the rafting was simply great!" Heath agrees, saying "I absolutely loved it" – but she remembers being taken aback, as one of the group's leaders, by the sexist attitudes of the owners of the outfitting company who led the trip. "They wouldn't let the women do anything other than the cooking," Heath says.

Back on campus there were no complaints about the cooking. Theodore Gardiner, Radford's Director of Food Services, made sure the Unitarian Universalists enjoyed delicious all-you-could-eat, cafeteria-style meals – a welcome change from dining at Fontana and Appalachian State. The "Nomad Years" were quickly fading into the past, and when it was announced at Friday morning's theme talk that Radford had invited the Institute back for the following year, those in attendance burst into applause and cheers, some even weeping tears of joy.

SUUSI had found its home.

Settling In (1976-1979)

With the resounding success of that first year at Radford behind them, participants went back to their congregations inspired to spread the good news of the reinvented Summer Institute. SUUSI-themed worship services and presentations took place at churches from UUCA in Atlanta to First Unitarian in Richmond to congregations all over Florida. Those who had experienced what it was like to spend a July week in the mountains with like-minded spirits, comfortably accommodated on the campus of a lovely little Southern college, encouraged their friends and family members to come join in the fun. Such spontaneous, organic evangelism paid dividends, as 695 registrants – the second-largest Summer Institute up to that point – gathered in Radford for the second summer in the bicentennial year of 1976. Among that number were a whopping 269 children. One participant came from as far away as Arizona.

The theme in 1976 was "The Price of Liberty," in keeping with the bicentennial spirit that consumed the nation all summer. The Institute logo prominently proclaimed "76" and featured stars and stripes, with a profile of an American eagle's head (facing left, of course) as a chalice flame burned brightly in its eye. Theme speakers and worship leaders addressed the rights and responsibilities shared by members of a free society, and elections were the predominant topic of conversation. Jimmy Carter, the popular former governor of Georgia, had become the Democratic nominee for President of the United States just two weeks earlier.

Meanwhile, at the invitation of Morris Hudgins, candidates for President of the UUA came to Radford to experience (and campaign among) what turned out to be the largest gathering of Unitarian Universalists in any one place that summer – larger even than that particular year's General Assembly.

SUUSI also held its own election in 1976. Responsibility for managing the Summer Institute was being transferred to a newly formed Board, composed of two members appointed by each of the three districts in the Southeast – Thomas Jefferson, Mid-South and Florida – as well as three at-large Board members to be elected by Institute participants. SUUSI's first Board election was an exciting affair, with a diverse slate of candidates ranging from Wally Vockroth of Richmond, who had missed only two Summer Institutes since 1951 and unabashedly described himself as the "Institute Patriarch," all the way to 11-year-old Marty Leary of Greensboro, who wrote in that year's newsletter, the "Radford Ravin'," that he believed "it is time we have a representative of [the] non-adults" helping to make policy for SUUSI.

Though he made a compelling case, young Leary was defeated for the one-year term on the Board by an adult, John Durham. Ben Edwards won the two-year term. Meanwhile, some election-night intrigue created a runoff among the top two candidates for the three-year Board position. Apparently, late returns from the late-returning whitewater rafting trip participants initially were not counted – and when they were, the result was a *tie* between Carol Taylor and Sonya Prestridge. Taylor won a runoff the following day.

*The entrance to Muse Hall, a popular SUUSI
gathering spot in the late 1970s*

When the new Board met at the end of the week, on Saturday, July 31, 1976 – under the leadership of SUUSI's first Board President, Roger Comstock – the bylaws were amended to include the following: "Article I. Name. The name of this organization shall be Southeast Unitarian Universalist Summer Institute. Article II. Purposes. The purpose of the Southeast Unitarian Universalist Summer Institute shall be to devote its resources to religious and educational activities, and to sponsor a week-long summer program for adults and children." (Compare this statement of purpose with that from 1952, quoted near the beginning of Chapter 2.)

The Institute's official name was now established, and the acronym SUUSI was beginning to catch on (despite the fact that two entirely different acronyms, SESI and UUSI, both appeared on the same page of the 1976 confirmation newsletter). Another important – and permanent – change in nomenclature took place the same year, when Sue Leonard, who had succeeded Brad Brown and did not wish to be called a "Chairman," indicated she preferred to be known as the "Director." The term has been used ever since.

Leonard's year as Director was marked by many programmatic innovations that became long-standing SUUSI traditions. Among them was a new offsite picnic, held Wednesday evening at Claytor Lake, about 15 miles southeast of Radford. Food for the picnic was "carted, cooked and cleaned up" by a volunteer crew of SUUSI-ites that included Tom Harty, Chuck Wells, Chuck Ford, J.P. and Judy Newell, Joe Traugott, Sue Schaefer, Margaret Thompson, Lynn Wheal, Ed Stephens, and John and Joan Preston. In addition to good food, Athletic Director Jack Hurley organized several engaging activities, including a hotly contested dorm volleyball tournament which saw the "Floyd Flames" defeat the "Peery Pagans" in the finals.

The Fair was another popular intergenerational event introduced in 1976. To conclude the week, Margaret Thompson put together a family friendly evening of entertainment with music, clogging, folk and belly dancing, including a "special presentation" by the male "belly" dancing trio of Phil Nungesser, William Benedict and John Durham. There was also more traditional Fair fare like sack races, a watermelon-seed spitting contest, lemonade and ice cream, as well as a cupcake walk (cupcakes courtesy of Radford Food Services). The event was emceed by Brad Brown.

John Buehrens started an afternoon drop-in workshop that

steadily grew in popularity. "The Wisdom Tree" gave participants an informal opportunity to learn and share thoughts. "I took the idea from one of my mentors, Jacob Trapp," Buehrens says. "He taught me an old Hindu proverb that goes, 'One must not cut down the wisdom tree'." Buehrens would sit underneath an old tree at the edge of a lovely garden tucked away between Preston and Reed Halls on the east side of campus, and gently guide conversation for anyone interested in exploring philosophy and religion, and their relevance to modern life. Crowds increased each day, and by the end of the week, Buehrens was asked to do the workshop again the following year. He continued as facilitator until 1981, and was followed by colleagues such as Terry Sweetser, John Burciaga and Gary Blaine, among others, each of whom carried on the Wisdom Tree tradition until 1989, when the tree was felled one night by lightning – during SUUSI – just as the Summer Institute was about to move to Virginia Tech.

Other innovations in 1976 included a "Quiet Serendipity," held upstairs at Heth, where reading and conversation, soft music, and games of bridge or checkers offered an alternative to the more boisterous party taking place downstairs. Programming – now adult led – was beginning to return for teenagers following the demise of LRY. The evening teen hayride proved to be a hit. And 1976 marked one of the first times a woman led a worship service at SUUSI. Linnea Pearson, minister in Gainesville, Fla., opened the week with a Monday night sermon titled "God Talk and Power."

"That was the first time I had ever heard a woman preach," recalls Kay Montgomery, who would later become Executive Vice President of the UUA. "It was a life-changing moment for me. In 2011, when Linnea retired at General Assembly, I got the chance to tell her how much that one sermon had affected me. It was a very special moment." The following year both Rev. Frances West from Atlanta, and Religious Education Director Mary Nelson from Knoxville led worship services.

Among the more popular workshops in 1976 was one called

"New Women Are Also Assertive," facilitated by Estelle Schwarz and Ron McMullin. Its description in the catalog invited registrants to "learn behavior skills to express your feelings, thoughts and ideas in situations where you ordinarily don't. Focus will be on diminishing anxiety in standing up for yourself."

Paul Carnes, Brad Brown and Frony Ward in 1976

Other workshops included one on hypnosis, where participants could learn about – and then experience – the technique. Billy Joe Nichols, the controversial minister from Texas, was back at SUUSI with a workshop promoting commune living titled "Unitarian Communalism."

Children's programming was once again under the direction of Pam Cline Phelps, who was now working with an expanded 15-person staff. Lee Knight, a singer-songwriter from Columbia, S.C., was brought in to add music to the children's program (he also performed at evening worship services and offered an afternoon music workshop for adults). Each morning began with ingathering and the singing of "Father Abraham." Then there were arts and crafts, games and swimming (at Peters Gym), as well as folk dancing and clogging. A train trip to the Mill Mountain

Zoo in Roanoke was on the agenda one day. Meanwhile, kids age 5 and under were cared for in the McGuffey nursery, with age appropriate games and stories, playground time, and of course, naps.

"The glue that held SUUSI together in those years was the wonderful kids' program run by Pam Cline," Roger Comstock recalls. "I remember being there with my three kids and not seeing them for almost a week. Then one day, they ran by saying, 'Hi Mom. Hi Dad. Can't stop! We gotta get to Dirty Day.' What a wonderful feeling it was to know the kids were safe and well taken care of, having a good time, and that we could be free to be adults... Of course, the kids came back filthy – but happier than I had ever seen them!"

Such fun does not come without its costs, however. Kate Couch, who was just beginning a long stint as SUUSI Nurse, reported by the week's end in 1976 that she had seen more than 100 persons, for injuries ranging from a skinned elbow on the playground, to a diving board accident, to a back injury from a nature trip that required a trip to the emergency room. Apparently skateboards were popular in 1976, with many minor injuries suffered and more than one notice posted admonishing young and old alike not to skateboard in the hallways.

At the end of the week that bicentennial year, the newly elected "Tri-District Board" charged Ted Machler with looking into the possibility of incorporating SUUSI in the state of Florida. On March 1, 1977, the Southeast Unitarian Universalist Summer Institute, Inc., was incorporated as a "non-profit corporation in accordance with the laws of the State of Florida," with the membership of the corporation to "consist of all duly registered participants in [the] Summer Institute of the most recent previous year." The incorporation papers went on to say, in Article IV, that "This corporation shall have perpetual existence." The three signers on the document were all Tallahassee residents: Richard R. Lee, Secretary of the SUUSI Board; Pamela Cline Phelps; and Margaret Ann Link. The President of the Board was listed as June

Preston and the Treasurer was John (now Alexis) Jones.

When participants arrived at the newly incorporated SUUSI in 1977, they were pleased to find an even smoother check-in procedure than the year before. Registrars Judy and J.P. Newell of Miami had as their motto that year, "Each person in and out in less than 30 minutes." Thanks to careful planning, they met their goal.

The couple had spent the preceding months organizing mailed-in, paper

Children playing on the large tree stump at Claytor Lake in 1976

registrations and checks, sorting them into multiple stacks in order to make housing and workshop assignments. It was a good thing they did – an all-time record attendance of 763 filled the dorms in the Governors Quad to capacity, and an announcement was sent out to all registrants in June that "SUUSI 77 is full! Spread the word! If you have acquaintances who planned a late registration, let them know there is no bed space available!" Nonetheless, "Seventy unregistered persons came with individuals who were pre-registered," according to the records, "severely impacting the program, especially Youth."

The Newells continued as SUUSI registrars for more than a decade, and were thus among the first smiling faces at Radford to greet and welcome countless "newbies" into the SUUSI family. In an era when computers were still a rarity, they created an "alpha list" (short for "alphabetical") of registrants that could be used throughout the week to facilitate administration. At the end of the week, a limited number of copies of the alpha list, in the form of "rosters" (no photos), were sold to participants for $1 each.

The Newells made use of dormitory floor plans to create and change room assignments (as J.P. judiciously puts it, "Back then there was a lot of fluidity in rooming arrangements!"). They created multiple "stations" in the ballroom at Heth to facilitate Sunday arrival and check-in, speeding up the process even more. Before driving to Radford, they put nametags on the outside of each arrival envelope, and placed room keys inside the envelope,

Pam Phelps and Ted Machler

then arranged the envelopes alphabetically. "That little trick, which seemed like common sense to us, for some reason really amazed people," says Judy. In short, in the late 1970s, the Newells devised and organized a registration and check-in system that, although now computerized, remains largely unchanged to this day.

The theme in 1977 was "Family." Co-Directors Larry and Mo Wheeler wanted SUUSI to be a true "family camp," and brought that perspective to all aspects of Institute life, beginning with an intergenerational Sunday evening Ingathering. Called "Meeting Our Family – New and Old," it was led by Gene Navias of the UUA, and the popular Lee Knight. The following evening, "New Games" were introduced to the SUUSI community by Roger and Faith Comstock. The cooperative games for all ages – without the competition – were instantly popular, as were the giant earth ball and a multi-colored parachute.

Roger recalls, "I had been trained in leading New Games the year before, and thought what better place to try them out? ... We played Catch the Dragon's Tail, and Snake in the Grass, and the Amoeba Race and ... Earth Ball... You put the ball in the middle of the field, and divide up into two teams. The object is to push the ball to the other team's end of the field. But during the game, if the ball starts moving too far in one direction, some folks suddenly change sides and help push it back in the other direction! That's what the games are all about: You can be competitive and expend a lot of energy, yet there are no winners and no losers. Kind of a symbol of the way SUUSI operates!"

The Claytor Lake picnic returned on Wednesday with the addition of a new, much more competitive tradition – the tug-of-war. An even bigger and better Community Fair on Friday night closed out the week with new activities like a water balloon toss, an obstacle course, bobbing for apples, body painting, a kissing booth, and a visit from Clarabelle the Clown (aka Don Blanchard). After the Fair, everyone adjourned to a "family worship service" that concluded the week.

Even the logo, designed by William Benedict, captured the

extended family feel of the 1977 Summer Institute, depicting a row (extending off into infinity) of stylized human figures of various sizes, all holding hands. Variations on Benedict's "SUUSI People" became almost synonymous with Radford itself, appearing on the cover of all but one annual catalog and logo through 1988, and on almost all promotional material and SUUSI letterheads produced over the next decade.

The theme speakers in 1977 were a couple from the UUA in Boston, Hugo and Barbara Holleroth. Hugo, known as "Holly," had been the Director of Curriculum Development for the UUA for several years, and Barbara was a licensed therapist and Director of the UU Pastoral Counseling Service. They shared the podium each morning before standing-room only crowds that crammed into the upstairs lounge at Heth, speaking on "What is family? Do you need one? Do you have one? Do you want one?" Marti Toms (then Sanders), a first-time attendee from Kingsport, Tenn., remembers how the couple presented the material in "just an amazing way, using different aspects of Peter Rabbit" to make their points.

Families were omnipresent in 1977, and could be seen in large numbers, three times each day, in what came to be called "the great migration" – walking in groups and pushing strollers across what they called "the Commons," a large open quadrangle between Heth and Muse, the tallest dorm on campus, where meals were now being served.

"SUUSI was a very different experience for families," says John Burciaga, who was then at the beginning of what would be a 20-year ministry in Clearwater, Fla. "For parents, it was very liberating to eat meals with the children, then be comfortable leaving them in a high quality, safe, age-appropriate environment. Pam Phelps had set up an outstanding kids' program, which shared wonderful UU values and helped the kids make connections."

Without exception, parents (both couples, and an ever-increasing number of single parents) sang the praises of the Youth Program. When Phelps retired as its director at the end of the week in 1977, the Friday newsletter offered the following testimonial, under the headline "Hot Damn! Thank You Ma'am!":

> There's a wonderful woman named Pam Cline Phelps,
> Who for six years now has run a program for whelps.
> For doing a job so incredibly tough
> Just saying thanks seems not quite enough.
> Our children all feel her strength, love and care;
> The programs are tops, the best anywhere.
> She has the wisdom of Isis, the strength of Shazam.
> We see what you've done – and we thank you, Pam!

Phelps' last year as Youth Director was a memorable one, including SUUSI's first field trip to the world-renowned Lakeside Amusement Park in Salem (which featured the nearly mile-long Shooting Star roller coaster with its 84-foot vertical drop; when the Shooting Star had opened in 1968, it was said to be the fastest roller coaster on the planet). The children also enjoyed their own hike in 1977, as well as a picnic and swim at Cascades, and evening bowling, Putt-Putt and skating. The Youth Staff continued to grow, and now sported their own special T-shirts.

The Teen Program (still under the auspices of the Youth Program) was also growing, as children who had been coming to SUUSI for several years were aging up. A new "Teen Center," featuring "music, cards, ping pong, TV and refreshments," was open every day from 2 p.m. on. The Monday newsletter reported that there was "No curfew for responsible teens. Definition of responsible: adj., stay[ing] within the dormitory quad ... or central campus up to the fountain in front of Muse; QUIET; considerate of others." The teens, many of whom had participated in their younger years, were also allowed to take part in Dirty Day in 1977.

Newly elected UUA President Paul Carnes flew in to spend two days on campus, fulfilling a campaign promise he had made at SUUSI the previous year. He held an open community dialogue on Thursday night. Worship on Monday night reflected trends in

Unitarian Universalism at the time, with Bob Karnan, minister of the Northwest UU Congregation in Atlanta, reading poetry from an eclectic array of socially engaged poets, and including music from John Denver, Stevie Wonder, the Moody Blues and the Beatles.

Workshops – now under the direction of Kay Montgomery and Jean Highsmith – focused on various aspects of family, with John and Gwen Buehrens offering "Understanding the Family System," Faith and Roger Comstock facilitating "Couples Communication," Pat Bowen leading "Single Parenting" and William Benedict, who was a founder and resident of Greenhouse, an intentional community of 10 adults and half a dozen children in Knoxville, leading "Community: Or, Do I *Have* to Cook for 16?" Individual exploration continued to be popular as well, with multiple yoga workshops being offered for the first time, hypnosis returning by popular demand, and a variety of different massage workshops on the menu.

Of the 17 ordained ministers on campus in 1977 – more than ever before – three were women. Rev. Leslie Cronin of the UUA Department of Ministerial and Congregational Services led an engaging social action workshop titled "Women in Action." Participants drove a caravan to Blacksburg to attend an Equal Rights Amendment rally, collected SUUSI signatures on a petition to President Carter expressing concern about legislative efforts to roll back *Roe v. Wade*, and saw a powerful slide presentation, open to the SUUSI public, on "Women Against Violence Against Women."

Not everything was serious, of course. As Elle Long put it, "During the day, we were thoughtful. At night, we just wanted to *have fun*." Serendipity had become the place to be once again. Attendees dressed up for much of the week, but really let their hair down on Friday night at the eagerly anticipated costume party. Fun and games were also encouraged by an increasingly active group from the Eno River UU Fellowship in Durham, N.C. The group came ready to take on all comers, having "stolen" from the defending dorm volleyball champion Floyd Flames four of its top players through "free agency." They threw down the gauntlet in the Monday edition of the newsletter (that year simply called "The Newsletter"), inviting any team brave enough to take them on to "leave a note for Bill Slebos, 118 Stuart [with] your name, local address, name of team and desired time of humiliation." Their victims proved to be (Arthur) Saltzman's Spikers, who at midweek went down to defeat two games to one at the hands of the Eno River Rockets. Trash talk continued the remainder of the week.

The number of nature trips continued to grow. "I could no longer even go out on trips myself," recalls Nature Director Chuck Harty. "It became all about organizing, coordinating, and arranging transportation." In those days, many nature trips were carpools, with individual participants volunteering to drive three or four other

SUUSI rock-climbing

people to off-campus sites for hikes, rock climbing, canoeing and so on. Horseback riding, at a 600-acre competition riding stable outside Radford, was added to the program; the more sedate campers were able to register for bird-watching. There was even a trip to a "working solar energy installation" to learn about what was being touted as the energy alternative of the future.

Sue Folk (formerly Leonard) was elected to the one vacant seat on the Board, and Larry and Mo Wheeler were asked to return as Co-Directors (1978 Director-Elect Brad Brown was about to move to Texas). Thus the Wheelers established the precedent of what would eventually become standard practice –

two-year SUUSI directorships. They also created a "flow chart" and reorganized the Staff, which was growing larger and more complex with each passing year. Minutes of a Board meeting indicate that it was a "change from a flat hierarchy, with perhaps 16 persons reporting to the Director, to a more vertical structure, with 7 persons directly reporting to the Director and others reporting to an intermediary, including the Director-Elect." While the Wheelers would remain Directors another year, Kay Montgomery was appointed Director-Elect for 1979.

By the summer of 1978, SUUSI had grown so large – reaching a registration of 850 – that participants could no longer all be housed in one compact square of dorms. Adult singles and some couples without children were accommodated in Pocahontas Hall, just a short distance from Heth and still on the same side of campus as the Governors Quad.

Included in that record registration was a group from South Florida that had actually chartered a bus – complete with professional driver – for the week. "SUUSI was a very big deal at the Miami church," says Jill Menadier, who, as a teenager, was in charge of taking a head count to make sure no one got left behind each time the bus stopped for a bathroom break. According to Kip Barkley, that was not very often. "We left Miami Saturday morning, swung by the Fort Lauderdale church to pick up some of their people, and then rode about 22 hours straight. There were coolers of beer in the back, and round-the-clock guitar music and singing. We only stopped for potty breaks once the bathroom in the bus got too nasty."

The bus trip from Miami was Susan Mahar (now McAlpin)'s first experience of SUUSI. "My first SUUSI was 1978," she recalls. "The ride was long! My friend Kip [Barkley] describes it as a sort of 'rebirthing experience.' I certainly felt as if I was going home, in more ways than one, since I had spent my childhood in neighboring West Virginia." The Floridians who rolled off that bus on Sunday must have felt particularly grungy, because McAlpin says that "upon arriving, I was literally thrown into a shower. It was the days of 'save water – shower with a friend!'"

The Miami bus seemed to be a tangible symbol of just how big a deal SUUSI had become – and it was met with great fanfare when it arrived in Radford. Karyn Machler, who herself had come up from Clearwater in her parents' camper, recalls sitting on the steps of the Heth Student Union, awaiting the arrival of the Miami bus, eager to see all her friends and hear about their trip. A cheering crowd greeted the bus and its occupants when they at last reached the hallowed ground of Radford.

Larry Wheeler and Judy Newell look over a registration form during 1978 check-in

Later that Sunday evening, the 1978 Ingathering featured Michael and Terry McGee from Meadville, Pa., offering further evidence that SUUSI's reach was beginning to spread beyond the Southeast. Other participants came from as far away as Missouri, Minnesota and even California.

What they found were nearly a hundred different workshops for adults and 55 nature trips (it was to be Chuck Harty's last year as Nature Director; his staff had now grown to 30 people). In addition, special nature trips were being provided for teens – one all-day adventure outing per day, Monday through Friday. There was an Appalachian Trail hike, spelunking, canoeing, rock climbing and a hike on Rocky Knob trail. The trips were advertised as "strenuous activities," only for those teens "in good physical condition," as an alternative to the regular daytime programming.

For other teenagers, such as Dianna MacPherson, working on Youth Staff – with perks such as special T-shirts and staff credit toward registration fees – was even more appealing. Trips to the

7-Eleven were becoming a part of the teen experience as well. The theme in 1978 was "Today's Tomorrows," and there was a growing awareness within the adult community of the importance of the next generation of Unitarian Universalists. The catalog proudly proclaimed, "After a period of discontent, our youth are again becoming committed to the life of the church. How can youth and adults support one another in their religious journey? This subject will be explored in a youth-adult dialogue" as part of the week's theme activities.

Sometimes, intergenerational dialogue was fostered unintentionally. According to John Goodhart, some women in the community had taken exception to the fact that the previous year's "alpha list" of registrants had included each person's age. In protest, a few – including his wife Diana (who at the time was in her 50s) – had registered for 1978 as simply "over 21." The result was that the Goodharts were inadvertently housed on the third floor of Peery with a large group of young adults!

Music was becoming another important aspect of the SUUSI community. In 1978, renowned hammered dulcimer player John McCutcheon came to SUUSI, performing with Lee Knight on Thursday night and offering a dulcimer workshop on Wednesday and Thursday. Landing McCutcheon was quite a coup for the Summer Institute. Another SUUSI rising star was Boomslang Meade, who guaranteed his place in SUUSI history in 1978 by rewriting the words to a Tanya Tucker hit, creating the instant SUUSI classic "When I Die I Want to Go to Radford" at Ingathering:

Boomslang Meade
performing at Radford

When I die I may not go to heaven;
I don't know if they let liberals in.
If they don't then let me go to Radford,
Radford is as close as I have been.

By the next summer, bumper stickers proclaiming "When I Die I Want to Go to Radford" were beginning to appear on SUUSI vehicles.

Themed T-shirts also added a special feel to each SUUSI. In 1978, "Summer Institute" shirts were popular items at the new Craft Fair, where SUUSI artisans could sell their wares in a bazaar-type atmosphere. A staff department called "Commercial Enterprises" oversaw the Craft Fair, UUSC Sales and the Bookstore.

Sue Male was in charge of worship in 1978, and invited Rev. Josiah Bartlett from Berkeley, Calif., to lead a service one evening. The popular John Burciaga from Clearwater was another worship leader. Choir music and even a mime were added to the worship roster, as was one SUUSI newcomer – Stephan Papa, the new minister of the Fort Lauderdale church. Papa had caught the SUUSI fever from his congregation. "There was a big contingent of people from the church who were just very devoted to SUUSI," he says. "SUUSI was the biggest event of the year in our congregation. Folks got a very special feeling by being part of something much larger than they could see just in Fort Lauderdale. And I loved worshipping at SUUSI, in that [Tyler Memorial] chapel. It was a real centering piece of each day – a good reminder of the fact that we were a religious community."

SUUSI had also become a big deal at UUCA in Atlanta, and in 1978 Mary Nell McLauchlin gave in to peer pressure and made her first trip to Radford. She didn't sign up for much, but did take a four-day workshop titled "Awareness of Dying in Living," led by Carole Selvey, a psychologist who was also from Atlanta. "I had been in a car accident over Memorial Day, in which someone had died," McLauchlin says. "That workshop was incredibly healing for me. The week was simply wonderful, and I've been coming [to SUUSI] pretty much ever since."

Mary Ann Somervill tells another tale of the magic of SUUSI from about the same time. Her son, Charlie, had been badly injured in 1977, losing the lower half of his left leg. SUUSI was the first time he had been among strangers since the amputation. Mary Ann gratefully recounts how welcoming and helpful Chuck Harty and his Nature Staff were in accommodating Charlie, and how open and embracing the SUUSI teens were to Charlie as well. Both groups encouraged Charlie to stretch himself and push his limits, but in a safe and loving way, always ready to catch him, either physically or emotionally, whenever he needed help.

"The warmth and acceptance of the teens and the nature folks made what could have been a nightmare a joyous week for Charlie," says Mary Ann. "That SUUSI was his first true UU experience, and it meant the world to him." Indeed, it made him a Unitarian Universalist for life; Charlie Somervill is currently the Director of SWIM, and is also a youth group advisor and Sunday School teacher at his local church in Asheville.

Not only were there miracles in abundance at SUUSI 1978, but the whole experience was quite a bargain. Those who have been coming since the late 1970s will be amazed to recall that adult registration fees at the time were only $40 ($30 for children and teens). Room costs were $32 per bed for the week, and meals (for those age 15 and up) were just $37. It was a very good deal for those lucky enough to be there – some of whom were surprised to find their picture on the cover of the *Unitarian Universalist World* magazine in September, when a cover story on the popularity of summer camps and conferences appeared in the denominational newspaper. "SUUSI was becoming the standard for UU summer camps," says Terry Sweetser, then the minister in Charlottesville. "Over time, it had a huge impact on how we understand the creation of large-scale community as Unitarian Universalists."

One of SUUSI's most lasting legacies has been The Mountain. At its end-of-the-week meeting in 1977, the Board had initiated "a feasibility study to consider the need for a year-round camp and conference center" in the Southeast. Ever since the disagreements with the YMCA Blue Ridge Assembly had led Wally Vockroth to write to the UUA about his hope of Unitarian Universalists owning, rather than renting, summer conference space, people had been talking about the possibility of a "landed camp" in the Appalachian Mountains, one that would *belong* to Unitarian Universalists. The feasibility study revealed that there was considerable interest, in the Atlanta area and all around the Southeast, in such a project – and so, between the summers of 1978 and 1979, the SUUSI Board doggedly pursued making the dream a reality.

Roger Comstock, along with Larry and Mo Wheeler, located an ideal, 85-acre site in Highlands, N.C., on Little Scaly Mountain. The camp had 21 cabins, a six-bedroom lodge, a dining hall, a recreation center, tennis courts, stables and more. The asking price was $500,000. Up to $250,000 more was expected to be

Walt Pirie, Jake Haun and Larry Wheeler

spent on necessary renovations and equipment upgrades on the long-unused facility.

The Board met at the site in April 1979, and immediately fell in love with the place. Comstock remembers the group sitting on what has since come to be known as Meditation Rock, looking out over a view of three states' worth of gorgeous, rolling mountains. They decided, then and there, to purchase what would become The Mountain, agreeing to make an earnest offer of $5,000 from their own personal funds and enter into negotiations to purchase the property.

At SUUSI that summer, there were many questions about the plan. The week-long Summer Institute had already grown too large to be accommodated at the proposed conference center (more than 950 people had registered for SUUSI 1979), but a heavily promoted Wednesday night information session was attended by about a hundred people. Those present were offered assurances that potential summer-long and year-round UU family programming possibilities would only serve to "supplement the present program at SUUSI." It was announced that the realtor had agreed to have an open house for those SUUSI participants wishing to see The Mountain for themselves, on Saturday afternoon following the close of SUUSI. In addition, a "dry run" of what it might be like for a large group of Unitarian Universalists to meet at a place such as The Mountain was scheduled for a month later, Aug. 19-25, in Valle Crucis, N.C., near Boone. This gathering was billed as "a one-week opportunity to discover and to explore your place and your space – your intra-personal space, your inter-personal space, your spiritual space and your place in space... You and other UUs – together for a week of discovery."

By September, The Mountain had been purchased (with generous help from the Veatch Foundation and countless individual Unitarian Universalists and congregations throughout the Southeast). Though the motivation, the legwork, and the funding had initially come from SUUSI and in particular the SUUSI Board, it was recognized early on that the two entities needed to operate independently, and so The Mountain was set up as a separate non-profit, with its own Board of Trustees, financing and operations.

The excitement surrounding the possibility of purchasing a camp and conference center might have dominated the mood in many other years, but 1979 was a particularly memorable, even pivotal, year for SUUSI in many other respects. Director Kay Montgomery had chosen "CHANGing" as the theme, and the

UNITARIAN UNIVERSALIST WORLD

Vol. 9, No. 13   The Journal of the Unitarian Universalist Association,   25 Beacon St., Boston, Ma 02108   September 15, 1978

IARF looks at limits of toleration

When Charles I held court in Oxford during the religious wars that led to England's Toleration Act of 1689, Oxford already was older than any now existing city in the United States or Canada. So it's not surprising that North American UUs attending the IARF's (International Association for Religious Freedom) 23rd Congress, "The Limits of Toleration Today," came home saying they felt a sense of history.

The North American delegates joined religious liberals from India, Japan and Eastern and Western Europe in worship services, panel discussions and informal meetings in a search to find a way to counteract the intolerable injustices and the intolerable indifference encountered in the modern world.

The 400 men and women representing 43 member groups in 20 countries with 15 languages on every continent sought and agreed on a definition of genuine toleration, and what toleration is not. They honored a Belfast minister who stands for tolerance in the midst of intolerance, hatred and violence in Northern Ireland, and many made a tangible commitment to the IARF's service project there.

They agreed toleration is not indifference to evil or an academic exercise for religious thinkers, and that it grows out of a firm basic conviction achieved by

Continued on Page 3, Col. 1

At 23 camp and conference centers around the continent this summer thousands of UUs found themselves among joyous gatherings like this one at the Southeast Unitarian Universalist Summer Institute (SUUSI) at Radford College, Radford, Va. Here pictured are some happy campers picnicking at a nearby State Park. Attending the summer get-together, a Southern UU event for nearly 30 years, which, except for the General Assembly, is the largest annual gathering of UUs, were 540 adults and 310 children. The fast-rising attendance rate is at least partially attributable to a strong emphasis on family. Full-day children's programs for various age groups offered a balance of nature experiences with arts, crafts and sports. For adults SUUSI had more workshops than most summer camps and conferences, but it was typical in its offering of a well-rounded program of activities that build the body, stimulate the brain, nourish the soul and exercise the muscles that make UUs smile. (Wallace White photo)

Three-year program aims to eradicate sexism

Ms. Cronin

"The 1977 General Assembly Women and Religion Resolution asks us to look at the ways our religious beliefs cause us to undervalue and overlook women.

"It asks us to look at the relationship between our religion and sexism.

"It asks us, as Unitarian Universalists, to 'clean house.'"

With these words the Rev. Leslie Westbrook Cronin opened the 1978 UUA General Assembly hearing on Women and Religion and launched a projected three-year effort designed to initiate a UUA housecleaning of sexism in thought, word and action.

This is an effort conceived by a small working group of UU women; introduced in Lexington, where the "shot heard round the world" was fired; submitted as a resolution to the 1977 General Assembly by 548 members of 57 active member societies; mandated unanimously by the '77 GA; shaped by the staff at 25 Beacon Street; ordered by President Paul N. Carnes; and endorsed by UU women and men all over the continent.

Delegates to Unitarian Universalist General Assemblies for the past two years, in Ithaca and Boston, have eagerly proclaimed that they are ready to examine the religious bases of sexism. And President Carnes has made a continuing commitment to implement the 1977 resolution.

With the President, the Rev. Ms. Cronin has the denomination's major responsibility for programs to im-

Continued on Page 2, Col. 1

Public television explores world religions

Page 6

week lived up to its billing. Magical moments and life-changing experiences made 1979 one of the most talked-about years in the history of SUUSI.

Nothing was more memorable – either for those who did it, or for those who simply heard about it – than SUUSI's first-ever parachuting workshop. When participants opened their catalog in the spring of 1979, they found the following entry included in a greatly expanded listing of nature trips being coordinated by new Nature Director Walt Pirie:

GERONIMO-O-O
PARACHUTE JUMPING

This one-day course consists of 3-4 hours of thorough instructions in techniques and safety, practice jumps from a mock airplane, and ends the day with the real thing: a static-line jump (automatic chute opening), carrying a reserve chute. Parachute jumping is exciting, challenging, and carries an obvious degree of risk. It's a thrill that can't be experienced vicariously. Participants should be in good physical condition and, if over 45, provide a physician's statement to that effect...

Leader: John Stanford, director of the New River Valley Parachute Center, is an FAA designated parachute rigger-examiner and a USPA Instructor/Examiner. He personally has made over 2,000 jumps and trained over 1,800 first-time jump students. NRVPC has one of the best facilities and safety records in the country.

Early on the morning of Tuesday, July 24, 1979, the ultimate SUUSI extreme sport began with a dozen or so apprehensive Unitarian Universalists leaving campus for the adventure of a lifetime. There was nervous joking and false bravado, but as Stephan Papa, minister in Fort Lauderdale, recalls, "It also seemed as if everyone had some very serious *reason* for taking this particular workshop. They were dealing with something in their lives – something they needed to let go of, something to leave behind."

One participant in the group recounted having slipped off the edge of a cliff, years earlier, and literally clinging for dear life to some roots. After hanging on until a helicopter arrived, this person then had to *let go* of the roots in order to reach for the rescue basket hanging from the helicopter. Parachuting at SUUSI was a way of overcoming the visceral fear embodied in that memory.

Someone else was going through a divorce. Still others were contemplating changing careers or marriage partners.

The day began with several hours of on-the-ground training, which itself included at least one injury. One participant, Charlie Simpson, broke a rib jumping off the four-foot high training platform, but told no one about the pain until having completed the actual jump.

After practicing on platforms and watching videos of all the things that could go wrong in the air, the brave UUs at last divided into groups of three (the capacity of the plane) for their jumps. Terry Sweetser, minister in Charlottesville, volunteered to be in the first group. He remembers:

> Once we were up in the plane, we were looking at each other like *"This is really happening!"* One of the instructors went first, so we could see how it was really done. I remember feeling responsible for showing some leadership, since I was a minister, and so I stepped out on the wing of the plane. I can only describe the feeling that came over me as sheer terror. I wanted to turn back, but the wind was very strong. After a while, I finally let go.
>
> For a long period of time, as you're just floating free in the air, it's simply wonderful. But then you begin worrying about landing. For me, I was most

concerned about landing in the trees. I didn't, but I did hit the ground quite hard, and hurt my back a little bit.

Having done it, I can only say that it was a very special rite of passage. When we got back to campus, we felt like we were an elite group of people. We got the feeling of having a red badge of courage.

Another jumper, Tom Moore, was moved to write a poem that appeared in the Friday edition of the 1979 newsletter, "The Daily Plan-It." The following are excerpts from that poem:

Let me tell you about my jump.
In fact, hold still, will you?
        Listen.
I've <u>got</u> to tell you.

It's not really a jump.
        It's actually more like a step.
                A "mere" step...

"Cut!" the jumpmaster called to the pilot.
The engine lowered its voice:
a rather ominous tone of respect
        for the soon-to-be-deployed soul.
        No more was I concerned about whether
                Truette or Elle,
                who had jumped within minutes
                before me,
                        had already floated to safety.

"Get in the door!"
        Yes, that's me he's talking to.
Place left hand on right wing strut.

Okay, it does feel automatic.
But wait. "Geez," I inwardly cry,
　"my damn right foot won't stay
　on the step." The driving air
　easily blows it right off.
　"I don't want to tumble out head
　over heels."

"Get out!" the jumpmaster directs.
"Oh Lord," my brain roars. "Am I really
　doing this? I have a wife and
　three kids..."

...A big, beautiful circle over my head.
　No line-overs.
　　No holes that aren't supposed
　　to be there.
　Just a couple of twists in the lines
that are already disappearing as the
chute turns me full circle: once, twice...

...Oh ageless mountains.
Gorgeous, green Virginia.
　What a truly marvelous sight.
The step is over.
　Now just enjoy it.

And one of the most remarkable tales of that day is told by
Stephan Papa:

It was a static-line jump, which means your
parachute opens automatically. During training,
though, they had to teach us what to do if your
chute *didn't* open. That really got our attention.
They also taught us how to jump – all the

instructions. I did everything just as I had been told. I remember jumping, and screaming "Oh my God" – but that's the last thing I remember. *I fainted.* I didn't know it at the time, but I have a condition called "vasovagal syncope," in which there's a nerve in the autonomic nervous system that responds to a stressful experience by making you pass out.

The forceful opening of the parachute jerked me back to consciousness, and I was confused for several seconds. But then – the rest of the way down – it was just marvelous! The wind on your face, and how far you could see. It was amazing.

We had been taught how to steer the parachute, and there was a target, a circle, on the ground that we were to aim for. I actually got the closest to the bulls-eye! I got a little prize for that.

Another participant was not so lucky. Unable to steer his parachute (there were sudden gusts of wind throughout that afternoon), he was blown completely past the airport. After coming uncomfortably close to a building and some electrical lines, and nearly landing in a large pond, he finally came down in the front yard of a home about a mile from the designated landing area. The couple who owned the home happened to be sitting on the porch at the time, and after getting over the surprise of seeing someone with a parachute land in their yard, offered him a ride to the airport. He thanked them for their kindness, but said he preferred to walk back.

And then there is Nancy McDermott's 1979 parachuting story – a tale that has become the stuff of SUUSI legend. McDermott, too, was caught by a gust of wind, just as she was landing, causing her to hit the ground hard and then bounce on her hip. She says she knew immediately that she was hurt, but didn't think it was too bad. She even went out dancing that night at Serendipity –

albeit, limping, on one foot. However, McDermott was awakened early the next morning by excruciating pain, and had to be carried by paramedics down the stairwell from her room to a waiting ambulance. She spent the remainder of the week in the hospital.

This is how McDermott describes her experience:

> That year was my "leap into life." It was my first time at SUUSI, and I had recently left a job I had held for a long time. I wanted to challenge myself – to confront my fears. I had always been afraid of falling, so of course I went on the hike to Dragon's Tooth [an 80-foot high cliff] the very first day. We rappelled down, but then had to climb back up. And the next day, I went parachuting.
>
> It was the scariest thing I ever did in my life. They tried to teach us in one day what you spend a couple of weeks learning how to do in the military. When it was my turn, and I got out on the wing, the jumpmaster told me to jump, and I tried to climb back in the plane. That's how scared I was. But I did jump, counting like they told us – one one-thousand, two one-thousand, three one-thousand. It was such a relief when the parachute opened, and I actually did enjoy the rest of the time in the air.
>
> Then, just like they taught us, I steered to my landing, and landed on my feet – but a gust of wind flipped me onto my hip, hard. It hurt, but I was able to pick up my parachute, walk back to the group, even enjoy the celebration and then go out dancing later that night. But I spent the rest of my SUUSI in the hospital. I had come up on the Miami bus, but had to fly back home.
>
> I've been coming to SUUSI ever since – but I never went parachuting again! I'll say this: It was a

rite of passage, and I'm glad I did it. It was a good experience for me.

There were other leaps of faith taken at SUUSI 1979. Mary Ann Somervill and Scotty MacDiarmid got married on Thursday night in the lounge at Muse (which for the first time that year was housing SUUSI participants as well as serving them meals). With their SUUSI friends and family (including Mary Ann's daughter, Laura, and son, Charlie) looking on, the happy couple – who for years had led workshops together at SUUSI – said their vows in the most unusual, and yet most appropriate, of settings. Stephan Papa, walking straight to Muse after leading a worship service in Tyler Chapel (and just two days removed from passing out while parachuting), performed the ceremony.

Mary Ann Somervill and Scotty MacDiarmid light a unity candle during their 1979 wedding in the Muse lounge

Another very busy denominational figure at SUUSI that year was Dick Scobie, Executive Director of the Unitarian Universalist Service Committee. The UUSC had enjoyed a strong presence at SUUSI for several years, selling crafts and other items and frequently putting on workshops or staffing informational tables. Carolyn Taylor and Nancy Bartlett were active in promoting the UUSC at SUUSI.

Attending his first SUUSI, Scobie led three different one-day workshops focusing on current UUSC causes ("Stopping the Prison Epidemic in America," "Population Control" and "Human Rights and Hunger"). He also offered the Tuesday night theme talk – titled "Change the World! A UU Imperative" – and on Friday night co-hosted a SUUSI version of the "UUSC Follies," a popular event at General Assembly. Of his first time at Radford, Scobie says, "I was bowled over by the size of the conference. There was nothing like it other than G.A... I remember telling Kay Montgomery [that year's Director] how impressed and respectful I was of the 'institution' they had built at SUUSI, and of her leadership in that process... The wealth of the offerings in the program was incredible. I was also delighted by the musicality of so many of the participants, and I quickly attached myself to the circle of musicians who already knew each other."

In fact, it was through music that Scobie left his mark on SUUSI, in the process becoming nothing less than a SUUSI legend. An accomplished bagpiper, Scobie would stand on the open-air penthouse of Muse each morning and play his bagpipes to summon the SUUSI community to breakfast. Those who were there speak almost mystically about the experience, using words like "surreal" and "profound" ... "it gave me goosebumps then, and even now" ... "one of the most spiritual experiences I've ever had." Both those who were young then, and those who were older, remember the feeling of making that long walk across the Commons to breakfast, early in the chilly Radford morning, the sun just rising and a mist in the air, as the sound of bagpipe music drew them forward into sacred community, and another day of SUUSI love and adventure.

For the next four years, Scobie and his bagpipes were one of the most enduring memories of the SUUSI experience.

Dick Scobie playing bagpipes atop Muse

The UU Service Committee wasn't the only social action outlet at SUUSI. The struggle to pass the Equal Rights Amendment played a more prominent role in the life of the community than it ever had before. After initial momentum had resulted in 30 of the 38 states necessary to amend the U.S. Constitution ratifying the ERA, by 1979 progress had stalled, particularly in the South. SUUSI supporters sought to sway the last few states needed for ratification – one of which was Virginia. During the preceding 12 months, at the behest of the SUUSI community, the Board of Trustees (while at the same time pursuing the purchase of property for a permanent camp and conference center) had written governors and key legislators in Southern states urging ratification, and indicating their desire to take SUUSI – and its business – to a pro-ERA state. Virginia was seen as a key swing state for the entire Southeast in terms of ERA support.

Further fueling the fire was the fact that the UUA General Assembly had passed a resolution prohibiting UUA staff from participating in meetings (including conferences such as SUUSI) in non-ERA states beyond the end of the decade – thus calling into question SUUSI's ability to bring in "big name" UU speakers and leaders beginning in 1980. An ERA information and advocacy table was set up each day during SUUSI 1979, and signatures were gathered on a petition to Virginia Gov. John N. Dalton.

Following in the footsteps of Chuck Harty, Walt Pirie became Nature Director in 1979 and promptly took that program literally to new heights – beginning, of course, with the parachute jumping workshop, but also including a rock-climbing trip and a couple of innovative week-long immersion experiences (which could be taken either all together, or on a daily basis). Every day, Monday through Friday, a different caving experience was offered ("Underground Virginia, No Relation to Underground Atlanta"). Similarly, "A Week of Waterfalls" included a daily hike to five different area waterfalls.

For the second year in a row, the "Florida Bus" was commandeered to accommodate the high demand for spaces on the whitewater rafting trip to West Virginia. Susan McAlpin recalls that while on the river, participants were allowed to leave the relatively safe confines of their raft and "body surf the rapids. Our guide instructed us to go feet first!"

Upon their return to campus late that Wednesday night, after a day that had begun before the rise of the sun, the whitewater trippers were treated by the Nature Staff to a full-blown Italian meal, as the basement of Trinkle was transformed into "Alfredo's." There were white table cloths, candlelight and live music. Wine was poured into real wine glasses by well-dressed waiters with cloths over their arms. Thus began a tradition that became synonymous with the whitewater trip. Over the next several years, more than one romance had its start in the candlelight at "Alfredo's" – including that of future husband and wife Myles Smith and Ortrude White.

Another very important SUUSI tradition began in 1979. Millicent Simmons, a dance movement specialist with the National Endowment for the Arts and a performer and choreographer with the Birmingham Creative Dance Company, offered a week-long workshop that she called "Way Off Broadway." The course description in the catalog promised that participants would "learn some dance routines and songs from shows like 'Oliver,' 'A Chorus Line' and 'Sweet Charity.' It doesn't matter if you've got no experience or are a seasoned pro – there will be a place for you."

Simmons says that when she proposed the workshop, she had no thought that there would be a *performance* involved – but by the middle of the week, "everyone wanted to let the whole of SUUSI see what they had been doing." So on Thursday night at the Fair, "The Daily Plan-It" reported "the debut of the Way Off Broadway workshop production ... [featuring a] vivacious, energetic cast of future stars – 40, count 'em, 40! – directed by Millicent Simmons." The title of that first Way Off Broadway was "Oliver, A Medley."

By 1979, Serendipity had grown into one of the biggest events of the week. Inspired by the recent hit movie *Animal House*, many participants danced in "togas" (actually standard-issue Radford dormitory linens). Other forms of Serendipity-inspired creativity abounded. Monday night included a "Service Auction," with items that ranged from kisses by popular SUUSI leaders to a skinny-dipping outing, and "several wholly tasteless items from Frederick's of Hollywood." Tuesday night, Mary Ann Chew wrote and directed a dead-on, hilariously accurate "Serendipity Spoof."

The week closed with "X-Rated Jokes" from Chuck Larkin on Friday night, and a "feminist response" from blue joke teller Carol Sheridan. The Daily Plan-It reported late in the week that "We're having a problem with [Serendipity] security. Lots of underage and non-SUUSI gate crashers are attending. The only way to maintain control is to require a SUUSI nametag for admittance."

In that era, various groups ranging from Nature Staff to different congregations sent emissaries into the Heth ballroom early in the evening to set up and reserve their own tables for that night at Serendipity. One such group were the folks from the Greensboro church, whose table "hostess," Martha Shelton, was renowned for putting on a great party, complete with themes, decorations, and party favors.

Poncho Heavener met his future wife, Zeida Lamothe, at Serendipity in 1979, when she asked him to dance – something still relatively unusual at the time. From that experience, Heavener was inspired to offer a workshop titled "Serendipity Survival," offering participants tips on how to make the nightly dance less intimidating and socially awkward. "Serendipity could be such a great way to connect with people," he says, "but folks were hesitant to ask someone to dance. I noticed there were always a lot of people standing along the walls. I wanted to give them permission to get involved – to dance with whoever they wanted to, or with no one at all. To take the initiative and be in charge.

"It seemed like it was something folks needed. When I got there the first day, I was stunned to see 50 people in the room. I thought I had gone to the wrong place!"

Also from 1979:

- Planning took place for a "Cruise for UUs," departing from Charleston, S.C., in October.

- Coordinated by Diane Hamrick, an effort was made at Sunday dinner to have SUUSI veterans assigned to eat with each newcomer, thus easing the transition into what sometimes can be an overwhelming new community.

- On Tuesday, The Daily Plan-It revealed that the Radford Soccer Club had issued a challenge to take on "all Unitarian Universalists" in a soccer match. The next afternoon, a few dozen SUUSI-ites took them up on their offer – literally – in a "blood and guts match ... on the Commons." According to the post-game report, the "SUUSI Angels beat the Radford Rowdies 8-5 in a thrilling match that pitted skill against numbers. The amazing antics of the Rowdies were no match for the swarm they struggled against but could not escape. In the end, [we] thank the Radford University students for the hospitality and sportsmanship they displayed in this grand event."

- There was an LRY reunion to mark the 25th anniversary of the formation of LRY. Meanwhile, current teens were divided, for the first time, into two separate age groups – 12-14 year-olds and 15-17 year-olds. Pete Tolleson taught Dungeons and Dragons, which was all the rage that year.

- The 5-8 year-olds made their own rules for the week, which they called the "Thirteen Commandments": Raise your hand. Have patience. Be quiet and listen. Be considerate of others. Make friends. Don't talk back. Stay with the group. Don't run inside. Don't talk unless you have something to say. Go to a staff person for help. Respect others. Share. Be nice.

By the time it was all over, many were declaring SUUSI 1979 the "best ever." In her closing remarks, Director Kay Montgomery noted that "The miracles happen: the bagpipes in the morning, the song written for a beloved member of our community, the nurse who smiles and nurtures as she is wakened night after night, the child who blossoms, the rainbow, the new and lasting friendships... I cry and smile for the joy of having shared it with you."

Looking back a few years later, Montgomery said being SUUSI Director had been "one of the few things I've ever done where the rewards were clearly greater than the effort. But after all the shouting, the thing that I remember most clearly about that week was making coffee every morning with Karen Chandler. Everyone else would still be sleeping, [and] we'd pass one another, carrying water, or clean up the Stuart lounge for the staff meeting... Then sometimes we'd just sit on the outdoor steps for a minute. The simplest kind of communal housekeeping. Nothing special. But that's what I remember best."

The Eighties

As a new decade began, SUUSI was at an interesting crossroads in its institutional development. The Summer Institute had grown to become an ongoing community of a thousand or more members, now quite comfortably settled into Radford *University* (which had itself made the transition from being Radford "College" in 1979). Many workshops and nature trips were annual favorites. Several programs – from the nursery and children's activities to adult nightlife and Serendipity, from story-telling and song-swaps to the annual midweek picnic at Claytor Lake – were now not only eagerly anticipated each summer, but had become expected. A sense of routine was beginning to set in.

On the other hand, new and exciting offerings like parachuting, hot air balloon rides and Way Off Broadway had been added throughout the previous decade, quickly becoming cherished parts of the SUUSI experience. The Mountain was now open, offering Unitarian Universalist programming throughout the summer and indeed the year, and competing for the attentions of time and energy of many of SUUSI's long-time leaders. (At one point, in 1981, SUUSI's Director, the Director-Elect, the Nature Director, Board President and the theme talk coordinator were all active in leadership positions at The Mountain.) Meanwhile, in the broader culture, a decidedly conservative turn in America's political climate was alarming many in the SUUSI community, leading some to envision a more active role in collective social action for the Summer Institute.

It was against this backdrop that SUUSI began its next decade. For the first time ever, registration topped a thousand, as 1,071 people found their way to SUUSI 1980. Appropriately enough, the theme was "Belonging, Breaking Away and Returning."

Registration fees were increased by $10, across all age groups, to cover rapidly rising costs; meal fees also went up, but only by a dollar. Jake Haun, beginning the first of two years as Director, wanted to create challenging, high-quality programming that would be responsive to the needs and desires of all participants. To that end, he instituted a detailed end-of-the-week questionnaire to help guide decision-making for the following year. Feedback forms in individual workshops also were used.

Allaying any concerns that top-notch, national-level Unitarian Universalist talent might not attend SUUSI so long as it was held in a non-ERA state, Jacob Trapp, one of the denomination's most highly respected ministers and elder statesmen (he was 80 years old at the time), came to Radford in 1980 and gave not one, but three inspiring theme talks. He reflected, in order, on each of the three aspects of the year's theme. Beginning with "Belonging" on Monday, Trapp spoke with perhaps particular poignancy to members of the SUUSI community when he said, "Without community, there can be no real individuality... Community is the necessary sunlight in which the individual person can come to be." Later, Trapp went on to say, "We owe to our children a shared sense of belonging to the Great Tradition which, of course, has to be alive in *us*, to become alive in them."

One thing that helped knit the SUUSI community together in 1980, in a way never previously achieved, was the creation of "The SUUSI Mug Book." Here, in one place, for the first time since the group pictures of the 1950s at Blue Ridge, were the faces of everyone who was part of the SUUSI family. Participants were overjoyed to have, at their fingertips, the names, addresses and phone numbers – as well as individual photos – of each person who comprised the SUUSI community. Though there was some grumbling about the long line in which one had to stand to get one's picture taken, at the end of the line a hug awaited – and at the end of the week there was a treasured keepsake whose value few could have imagined during the hectic moments of check-in on Sunday.

The first mugbook

It was Jake Haun who had the vision to imagine the wide-reaching, positive impact such a "mugbook" could have on the SUUSI community. It would come to strengthen the kind of year-round connections that until the 1980s were much more difficult to maintain. Haun had shown SUUSI photographer Vonnie Hicks his own children's school directory, which included pictures along with names and addresses, and asked Hicks if SUUSI might be able to create something similar. "Alpha List" rosters were already being sold for a dollar each at the end of SUUSI, but Hicks knew that a photographic directory would be much more expensive – and difficult – to produce.

"I did the research, and found out we could do a mugbook, using a process developed by Kodak that involved dot-screening. I learned the process and put together a pilot version to take to the spring staff meeting," says Hicks, "and they loved it! So that summer [1980] we did the first mugbook. A printing press in Christiansburg produced the first one, but it took us a few years to find the right printer and get the process down." Included in the 1980 mugbook was the first known written history of SUUSI, a one-page summary of the Summer Institute's first 30 years.

Another innovation in 1980 was the SUUSI Forum, which followed evening worship and provided a bridge between those services and the nightlife of Serendipity, Quiet Serendipity and the like. Facilitators led discussions on a variety of subjects, each beginning at 9:45 p.m. Topics included "Money, Contracts and Marriage," "Southern [Human Rights] Issues," "Step-Families," "How to Lobby Your State Legislature" and "The Highlands Camp and Conference Center [The Mountain]."

Kay Montgomery floating back to earth during her 1980 parachute jump

Back for a second straight year were the hugely successful parachuting adventure and Way Off Broadway. Kay Montgomery, past SUUSI Director, was one of the parachuters in 1980, along with co-registrar Judy Newell. "Judy had been a dancer, and she was blessed with such

*Kay Montgomery, Judy Newell and Mary Feagan back on
the ground after their exhilarating jump in 1980*

incredible body wisdom," recalls Montgomery. "She jumped out of the plane right before me, and did it with such grace. For my part, I was simply *terrified*. It took me a while to get out on that wing. But I remember thinking – literally – that I would rather die, than be embarrassed. So eventually, I jumped."The experience was so special for her that Montgomery, who from 1985-2013 served as Executive Vice-President of the UUA, kept on her office wall in Boston a framed photograph of herself, dangling from a parachute in mid-air against a backdrop of Virginia mountain clouds. It was a reminder, she says, of what is possible.

Over the years, countless SUUSI-goers have discovered what they are capable of through the magic of Way Off Broadway and later its offshoot, Teen Way Off Broadway. In 1980, after the smashing success of "Oliver, A Medley" the year before, Director Millicent Simmons invited to SUUSI a choreographer with whom she had collaborated in, of all places, Argentina. Marj Nordstrom and Simmons had worked together, as fellow expatriates whose spouses were living and working in Argentina, on a production of "Godspell." Simmons managed to talk Nordstrom, "a nice, sweet, Protestant lady," into joining her at SUUSI for an encore. (Coincidentally, years earlier Simmons and Nordstrom had also met and gotten to know future SUUSI bagpiper Dick Scobie – *in Argentina.*)

"Marj was simply a lovely woman who could sweet talk anyone into getting on stage," says Simmons. "One year we even had a guy who played the saw in the orchestra." The 1980 production of "Godspell" – which had been moved into the theater and into "prime time" on Friday night – sold out, and the following year, two shows were offered. Way Off Broadway had become a smash hit at SUUSI, and would continue through the remainder of the decade, providing a vehicle not only for those of all ages to shine by singing and dancing on stage, but also for an eclectic array of SUUSI musicians who formed an orchestra during the week each year and performed all of the show's music – live.

As Jake Haun put it, SUUSI had become "a community whose people expect, and find, the best in each other."

But questions remained about *where* that community should come together. Despite having enjoyed an ideal, even "idyllic" home now for six consecutive summers, there was deep consternation about the fact that Virginia was a non-ERA state. Even before SUUSI 1980, it was announced to the community that "there are 13 places where SUUSI might be held in 1981 – 11 [of them]... in Tennessee" (the Volunteer State being the only one in the Appalachian target area that had ratified the Equal Rights Amendment – in 1972 – though it later rescinded that ratification). As they departed Radford on Saturday, Aug. 2, 1980, some among the more than 1,000 participants were wearing T-shirts that bore the motto "I will return, for I like myself when I am with you" – but none knew for sure how many more years that return would be to Radford.

When the Institute did, indeed, reconvene in Radford on the last

Sunday of July in 1981, participants learned that SUUSI would be staying at Radford University for the foreseeable future. During the previous months, a Site Search Committee had evaluated many potential locations, including past locations such as Boone, Sewanee, Blue Ridge and Brevard. Radford had come out on top, scoring much higher on a list of criteria than the closest runner-up, Appalachian State. Of the primary contender in Tennessee, Pam Phelps, Board President, wrote in the 1981 catalog, "We ... made a special trip to Sewanee... With five of the staff, we toured The University of the South, and found it inadequate for SUUSI."

The evaluation form used in the site search reveals the competing interests SUUSI leaders were trying to juggle in making their decision:

1. Is it located in an ERA-ratified state?
2. Will it accommodate 800-1,000 people?
3. Is it located close to a population center in the Southeast? The mountains?
4. Would the cost be in keeping with a family vacation?
5. Do the characteristics of the site enhance and encourage community and family participation?
6. Is the site conducive to a good nature program?
7. Are there adequate facilities for the nursery? The youth program?
8. Are the facilities and laws adequate and conducive to a good adult program? A safe, enjoyable Serendipity?
9. Are the facilities suitable for participants who are handicapped or have special physical needs?
10. Is there an attitude of positive acceptance toward our philosophies and religious concepts?
11. Is the site desirable in the opinion of participants?

Just as SUUSI was committing to Radford, the Equal Rights Amendment died, having failed to achieve the necessary number of states for adoption. There would not be another SUUSI site search for nearly a decade.

SUUSI 1981 began with a "UU Revival" on Sunday night, led by Clearwater's John Burciaga. Clearwater was becoming the largest and most organized congregational presence at SUUSI, and its minister's revival inspired many an "Amen!" and plenty of good-ol' gospel singing. "Amazing Place," in particular, had attendees talking: "Amazing place that we have found, a place we love to be; where hope and joy and love abound – our sweet community..." Regardless of whether they loved the idea of a revival or felt it was "too Christian," all agreed the opening night celebration was worthy of a community that was glad simply to be together again, and to feel settled once more in its Radford home.

Besides a revival, the week provided other challenges to some participants' comfort zones. For the first time, there was an open presence – and public witness – by gay and lesbian Unitarian Universalists. Bob Wheatley, director of the UUA's Office of Lesbian and Gay Concerns, led a week-long workshop titled "What Every Religious Liberal Should Know About Being Gay." Each day a different aspect of this heretofore taboo topic was examined:

Monday: "Being homo- or bi-sexual in a heterosexual world. What's it like to be left-handed in a world of right-handed nuts? Some personal and professional views."

Tuesday: "Homosexuals and Bible Belt religions. Scripture-based homophobia, hatred and rejection can never lead to acceptance and understanding of lesbians and gay men. A look at how it all began."

Wednesday: "Gay couples and wedding ceremonies. What every UU minister and local church board member should know about a growing issue. Should we or shouldn't we perform such services in UU churches?"

Thursday: "Being parents, relatives or friends of gays and lesbians. Whether you know it or not, you *do* know someone who is one. How do you handle it?"

Friday: "Not in our church! On hiring openly gay/lesbian ministers, DREs, denominational officials and other assorted leaders. Oh WOW!"

Wheatley's workshop sparked some amount of controversy. On Thursday night, a two-hour discussion titled "Loving Someone Gay" was held in Muse Lounge prior to Quiet Serendipity. One participant wrote in the next day's newsletter, "In my opinion the activities of the Lesbian Gay Caucus reflect discredit on the denomination in the eyes of the public. I wish to express my disapproval of the Institute's policy of allowing their advertising." Nonetheless, the following year, there was a nightly "Conversation on Lesbian and Gay Concerns," as well as a new "Support Group for Lesbian/Gay/Bisexual People." SUUSI was taking its first tentative steps toward becoming a truly welcoming community.

Wheatley wore two hats on behalf of the UUA at SUUSI 1981. As Associate Director of the UUA Office of Social Responsibility, he led another group in formulating a "SUUSI Social Concerns Resolution," which he forwarded to UUA President Eugene Pickett (formerly the minister for churches in Miami, Richmond and Atlanta). Signed by four dozen SUUSI participants from six different states, it was titled "Religious Liberals and the Far Right." With Reaganism on the rise, the signers decried an agenda of "anti women's choice regarding abortion, anti ERA, anti small-gun control, pro teaching of creationism, pro school prayer" that it said was "contrary to views and standards held by many Unitarian Universalists."

"Be it therefore resolved," the resolution continued, "that we, the undersigned attendants [*sic*] at the 1981 Southeast Unitarian Universalist Summer Institute do, indeed, view with alarm the aforementioned developments, and recommend ... that national

Unitarian Universalist leadership prepare a white paper describing and defining the recent religious extremist phenomenon; that this white paper be distributed to all Unitarian Universalist ministers; call upon our ministerial and educational leaders to inform themselves fully of these facts and forthwith begin programs of information and education to alert their memberships of the issues involved... [and] call upon individual Unitarian Universalists everywhere to join in actively opposing these forces of extreme religious conservatism which we, in good conscience, feel we must resist if we are to protect precious freedoms and prerogatives gained for us in other times by like-minded liberal religious pioneers, of whose heritage we are now the recipients."

President Pickett responded positively, writing on Sept. 4, 1981:

Dear SUUSI Friends,

Bob Wheatley has brought to my attention your recent resolution on "Religious Liberals and the Far Right." I am pleased that you devoted some of your Summer Institute time to this important subject.

I want you to know that we take your concerns seriously. I understand that our Section on Social Responsibility is in the process of producing a comprehensive mailing for all of our churches with analysis of the New Religious Right and suggestions and resources for countering their efforts. We have been very active, in addition, in urging our congregations to oppose the Family Protection Act which threatens all of us...

Sincerely,
Eugene Pickett
President, UUA

Amid the serious work for social justice, there were several new recreational activities at SUUSI in 1981, including the first annual "Fun Run," the brainchild of Avery Henderson. Winners in the three-mile division were Dave Smith (men), Bobbie Pohl (women) and Shane Benedict and Neal Cline (youth). Dave Smith also won the one-mile race. All participants received treasured "By Damn I Made It" awards.

Canoeing, taught by Neal Sanders and Jack Hart, as well as kayaking and other active water adventures were also popular. In those days, SUUSI's canoes were borrowed from The Mountain and driven to Radford by various members of the Nature Staff. Trips themselves – whether canoe outings or hikes, tubing or a trip to go horseback riding – involved participants piling into one another's cars for the drive. Drivers and riders were coordinated during meetings the night before the trip. The only bus on campus was the "Miami bus." Nature vans were still in the future.

The 1981 whitewater rafting outing was so popular, in fact, that even with the use of the Miami bus some participants had to carpool, following the bus into the backwaters of West Virginia for the annual day of challenge and fun (which culminated, once again, with the now-traditional Italian feast back at "Alfredo's"). For those inclined to more gentle explorations of the natural world,

SUUSI whitewater rafters

a wide variety of Interpretive Field-Study Trips were offered, including a day trip to an archaeological dig, mushrooming, bird-watching and fossil-finding. Of course, a peaceful float down the New River in an inner tube was also possible, with tubing trips designed for just about every demographic and interest group, including Teens.

Dirty Day had grown so popular with the kids (and their parents) that an "Intergenerational Dirty Day" was scheduled to complete the week's nature offerings on Friday afternoon. For a $3 fee, adults were challenged to "see if you can relax your adult restrictions about getting dirty and join in the fun." Though there is no record of which adults took the dare (or if there was an adult version of the "Dirty Dozen"), the twelve youth winners of that esteemed honor were Kristen Malling, John Wheelan, Patrick Pohl, Mark Harris, Stephanie Clark, Arnold Miller, Peter Benedict, Douglas Bell, Lisa Zander, Teak Shore, David Bessel and John Felts.

There were as many different ways for young people to have fun at SUUSI in 1981 as there were young people. Pranks ranged from putting Vaseline on door knobs to setting off dorm fire alarms to rolling toilet paper out upper floor dorm windows. In fact, defenestration of just about any object one could lay one's hands on seemed to be a rite of passage, aided by the fact that in those days open windows (with constantly running fans and the window screens removed) were the norm for all SUUSI dorm rooms. And annually, for many of the early years at Radford, there was also at least one loud outburst of a long string of firecrackers at some unexpected time and location on campus – always carefully timed to coincide with a large gathering of people. Years later, Allen Bergal confessed to being the firecracker artist.

For the first time, there was a Young Adult program, offering community and activities for those aged 18-25. Tracey DeVol came up with the idea and coordinated the program. Also for the first time, Way Off Broadway gave two performances on Friday night to accommodate demand. Since the show featured the music of "Hair," the cast gave an early show that was rated "K-P" (for kids and parents) and a late show rated "H-C" ("hard-chord"). After the final curtain, the cast went en masse to the final night of Serendipity – in costume – and led a sing-along with music from the Sixties.

One memorable theme talk was titled "Womanstruggle." Former Director Kay Montgomery recounted struggles both deeply personal and socially universal. "The goal hadn't been to join the men's society," she said. "The goal had been *transformation* for both men and women... [Now] once more, this time with a little more humor and a little more humility, we're reshaping our lives. And so are men." John (Alexis) Jones sang "Bread and Roses" to make the morning complete.

At least one couple who is still together met at SUUSI in 1981. In addition to his duties as Director, Jake Haun played matchmaker that year, bringing together Myles Smith and Ortrude White. "Jake knew I was recently divorced," says Smith, "and he told me there was a lady I should meet, from Richmond. When I got to registration on Sunday, there she was, doing calligraphy of everyone's name on the nametags. I commented how beautiful her work was. Turns out we were both city planners, so we had something in common.

"Later in the week, I found out she was going whitewater rafting, and I asked Bill Spurgin, who was in charge of 'Alfredo's' that year, if I could serve her table. I got a lot of red wine into her, and then asked if she would go with me to Serendipity after dinner. The rest, as they say, is history!" Myles bought Ortrude a ring at the Artisan's Bazaar the following year, proposed, and they were married in February 1984. "It gives you a really special feeling about SUUSI when you have that kind of personal history," he says. "We've always felt a very strong connection to SUUSI, because SUUSI is the reason *we* are connected."

Some folks were moved to capture their memories of the week in melody or poetry. Suki Nickerson's rewording of the popular 1920s Eddie Cantor song "If You Knew Susie" became the unofficial theme song of 1981:

> If you knew SUUSI, like we know SUUSI –
> Oh, oh, oh ... what a trip!
> We come by buses, and make our fusses
> But gee whiz, aren't you glad we are usses?
> Registration: First we get mugged, it tries our patience,
> But we make it through and we get hugged.
>
> If you knew SUUSI, like we know SUUSI –
> Oh, oh, oh ... what a gang!
> Yes, by cracky, we're somewhat wacky,
> And oh gee, holy Moses, we get tacky!
> Pie-toss action gives us our kicks,
> And satisfaction comes from getting our licks.
> If you knew SUUSI, like we know SUUSI –
> Oh, oh ... what a gang!

On a more serious note, Maxim Tabory shared a poem in the Friday newsletter titled "The Song Shared in Our Hearts":

> the music
>   of our harmoniously beating hearts
>   fills the silent infinite with
> melody
>   and the loneliness with smiles.
> radiant
>   it flies beyond the boundaries of the
>   reasoning mind, and adorns our lives with
> beauty.
>   the song shared in our hearts is more deeply
> intimate
>   than any other closeness.
>   it slows down the race of the minutes
>   and brightens the grayness of our

                                        fleeting days
            with the diamonds of
    memories

And John (Alexis) Jones, in the Friday NUUS, reminded participants of the fact that it was *they* who had created those memories:

> At the risk of heresy, I want to say that SUUSI is not a special event. What we have done is to have entrusted a small group of people with the responsibility to create the *space* for SUUSI to happen. And what we did to be here is simply to buy a ticket and present ourselves. That's all.
>
> From my personal experiences, and those of loved ones I have known here, we sometimes go home – back to the routine we left – get depressed, feel lonely, and may or may not feel a need to contact someone we met [here]. What is missing, then, in our lives, is our *experience* of being here. What I want you all to know is that only *you* created your experience here. Radford did not. Your friends did not. The Staff did not. SUUSI did not. You did.
>
> And you can take this experience home with you. You can integrate it into your life – your family, your friends, your work, your environment – and, simply … into *you*.

Many participants sought to extend the SUUSI experience later into the summer, and into the fall, with a record number of "decompression parties." The Eno River (N.C.) Fellowship held a "SUUSI Celebration" picnic at Chapel Hill Lake, to go along with a Sunday morning service highlighting SUUSI memories. Folks in Richmond, Miami-Fort Lauderdale, Atlanta and Birmingham also reported highly successful decompression events.

People further up the eastern seaboard of the United States were beginning to catch the summer institute fever as well. Culminating nearly three years of planning in mid-July, 1982, more than 75 Unitarian Universalists hailing from Maryland to New York gathered at Lafayette College in Pennsylvania for the first-ever UUMAC (Unitarian Universalist Mid-Atlantic Community). Among them was Morris Hudgins, who some years earlier had become the minister in Media, Pa. Hudgins had inspired the UUs further north with his testimonials about the wonders of SUUSI (which he still attended religiously). Itself born of the inspiration of the *Southwest* Summer Institute, SUUSI had now given birth to three other separate and distinct Unitarian Universalist gatherings and gathering places – SWIM, The Mountain and UUMAC.

By 1982, SUUSI was truly settled into its own home at Radford. Age-centric, lifestyle-centric and affinity group housing were being offered, both officially and unofficially, to help the thousand-plus participants build closer connections with others amid a large, active and diverse population. Nature Staff lived, worked, played and partied together in Trinkle. Young adults now had their own space, in Floyd Hall, where they created a lounge called "Floyd's Place." And, for the first time in decades, teenagers were allowed to be housed together.

Lynn Wheal (formerly Thompson) had become Youth Director the previous year, and was slowly trying to resurrect a Teen Program from the ashes of LRY. "Having grown up as a teen at Summer Institute and then gone away for a few years as a young adult, when I came back to SUUSI it was disturbing to see what had happened to the Teen Program," she recalls. "There really wasn't much programming; the teens were largely being left to their own devices, unsupervised. I went to the Board and asked for a 'Teen Dorm' to provide some structure."

As Jan Machler, 1982 Board President, wrote in the catalog that year, "The Youth Staff presented a proposal to the Board offering teens (14 to 17 years old) the option of an alternative family experience – an extended family. Teens choosing this option will be living among peers and Youth Staff in Peery Hall. Freedom with responsibility is something we talk about a lot with our kids. The youth floor(s) will allow teens to be responsible, with freedom, in a safe environment. A midnight curfew will be in effect for all teens, whether choosing the program or not.

"After thoroughly considering all aspects of the proposed program, the Board unanimously approved the youth floor(s) proposal for SUUSI '82. Further, the Board set up a mechanism for monitoring the program during SUUSI '82, and for having an evaluation report presented by the Youth Director at the Fall Board meeting. The Board hopes and anticipates that this experimental program will help our teens feel more a part of SUUSI."

The Teen Program was thus reborn, and it quickly proved to be a huge success. Trudy Atkin, a friend of Wheal's from Richmond, was brought in to coordinate an extensive array of teen activities, which began each day after lunch and wrapped up late at night with midnight movies. Afternoon workshops included discussions ("rap groups") about life and death, religion and adolescence, and – literally – sex, drugs and rock and roll. There were leather crafts and T-shirt art, and a video game room which had been set up in the Peery lounge courtesy of, and staffed by, Radford. There was teen tubing and water skiing on Claytor Lake – and of course, teens could still participate in Dirty Day. Nighttime activities included the introduction of a mid-week hayride and a Friday night love feast. Parties in the Peery lounge featured rock and new wave music. Late-night movies ranged from *Easy Rider* to *Yellow Submarine* to *The Concert for Bangladesh*.

The program proved to be such a success that the following year, the teens occupied two floors in Peery, and warranted their own Teen Staff.

For the younger children, Wheal had engaged a staff that included several teenagers, helping them to afford their SUUSI experience with staff credit (not to mention the coveted Youth Staff T-shirt). Throughout the day there were a wide variety of activities, both indoor and outdoor, onsite and offsite, that served to create lasting memories for the children. Dick Scobie gave a bagpipe demonstration to a group of awestruck children who had previously only heard the unmistakable sound emanating from heaven in the mornings, on their way to breakfast at Muse.

When weather permitted (and even, sometimes, when it didn't), crafts and sing-alongs, watermelon eating and homemade ice cream for build-your-own-sundaes meant there was always something happening on the Peery patio, where the echo of

A tradition in the 1980s involved surprising the Director with a cream pie to the face sometime during the week. Here, 1982 Director Sonya Prestridge reacts after being "pied."

children's laughter created a SUUSI zone of joy. There were games of slip-and-slide or freeze-tag in the Governors Quad each day. Hot afternoons were cooled off with frozen bananas and grapes, or ice pops. A Slushee machine was never far away. Beloved Youth Staffer Audrey Hudgins brought a sense of adventure – and humor – to everything the youth did, whether it was a well-timed camp song when an overfilled van got stuck in some mud, or an ill-timed pie to the face of a fellow staffer. And there always seemed to be a youth trip underway. Outings to Cascades and Pandapas Pond (an active beaver pond), or tubing on the New River appealed to the nature lovers, while roller skating and the Lakeside Amusement Park served the needs of a different crowd. Radford University's brand-new Dedmon Center, located just across East

Main Street, provided new, modern recreational facilities like a weight room and a competition swimming pool.

It had been hoped that Ingathering would take place at the Dedmon Center in 1982, but at the last minute, that plan fell through. Gathering instead in Preston Auditorium for the eighth straight July, a thousand people were welcomed to SUUSI with the music and singing of Pam Phelps and friends (including clowns and a mime). Director Sonya Prestridge said it was her "goal for participants to experience [SUUSI as] a 'good people place' – an environment that fosters human fulfillment, enhances human rights and dignity, and reinforces the self-esteem of [its] people." Later that evening, for those new to SUUSI, long-time participant and workshop leader Don Male offered a Sunday night "Introduction to SUUSI," explaining jargon and explicating traditions and sacred cows.

On Monday morning, Eugene Pickett, President of the UUA, addressed a standing-room only audience in Porterfield Auditorium. Pickett, who had first attended the Southern

Activities at the annual Picnic included a "lap sit" game in which participants would see how many people could sit in a circle on each other's laps.

Unitarian Summer Institute 29 years earlier at Blue Ridge, began by stating the obvious, noting "both the Institute and I have come a long way!" Comparing his life with that of SUUSI, Pickett added it was "not without some difficulties during the intervening years." With pride he noted that "SUUSI has become the largest and most comprehensive Summer Institute in our movement."

Indeed, Director Sonya Prestridge pointed out that there were 108 workshops and 96 nature trips from which to choose. There were new nature offerings, including hang gliding, overnight camping, fishing, orienteering, water skiing, vertical caving and "night owl" canoeing. SUUSI programming was slowly becoming more round-the-clock.

No history of SUUSI would be complete – or completely honest – without mention of the practice of "skinny-dipping" that was part and parcel of the SUUSI experience for some participants from the late 1970s well into the 1990s. It all began with "private" Nature Staff outings that occurred before and after SUUSI proper, where staff members would "go to the lake" on the Saturday before campers arrived on campus, or "celebrate at Cascades" on the following Saturday after SUUSI had ended.

With such a free-spirited community – and the presence of several practicing nudists on the staff – it was not long before certain nature trips became "clothing optional" outings, sometimes much to the surprise of unsuspecting SUUSI participants. One person recalls signing up for a hike in 1982 "which looked like it was a regular part of the SUUSI program. It was listed just like the other nature trips in the catalog." He continues the story: "After hiking for a while, we reached the water and suddenly the trip leader, a woman, took off her clothes and jumped in the water. She looked at the rest of us and said, 'Come on in. The water's great!' Needless to say, I was pretty surprised. There had been *no* indication ahead of time that this was a clothing-optional trip. Some of us clearly knew what was going on, but others – including me – did not."

At that time, catalog descriptions used phrases like "we will take a short, refreshing dip" or "enjoy the most private swimming hole in the state," but in fact many hikes would, upon reaching any sufficiently secluded water or wilderness, suddenly become clothing optional. If one was not in the know, one was in for a potentially unwelcome surprise. After receiving some negative feedback regarding clothing optional nature trips in 1982, the Nature Staff in next year's catalog specifically indicated certain trips were open only to those "age 18 and up." Come 1986, two hikes – Dismal Falls Evening, and Bent Mountain Falls – were listed as "swimsuit optional," and by 1987, there were no less than five hikes that openly advertised "skinny-dipping."

It would be several years before public nudity was expressly prohibited at SUUSI-sponsored activities, and even then unsanctioned, "underground" skinny-dipping trips by various groups of participants continued well on toward the turn of the century.

The Talent Show returned to SUUSI in 1982. Thursday evening's intergenerational program was devoted to allowing singers, storytellers, skit-creators and artists of all stripes to "show off what they have learned and what they have done this week." The Fun Run moved to Claytor Lake, where it became a fixture at the Picnic for many years; the first winners at the much more challenging Claytor Lake three-mile course were John Felts and Barb Scherrer. The first annual Radford Staff vs. SUUSI Staff volleyball game ended with SUUSI taking a drubbing – despite the fact that the referee was a SUUSI participant.

General workshops ranged from computers to calligraphy. Eleanor Sableski led a new workshop titled "Sing Out at the O.K. Chorale," which would eventually evolve into the long-running SUUSI Cantatori. Graphics designer Ortrude White created a beautiful butterfly logo that adorned not only the 1981 and 1982 catalogs, but also SUUSI T-shirts, mugs and memorabilia on sale in the Bookstore, including a seemingly ubiquitous yellow frisbee. The masthead of the 1982 newsletter, "The SUUSI Network," even featured a smiling caterpillar and the wings of a butterfly, symbolizing the transformations that take place throughout SUUSI week. Brydie and Erdman Palmore of Chapel Hill, N.C., were the newsletter editors that year.

One of the newsletter articles reported that Bill Ranck and Bev Booth were married on Wednesday, with Eugene Pickett officiating and 300 friends and well-wishers attending. As Ranck said of having the UUA President perform his nuptials, "That's better than being married by the Pope!" In lieu of a honeymoon, the happy couple went canoeing on Claytor Lake.

The 1982 Forum offered multiple discussion topics each night of the week, at various locations around campus, ranging from politics to poetry sharing to religious education to "lesbian and gay concerns." Gene Navias, the UUA's new Religious Education Director, met with those interested in congregational R.E., and also offered a slide show about the new Unitarian outreach to kindred congregations in Transylvania, while Joe Chancey, a minister in Atlanta, facilitated those who wanted a safe space to discuss gay and lesbian issues.

Thursday's somber Forum topic was "How to Prevent a Nuclear War." The newsletter reported that earlier the same day, the 9-13 year-olds "thought, sang and talked about what a nuclear holocaust" could entail. The subject also had been raised in William Holway's theme talk on Tuesday, and it continued to be a topic of discussion for several years to come (two of the workshops in 1983 were called "How to Survive Nuclear Disaster in Non-Target Areas" and "The Threat of Nuclear War: From Facts to Feelings"). It seems President Reagan's nuclear buildup was never far from people's thoughts in those days.

With all the increased activity and programming, it was only natural that fees would increase. Registration (for an adult) cost $65 in 1982, with beds going for $38 for the week. Meals (for those age 15 and above) cost $51. Part of those costs were to cover the fact that SUUSI was continuing to give financial support both to The Mountain (from which it was borrowing considerable amounts of nature equipment) and to the Council of Unitarian

Rev. Tim Ashton leads a discussion under the Wisdom Tree

Universalist Camps and Conferences (CU2C2) – of which SUUSI's latest offshoot, UUMAC, was now a member.

More than one third of the 1,000-plus participants filled out an evaluation form in 1982, and the week received an average rating of 6.34 out of 7. Bruce Kitchell of Atlanta, SUUSI's first computer guru, crunched the numbers and reported that the overall satisfaction with Summer Institute was extremely high. The budget was approaching $200,000 annually.

Though there was now an expectation that Directors would serve for two years, the demands of work and graduate school led Sonya Prestridge to turn over the reins in 1983 to Florence Cohan of Miami, who had previously coordinated adult workshops and Serendipity. When a professionally produced catalog, with slick magazine-type paper, arrived in participant mailboxes in the spring, it heralded SUUSI with one word: "Celebrate." (Ever since, Directors have tended to prefer simple, easily memorable and understood themes that capture the essence of the spirit of

Chuck Larkin tells a story during the Picnic at Claytor Lake

SUUSI). Mirroring the simplicity of the 1983 theme was the logo – two joyously dancing, stylized figures against a horizon depicting a mountain range and a large, brightly shining sun.

The publicity materials prior to SUUSI 1983 encouraged Unitarian Universalists in local congregations to create banners representing their church, and to bring those banners to SUUSI for something new – a "banner parade." On Sunday evening, July 24, just after the "First Supper," hundreds of people of all ages, representing congregations from Florida to Pennsylvania to beyond the Mississippi River, milled around at the lily pond outside Muse, holding banners and greeting one another with excited hugs. At precisely 7 o'clock (more or less), they formed a line and began a procession that eventually stretched all the way from the steps of Muse to the steps of Preston Auditorium. The variety of colors, shapes and messages on the congregational banners demonstrated how wide was the net now cast by this Southeast Summer Institute. Looking back at the banner parade,

Sylvia Barnes exclaimed, "We've taken the spirit we have [every year] on Friday, and started the week with it!"

Indeed, inside Preston the feeling of joy and celebration was palpable during the Ingathering ceremony. Millicent Simmons started things off with a choreographed dance, followed by remarks from Board President Myles Smith. John (Alexis) Jones sang two songs – Ric Masten's iconic "Let It Be a Dance," and later "Love Is a Circle." Barbara Moore sang "Song of the Soul" to conclude the ceremony. In between, Chuck Larkin told the "story of SUUSI," while former Youth Director Wayne Starkey offered a skit with and for the children.

It was announced that for the first time, more than 1,100 people now comprised the SUUSI community, of whom roughly 300 – wearing special orange nametags that got them plenty of SUUSI hugs – were first-timers. Included were four generations of Saxes: patriarch Max, along with Bob, Bill, Beverly, Caroline and Helen, as well as Barbara and Robert Rosenberg and their son (Max's great-grandson) Richie. Barney Hurlbutt was recognized as having traveled the furthest to SUUSI after flying in from Hawaii. Don Male was honored for attending his 25th Summer Institute.

But not everything went as smoothly as Ingathering on that first day of 1983. Though registrants were photographed for the mugbook, as usual, at the end of their check-in, once mugger (and SUUSI frisbee phenom) Dane Victorine began developing the film on Monday, he discovered that none of the photos had come out. The community was alerted, and "Operation Re-Mug" began. Pictures were retaken outside the Muse cafeteria throughout the day on Tuesday and Wednesday, and – with the help of a veritable army of volunteers who were pressed into duty by the emergency – the mugbook was still completed in time to be distributed (although in some copies the way the pages were collated left participants alphabetically challenged).

Serendipity was thrown off balance in 1983 by a change in Virginia's drinking age. Until that year, 18-year-olds could legally drink in Virginia, but a change in the law that increased the age to 19 created a minor stir at SUUSI, particularly in the party zones at Heth. This did nothing, however, to quell the growing enthusiasm for two Serendipity traditions – highly competitive, over-the-top individual (and group) costumes on Costume Night, and the long and winding, raucously inebriated conga line that accompanied the playing of Ritchie Valens' "La Bamba" at the stroke of midnight each night.

One of those nights included a full moon, a fact that was not lost on the Teens, who at the time were out in the country at their ever-popular hayride. Gathered around the bonfire at Mr. Flincham's farm, under the full moon, there was much howling and screaming to accompany both marshmallow roasting and some less appropriate, though predictable, adolescent acting out. Yet perhaps nothing was more inappropriate in 1983 than the Young Adult underground newsletter. "The Inside Scoop" featured crude jokes, gossip about SUUSI personalities whose identities were only thinly veiled, and a barrage of double entendres. The YA's reputations were redeemed later in the week, however, when they were called in to help produce the official SUUSI newsletter, "The SUUSI Network," while its staff took a day off to "brave the rapids of the New River."

Though most nature trips went off without a hitch (participants in the post-SUUSI survey chose Nature as the "program of highest quality" in 1983), there was a minor parachuting injury. Jane Pointer of Knoxville broke her ankle in a hard landing and had to spend the rest of the week on crutches. Meanwhile, for those not inclined to jump, airplane rides had been added to the list of offerings, harkening back to the very first Summer Institute in 1950.

Worship, which just a few years earlier one minister had described as "akin to a fringe event at SUUSI," continued to expand its place amid the SUUSI spirit of celebration. John Burciaga offered early morning vespers services with meditation and poetry. He also led the increasingly popular Wisdom Tree

An early version of the Star Car allowed Youth Staff to transport small children around campus. Here, Bill Loomis delivers some kids to Floyd Hall.

afternoon workshop. Christine Robinson led an intergenerational worship service at the Claytor Lake Picnic. Other worship leaders were Kendyl Gibbons, and the Southeast's new Inter-District UUA Representative, Robert Hill of Auburn, Ala. SUUSI welcomed a non-UU as one of its theme speakers when United Methodist minister Jim Brewster of Niagara Falls, N.Y., spoke – underneath an array of beautiful congregational banners in Porterfield Auditorium – on the Transcendentalist and Unitarian Henry David Thoreau.

A growing awareness of earth-centered and Native American religious traditions – the early edges of the pagan movement within Unitarian Universalism – could be felt in programming. A "Celebration Rite" that began in 1982 for women only was expanded in 1983 to include men. The Youth Staff was energized by the addition of Floating Eagle Feather, a charismatic young storyteller and chanter from Honduras who engaged and entertained children of all ages, teaching them native songs,

Floating Eagle Feather

stories and dances and bringing an energy and spirit to SUUSI not seen before or since.

Eagle Feather was also instrumental in coordinating card-making and visits by the older children to two area hospitals. Early in his own life, Eagle Feather had been gravely ill, requiring major surgery that left him with a long scar down his chest. He tearfully confided to several members of the Youth Staff about how embarrassed he had always been by the scar – until he came to SUUSI, that is, where people were so free and accepting of their own bodies and others'. After that confession, for the remainder of his time at SUUSI – many happy years on Youth Staff, until health problems prevented his return – he wore a leather vest, opened at the chest to expose his heart, both literally and metaphorically. In a poem that appeared in the newsletter on Wednesday, he wrote:

> We become fearless as Love
> becomes greater within us,

and work to bring that love
to all, and brave easily
(with perhaps a few blisters)
the actions of those opposed
to One Living Society.

We find a pilgrimage
in telling a child a story
in open revolt to materialism,
as pure love is spun between us.
We fold cranes in folded pilgrimage
to a desire for all the children
to have long lives, filled with happiness,
and send them to those we feel are
oppressing us, or our brothers
and our sisters.

We wish these people long lives, happy lives,
for we know such a wish cannot come true
unless these folk also begin to work
to make long happiness possible for all Living,
and we help these people
find their own way of making
pilgrimage from fear to Love.

Floating Eagle Feather died of AIDS in 1991. When an impromptu, chalk-on-sidewalk version of the AIDS Quilt was created one SUUSI several years later, his name was lovingly inscribed there by his Unitarian Universalist community of the heart.

The spirit of celebration at SUUSI 1983 was also captured in another poem which appeared in the newsletter, by J. Carroll Simms of Richmond:

WHY I COME TO SUUSI
To climb a mountain,
See a waterfall,
Shed a tear –
Think in silence
Know you're here.
To laugh and sing,
To dance and play,
And just be near my friends –
Then closer to myself.
SUUSI's magic helps me understand,
Reminds me of the life within
We celebrate each year.

The newsletter was also home to complaints about the legendary height (or more accurately, lack thereof) of the shower heads in Radford's bathrooms. One person wrote, "Did you ever wonder, every time you stand 'under' the shower, why are all the Radford students under 4'11" tall?" [Or for that matter,] why 40% of your time is spent trying to lock and unlock your dorm door?"

Singing, from Boomslang Meade's "When I Die I Want to Go to Radford" to Lee Knight's "The Bells" to the Pete Leary song-swap – not to mention two rousing performances of "Oklahoma" by Way Off Broadway – made 1983 perhaps the most musical SUUSI yet.

Yet if one image of the year remains strongest in the memories of those who were there, it is *color*. Bright, vivid color. A long wire fence, about four feet tall, was placed in the middle of the Commons, and brightly colored streamers, ribbons and yarn were provided so that throughout the week, participants walking to and from Muse could weave together a colorful "rainbow fence." The fence was an ongoing, ever-changing work of art, attracting people of every age together in a massive, community-wide project that was simply spectacular to behold. Then amazingly, on Saturday morning at the newly dubbed "Out-Gathering," portions of the rainbow actually were sent aloft, tied to a giant helium balloon structure along with messages written by individual SUUSI participants that were SUUSI's message to the world. As the ribbons slowly rose into the morning sky, there was a sense of connection with the broader community to help carry participants back into their "real-world" life.

As reported in the *Floyd County (Va.) Press*, the UU message-in-a-bottle, which had included contact information for SUUSI, traveled some 25 miles south before being snagged in some tall trees on the property of the Turpin family. Juanita Turpin wrote:

> Dear Friends,
>
> We found your balloons in treetops about 100 feet high near our house. It was sighted Saturday evening by a neighbor who first thought it was an airplane that had crashed. It stretched over the tops of five pine trees. My husband climbed the trees and pulled all he could of it out...
>
> We have three children and they have really enjoyed this... From all the different children and places that we found on the balloons you must have a <u>big</u> organization. We also gathered that you are for peace and against nuclear war. We are also for and against these things. My husband is a minister for the Church of the Brethren. He pastors a small country church. Please let us hear from you.
>
> Love,
> Juanita Turpin

An interfaith correspondence with the Turpins developed, and some young SUUSI participants became pen pals with the Turpin children.

Having sent its message of peace and love out into the world, SUUSI reconvened at Radford in 1984 with the theme "Connections." New Director Karen Chandler built on the bright colors that had been seemingly everywhere the previous year. The 1984 logo featured a rainbow emerging from a chalice and arching over multi-hued mountains. "Each person who comes to SUUSI is unique and adds his or her special hue or tint to our joint adventure," she wrote in the catalog. "We invite you to help us create a rainbow of unity and become part of the great circle of connections that is our SUUSI family." To make that possible for those who otherwise might not be able to afford it, the SUUSI Board had established a scholarship fund, to be administered by Christine Robinson.

The banner parade to Ingathering was led by Lee Davis, who was taking up the mantle of SUUSI bagpiper (Dick Scobie's last year at SUUSI had been 1983). Following the call of Davis' bagpipes – and his contingent of 37 people from the Hagerstown, Md., church (more than half the entire congregation!) – participants gathered in one of the most popular Ingatherings ever held. Written by Mary Anne Chew in collaboration with Feriel Feldman and Kathee Williams, the evening had been laboriously rehearsed and choreographed during the spring in Atlanta, where most of the performers lived. There were intergenerational musical numbers, a mime troupe, and a script that "connected" everything together. Ingathering culminated with hundreds of participants singing along to "The SUUSI Connection" (based on Kermit the Frog's rendition of "The Rainbow Connection"), which quickly became one of two unofficial theme songs for the year. The other was an original piece titled simply "Connections," by Adele Abrahamse of Charlottesville.

To everyone's delight, the rainbow fence returned in 1984 – some of it literally. Bill Amos, who had taken several long pieces of ribbon from the fence home with him after SUUSI '83, drove back to SUUSI with the colorful streamers tied to his car's antenna, and then wove them back into the 1984 fence, thus starting yet another SUUSI tradition.

Director Karen Chandler created a 30-page staff handbook (with a rainbow on the cover, of course) that for the first time in a couple of decades clearly laid out the duties and expectations of the many volunteers who annually make SUUSI happen. She also suggested a 12-month SUUSI calendar, in which the first month of the "year" would be July. Photos of SUUSI activities and personalities were solicited prior to the summer, and the first SUUSI calendar was produced for sale at the Bookstore. In conjunction with the calendar, a "New Year's Party" was held as one of the week's intergenerational events.

Jill Menadier, who had been to the Summer Institute in Boone as a teenager but had not been back since, returned to SUUSI in 1984 and noticed a very positive difference from the early 1970s. "There was a lot more organization and structure at Radford," she says. "There were programs for teens. There was a nature program. There were organized events. Everyone gathered in the Quad every afternoon. Everyone ate together. There was just a much better sense of community."

A newcomer in 1984, Robby Greenberg, recalls immediately finding a group of like-minded souls within the larger community. "When I first came to SUUSI, I was very shy. Serendipity was hard. But after Serendipity was over, a bunch of folks would gather in a lounge in the dorm. It was hot; there was no air conditioning, and the windows were always open. We'd sit around and people would play music and sing. Pete Leary, Alexis Jones, Vonnie Hicks – we'd be there all night. The sun would come up and we'd still be there, singing, giving massages, talking."

Greenberg, years later, was the driving force behind the rich and diverse music program SUUSI now enjoys.

The two candidates for UUA President, one of whom would be elected at the General Assembly the following spring in Atlanta, both gave theme talks in 1984. William Schulz and Sandra Caron also appeared at a Presidential candidates' forum. Schulz, who eventually won the election, is remembered for selling tote bags ($2 each) promoting his candidacy.

In addition to inviting candidates for national office, SUUSI also remained committed to other denominational entities like The

Mountain and the UUA Program Fund, both of which continued to receive annual donations. An extra $1 per participant was added to registration fees to cover SUUSI's dues to the Council of UU Camps and Conferences.

Following the Tuesday night worship in 1984, a panel of half a dozen ministers, moderated by first-time SUUSI attendee Arvid Straube of Eno River in Durham, N.C., took the stage to discuss the state of Unitarian Universalism, which was in the midst of the two-year General Assembly process required to adopt its new Principles and Purposes. Panel members made statements, conversed and fielded questions from the audience. There were so many people waiting in line to ask questions and/or make comments that the panel was extended to a second night.

The much-loved Picnic was moved from Claytor Lake State Park – a 20-minute drive from campus – to Radford City Park, a 10-minute walk (at least, for those without children). Brightly colored balloons, which were rapidly becoming a SUUSI trademark (as Fred Thompson laughed, "Folks used to think we

The annual tug-of-war was a highlight of the mid-week Picnic.

were the Moonies; now they think we're the Balloonies!"), guided participants to the park, where all the usual Picnic activities awaited. The move to the park in town, however, was not popular. Many complained of missing Claytor Lake, and attendance at the Picnic dropped, with some people choosing simply to eat dinner in the cafeteria on campus.

Given the Orwellian significance of the year, it was inevitable that homage would be paid to the dystopian vision of *1984*. Sue Folk, who actually had met and spoken with George Orwell, offered an evening workshop titled "It's 1984, But Is *1984* Really Here?" in which she and other fans of the genre explored the societal concerns – and the harsh realities – of the tension between freedom and technology.

But leave it to Way Off Broadway to drive the point home, with humor and music. Friday night brought two highly anticipated performances of the original "Big Brother Is Watching UU." The same team that had produced the wildly successful Ingathering five nights earlier – Mary Anne Chew and Kathee Williams, along with Way Off Broadway creator and choreographer Millicent Simmons – pulled together some 60 performers and musicians to create an instant hit. Weaving well-known Broadway songs into a satirical tour de force that featured Big Brother and the Moral Majority, the Underground Union (UU), the Thought Police and various rebels, conspirators and lovers, they made an unforgettable evening as SUUSI 1984 drew to a close. The show's scenery and props were made by participants in a scene-design workshop that had been offered that week by Carl Lefko, Radford's Technical Director for the Porterfield Auditorium.

A playreader's workshop gave many others a chance to get bitten by the drama bug. Participants did a dramatic reading of "Sister Mary Ignatius" on Thursday night at Quiet Serendipity. Other workshops – there were 128 in all – focused on relationships, personal growth, health and fitness, and various aspects of Unitarian Universalism. Yoga had become popular, with multiple levels of courses offered. And although SUUSI itself still owned only one (Apple) computer, participants could, for the first time, choose from a wide variety of computer skills and usage workshops to enhance their own take-home abilities.

Nature had also grown to offer more than 100 choices, with trips leaving at all hours of the day and night. As a result, the program was becoming cumbersome, so to bring some organization to the system, Nature Director Phil Sterner introduced four "divisions" – Hiking, Outdoor Discovery, Aquatics and Adventure – with four division leaders who would be responsible for individual areas of programming. It was just one more example of the increasing complexity of the Summer Institute infrastructure that in 1984 would serve 1,188 people – more than a hundred of whom were teens.

Indeed, the Teen Program practically filled Peery in 1984, as teenagers were once again becoming a major constituency within the SUUSI community. The previous year, Heidi Lux had run, unsuccessfully, for the Board as a teen (Jake Haun was elected) – but she raised awareness of the need for teen representation in SUUSI decision-making.

The *Rocky Horror Picture Show* made its debut at SUUSI in 1984. Teens (and curious adults) flocked to the Peery basement to see two showings of the very hard-to-acquire film. Tickets were required to see the R-rated cult classic, with parents or guardians having to sign the ticket for their teen to gain admission. The windows of the Peery basement were blocked, and staff was posted at both doors, to assure that no one entered who shouldn't see the saga of Rocky and the cross-dressing Dr. Frankenfurter. Teens dressed up for the occasion, then re-used their attire for two nights of "Teendipity."

The Youth Program, meanwhile, was distinguished by a different kind of fashion statement – the widespread appearance of "deely-boppers" on the heads of staff members. Consisting of a headband and two springy antennae with all manner of colors, shapes and styles, deely-boppers were inspired by the "Killer Bees" costumes on "Saturday Night Live." Lynn Wheal and Trudy Atkin made

*Youth Director Lynn Wheal uses a bullhorn during an
outdoor "parachute game."*

them the trademark of the Youth Staff in 1984. By now the staff had grown to number more than 50, and the festive headgear helped distinguish them (as if that were necessary).

Some sense of order and safety – if not decorum – was maintained in the Youth Dorm by the presence of uniformed, off-duty Radford city police. The nighttime "beat" in the Governors Quad was patrolled by Officer Granville, a long-time favorite of both the SUUSI Youth Staff and the teens themselves. Granville got along well with the free-spirited Unitarian Universalists, and seemed to take pleasure in running off any "townies" who often had their sights set on causing trouble for SUUSI participants.

Perhaps the locals knew that things were well under control at night, because 1984 saw a couple of brazen daytime thefts hit the SUUSI community. A bicycle belonging to a 10-year-old boy was stolen from a bike rack during lunch one day early in the week, and a Harley Davidson motorcycle was taken from the front of Muse early one morning.

For the most part, however, SUUSI participants and local residents got along splendidly. The Tuesday edition of the newsletter included this article under the headline "UUs Will Do Anything to Keep from Missing a Meal":

> Did railroad track construction blocking the road stop our UU tube-floaters from getting back to campus [in time] for dinner? No way! With true Unitarian diplomacy, Gene DuGar and Jill Klein said to the construction crew, "We are a church group, and have to get back for supper and evening services." Never mind mentioning the denomination.
>
> Leaving the backed-up line of cars standing, the railroad crew moved their equipment and waved us through!

A heartwarming story appeared in the Monday newsletter, when it was revealed that Joe Soto – who was going around campus wearing an "I Gave My Organ Away" T-shirt – had recently donated a kidney to his daughter, Melissa. Though Melissa was still back home in Nashville recuperating, an outpouring of cards, phone calls and expressions of love from SUUSI were sent her way throughout the week.

Karen Chandler returned as Director in 1985, and the theme was "Directions." The beautiful logo, reminiscent of a Navaho sand painting, that adorned the front of the catalog (and the front of many T-shirts and even sweatshirts sold that year) was designed by Grace Iglehart of Durham. It featured a circle embracing multiple levels of symmetrical symbolism. In the center was a small flaming chalice, around which was a circle of the same kind of simple, stick-figure people, of various sizes representing all ages, that had been characteristic of SUUSI logos and letterhead for nearly as long as the Institute had been at Radford. Outside the circle of people were four trees, each depicting a season of the year, and around the trees were two skies, divided into day and night, with sun and moon and stars. The entire drawing was encircled by the first three colors of the rainbow. Taken as a whole, the logo included all "directions," all people and the natural world – all of the "interdependent web of which we are a part."

The Unitarian Universalist Association had just adopted the Seven Principles at its General Assembly in Atlanta the previous month, and the logo, as well as the Directions theme, spoke to those new, unifying ideals. Theme speakers each addressed one or more of the Principles. As Chandler put it in her own theme talk, "Dil Simmons came to my rescue [by suggesting the theme of 'Directions']... which beautifully captures the idea of taking [our new] Principles and deciding how we, as individuals and as a group, can make them a part of our daily lives." Workshops were offered that addressed the Principles, and two midweek evenings were devoted to a Forum on Theological Diversity, with a panel of ministers and denominational leaders.

A much more mundane meaning of the theme "Directions" became something of a running joke in 1985. With Muse unavailable due to renovations – and, for the first time, more than 1,200 registered participants – many SUUSI-ites were reassigned to new and different dorms. Moffett, Bolling and Washington became SUUSI living and workshop space for the first time, and Walker Cafeteria once more was the dining spot, as it had been SUUSI's first year at Radford (when there were about half as many mouths to feed). This time, there were long lines for meals throughout the week.

But Unitarian Universalists are nothing if not adaptable and creative. While waiting in the line at Walker, some folks began to sing. Backrubs were given. Short, impromptu workshops were held. In a similar vein, when a summer downpour soaked the campus, the Friday edition of the newly renamed "SUUSI NUUS" reported:

NEW BREED APPEARS
With the rain-drenching of SUUSI-ites on Thursday, a new life form has emerged – the Bag People. (Plastic

bags, that is). Clear dry-cleaning [bags], some with green and white slips stapled for the lapel. Heavy-duty Hershey-chocolate brown swiped from the ...cafeteria, et al. Versatility is the mark of these garments.

We spied an extremely lightweight creation at the Sufi dance class, featuring an easy-to-fold-into-pockets design... It makes a good conversation-starter, too. [And] the generic white cardigan, scoop neck, with pinked edges for that extra touch of elegance, was hard to beat!

However, one very tall, dignified young gentleperson topped the dashing designer's list with a battleship grey, thigh-high sheath with simple cap sleeve and stylish Italian neckline.

[In addition,] Sunday's sun umbrellas converted well into baby-stroller canopies. All in all, a veritable Easter Parade was dashing through the raindrops...

Another running joke in 1985 was "key dorking." This activity was described, by various sources including the newsletter, as "spending an inordinate amount of one's precious, limited time at SUUSI awkwardly bent over in front of one's dorm room door, attempting to either lock or unlock the door, with one's key affixed to a lanyard hanging around one's neck."

While key dorking was a harmless – if time-wasting – pursuit, the creation of excessive levels of noise was not nearly as benign. Each day's SUUSI NUUS in 1985 brought increasingly strong reactions – some more intemperate than others – to what appears to have been an excessively loud SUUSI. Mixed in with these admonitions for noise moderation was an occasional indignant retort from a camper who simply sought his or her inalienable right to express SUUSI joy without inhibition. Particularly offensive to late sleepers were the grunts and thuds of early-morning tennis playing on the courts (where Dalton now stands) just outside the windows of Peery and Floyd. There was also much outrage expressed at the inevitable post-Serendipity revelry, as dancers made their way back to their dorms late at night.

The tone may have been set on Sunday night, when the week got off to a particularly loud – and hot – start with SUUSI's first-ever rock concert. Suzy Saxon and the Anglos, a new wave band from Richmond, was booked to perform in Peters Gym to kick off a new dance venue called NANS ("No Alcohol No Smoking").

Youth Director Trudy Atkin at her desk in the Youth Office. Standing, at right, is Nancy Farese (Massel).

At the time, the circular end of Peters that faces Heth featured a small stage, a wooden dance floor – and no air conditioning. As the concert went on into the night, and as enthusiastic young people sweated more and more, windows were opened for ventilation, sending the amplified music all over campus.

Due to both heat and noise, NANS was moved downstairs to the Peters Basement for the remainder of the week.

The idea behind NANS (which the following year was changed to CACHE – "Clean Air Clear Heads Everyone") was to provide an all-ages alternative to Serendipity. For the teens – and for many young adults who were old enough to drink – Serendipity was seen as age-exclusive, alcohol-centric and musically outdated. The "La Bamba" tradition was particularly reviled by the younger set.

The mid-Eighties was also a time when indoor smoking was

becoming a bone of contention in the SUUSI community. A special "smoking section" was set up in the cafeteria during meals in 1985, and it would not be too many more years before SUUSI banned indoor smoking altogether – long before doing so became widely accepted in the broader society. A smoking cessation workshop was among the general workshops offered. Reflecting the tensions in the community around these kinds of issues, another offering in 1985 was SUUSI's first beer-tasting workshop, which was held at the same time an Alcoholics Anonymous group was meeting elsewhere on campus.

All this had the SUUSI Board busy working on policies – none of which was more needed, or more hotly debated, than the new policies for the Teen Dorm. The 1985 catalog included an agreement that teens, and their parent or SUUSI guardian, were required to sign and adhere to. Note the striking differences between this document and the LRY rules from Blue Ridge in 1965, twenty years prior (Chapter 2):

RULES FOR SUUSI TEENS

1. Local and state laws with regard to alcoholic beverage consumption must be adhered to – i.e., NO UNDER-AGE DRINKING.

2. Federal and state laws with regard to illicit drug use must be adhered to – i.e., NO SMOKING OF POT.

3. Youth must be in rooms or designated areas at CURFEW – 15 minutes after the last evening program.

4. Parents will be responsible for damages done to teen's individual room.

Bed checks will not be made by Youth Staff. However, after curfew Security Personnel will patrol the Youth Dorm and Quad areas.

Parents and/or guardians will need to establish ground rules and room curfews with their teens during non-programmed time. Youth Staff is responsible only for those teens who attend scheduled programming.

I, ___(youth)_____, understand that violation of any of these rules will result in my immediate removal from SUUSI.

I, ___(parent)_____, understand that if my child is caught breaking any of these rules, I will have to make arrangements to send my child home.

There was also a new emphasis on "waiver forms" for nature trips and other events where a participant, of any age, could potentially be injured.

Meanwhile, SUUSI Staff was also making efforts to be more intentionally welcoming to newcomers to the SUUSI community. Upon arriving in 1985, first-timers were invited to a Sunday afternoon open house. A welcoming reception was held on Monday. Thursday was designated "Visitors Day;" Unitarian Universalists from churches in the immediate area – those who were not yet SUUSI-goers – were invited to come to SUUSI for the day, for a $10 drop-in fee, in order to check out all that SUUSI had to offer. There were special, free workshops that day. Lee Knight shared the music of Woody Guthrie and Pete Seeger, while Dean Shelton led a workshop on "The Theology of Garrison Keillor." But the highlight of Thursday's Visitors Day, for many, was the debut of "Priestley Discomfort," a "UU Rock Horror Musical" by Serendipity lounge lizard and long-time SUUSI veteran Boomslang Meade.

Along with cohorts Eileen Davis and Phil Brault (collectively billing themselves

Lee Knight sings at SUUSI

as Archibald Candoux), Meade had long been writing and performing both satirical and more serious songs about Unitarian Universalism, including the wildly popular "When I Die I Want to Go to Radford." "Priestly Discomfort" was described by Meade as a "blues opera" that evolved from a workshop in which performers learned some of Meade's original songs that told tales of Transylvanian Unitarianism as well as the "secret life of Joseph Priestley." Priestley, it may be recalled, was a British scientist and Unitarian who discovered oxygen (and invented soda water). That Thursday night, Murray Kaplan played the title role.

In the SUUSI NUUS on the day of the performance, Meade wrote, "Anyone suspected of having <u>any</u> substantial knowledge of the life of the real Joseph Priestley will be stopped at the door." The show was a rousing success, and was repeated with even more fanfare (and attendance) the following year. Popular songs included "Closet Unitarian" and "Oh Blood."

Amid all the fun, however, the specter of nuclear war continued to haunt many participants. There were workshops on peacemaking and political realities sprinkled throughout the course offerings. The entire SUUSI community worked together to fold paper peace cranes, in the tradition of the Japanese child Sadako Sasaki, whose story was immortalized in the book *Sadako and the Thousand Paper Cranes*. At the end of the week in 1985, a thousand cranes were sent to Japan to be part of the August 6th Peace Day memorial service at Hiroshima, commemorating the 40th anniversary of the dropping of the first atomic bomb.

Trudy Atkin, who had succeeded Lynn Wheal as Youth Director that year, got the children involved in the project in a big way. The children's program had been growing by leaps and bounds, and Atkin quickly became the visible face of all things Youth. An active and enthusiastic participant in the broader SUUSI community, she was a beloved spokesperson for the needs and concerns of SUUSI's youngest members and their parents. Her motto during the "other 51" weeks of the year was "Remember the Feeling." Folks really took that gentle reminder to heart; many of

"Trudy's kids" and much of her devoted staff remain key leaders in the SUUSI community.

In those days, the Teen Program was still part of the overall Youth Program, thus falling under the auspices of the Youth Director. Youth Staff and teens lived together in Peery. Atkin recounts one story that captures the youthful spirit and staff camaraderie that characterized Peery Dorm in the mid-80s, and also serves as a reminder of another tradition from that era in SUUSI's history – pie fights. She says:

> It was midweek, and there was buzz among the teens, who were asking staff for rides to get groceries. With all of the other activities going on, I hardly gave it a second thought. The day's activities drew down, [and] the nightly movies in the Peery basement would soon begin. I had decided I would actually enjoy some quiet time watching the movie with the kids. While sitting in the cool quiet, enjoying my popcorn, I felt a tap on my shoulder. It was [Teen Director] Bill Gupton. In his wonderful Southern drawl, he said 'I think you better come upstairs.' He was bouncing around more than usual, and wasn't speaking in complete sentences.
>
> The second floor of Peery was the teen floor. There was a group of staffers halfway up the steps who stopped talking when I approached. What in the world was going on? There was a familiar, but strange, aroma. Bananas??
>
> Nothing could prepare me as I turned the corner and looked down the hall. As far as the eye could see, there was cream pie of all colors and flavors on every surface visible – sticky, slimy goo all over the walls, floor and ceiling. Every cream pie in Radford, Virginia was down that hall, and I was ultimately responsible for it all.
>
> Bill was hopping like a rabbit, and Bruce Fiene was gathering staff and grabbing buckets. I was speechless, literally speechless. Someone said 'Go to bed, and there

will be no mess in the morning.' I turned without a word and went to my room. Before dawn the next day, still in my nightgown, I went upstairs to see the alleged 'clean up.'

The place was spotless! – though banana odor still hung in the air.

Love was also in the air at SUUSI in 1985. On Friday, July 27, there was both a wedding (Rel Davis and Edith Sloan) and a proposal of marriage (Phil Sterner and Linda Berger). Phil and Linda had been taking a weeklong workshop together, titled "Eight Ways to Love," when Phil – at that point SUUSI's Director-Elect – decided the workshop's closing exercise would be the ideal venue in which to demonstrate his love by popping the question to Linda (who, of course, accepted).

As always, the week also included several examples of what are typically referred to as "SUUSI Miracles." Two old college friends who had not seen one another in more than 20 years – Ed Harris of Charlotte and Bill Austin of Cincinnati – ran into one another outside Preston Auditorium at Ingathering on Sunday night. When they had last spoken, neither was a Unitarian Universalist, much less a SUUSI attendee! Then on Tuesday, outside Walker Cafeteria, there was a reunion of three people who had last crossed paths thirty years before when all were involved in the Lexington Theological Seminary (Christian Church, Disciples of Christ) – Jeanne Traugott, Anna Louise Watts and Delos B. McKown.

In her Friday morning theme talk Karen Chandler concluded her two years as Director by examining the mysteriously interconnected web that weaves us all together. Chandler, who was about to move on to become Director of the Ferry Beach UU Camp and Conference Center in Maine, said to participants, "We are over 1,200 strong. Each of us has a unique perspective... We have so much potential for positively affecting the world. Let us go forth from SUUSI with a renewed energy and desire to effect change. Let us follow the great circle, the roundness of power, and let our lives be like a rainbow, whose colors teach us unity."

Phil Sterner became Director in 1986, and chose as his first theme "Community." Sterner was particularly skilled at coordinating the ever-more complex SUUSI staff structure while still maintaining the strong sense of community that had always been a hallmark of the Summer Institute. As one Core Staff member put it, "The management of SUUSI became stronger and more organized. The people in leadership were now business-type people, and ran a tighter ship. The head changed, if you will, but the heart always remained the same."

As Sterner wrote in the 1986 catalog, which now contained several advertisements for other UU camps and conferences, "We come together annually to share our being, our skills and our limits with unusually few inhibitions, yet with a sense of real responsibility, individual and shared... In this home away from home, at Radford University, we create a shared experience of what real communion and community can be."

He added that "the SUUSI Staff deliberately designs programs and services that meet both general and special needs." To that end, there were several innovations to serve the 1,200 participants to which the Institute was limited in 1986. (Due to space restrictions, including the fact that Peery and Floyd dorms were both unavailable because of remodeling, Radford limited the number of beds available to SUUSI.) In the end, an all-time record total of 1,208 people attended.

Sunday afternoon campus tours were created to orient newcomers to Radford and its facilities. First-timers were also given hearts to put on their nametags (a heart was prominently featured in the logo that year), identifying them as potential recipients of welcoming hugs. The hearts were also able to be "given away" to others later in the week, as the newcomer grew more at home at SUUSI. Paula Heusinkveld wrote short articles about different first-timers in the newsletter each day, as another way to introduce them to the community.

Ballroom dancing, under the loving guidance of Georgene Thompson, was added as a dance style alternative to Serendipity (and as a workshop). An "alternative worship" was scheduled each night, Monday through Friday, early in the evening. It included different experiences such as meditation, Christian communion and earth-centered rituals. The Nature Program, now under the direction of Bonnie Sheppard and Bill Spurgin, added scuba diving to its menu of choices. No simple "training run" in the Peters Gym Pool, this trip was an actual dive in the New River, where three different 40-foot underwater holes awaited those adventurous enough to take the challenge.

SUUSI also returned to Claytor Lake that year – if only for "beach" outings for the children. With hundreds of children in the community, and the primary youth dorm lost to construction, a service was added that was to prove crucial to parents' full participation in SUUSI ever since – a Childcare Co-Op. Coordinated by Louis Bregger, the Co-Op was an intentional grouping of families who had signed up to live in one area of Washington Hall. Parents worked out the details of shared babysitting and evening child supervision. Though there were some kinks to be worked out, and inevitably not everyone felt as if the responsibilities were shared equally, the Co-Op was a big success, and had a lasting effect on the SUUSI community.

The previous year's renovations to Muse had done away with the beloved lily pond that was located right in front of the tallest dorm on campus. The lily pond had become a popular gathering spot and meeting place for participants, so SUUSI decided to dedicate and reclaim the special space by turning the now bricked-in landscaping into "The Garden of Creative Expression." In the confirmation newsletter earlier that summer, people were encouraged to bring meaningful items from home – "a branch of the old elm tree, a scrap from Aunt Bessie's quilt, a drawing," etc. – and on Monday evening after dinner, these items were placed in the former lily pond. Lee Knight sang traditional SUUSI favorites, and SUUSI's Garden of Creative Expression was born. Each day and evening, folks added items to the creation, and at the end of the week, they were invited to take something home with them, as a memento of SUUSI 1986.

Alexis Jones was inspired to offer another way participants could "remember the feeling" throughout the year. In 1986 he compiled and produced a cassette tape of the "Sounds of SUUSI," designed to "reflect the sense of family which I experience at this gathering." His cassette remains one of the few definitive musical and spoken word recordings capturing the rich variety of expression that characterized the SUUSIs of that era. The tape includes selections from "Priestley Discomfort" (which returned in 1986 to rave reviews), Lee Knight's "The Bells," Adele Abrahamse's "Connections," Jones' own version of "Let It Be a Dance," storytelling by Chuck Larkin and music by both the Way Off Broadway cast and the SUUSI Cantatori. There are also excerpts from sermons and theme talks, and of course the traditional Blue Ridge Assembly wake-up song, Mitch Miller's "Carolina in the Morning."

Musically as well as in other respects, SUUSI's ongoing evolution continued. The "Lounge" had become "Cabaret," offering a stage for many of the same performers featured on the "Sounds of SUUSI" tape. Meanwhile, just downstairs from Cabaret (and across the hall from Serendipity in Heth), the new alcohol-and-smoke-free nightly dance, renamed CACHE, was the happening spot for teens in the Highlander Room. "Puttin' on the Lips," a CACHE lip-synch contest, became an instant hit.

For those who were theatrically inclined, the year's Way Off Broadway was a production of "West Side Story," which included SUUSI Board President Dil Simmons, the only person to have appeared in every Way Off Broadway production. Bob Hill, the Southeast's UUA Inter-District Representative, shared an original performance titled "Salad Days in Mt. Gonebeyond," a satirical stab at Garrison Keillor's "Lake Woebegon." Included in Hill's "sermonlogue" were references to that "small city near where Unitarian Universalism is the majority religion."

Workshops ranged from clogging to conflict resolution to computers. Particularly memorable for Marti Toms was a

A scene from "West Side Story," Way Off Broadway 1986

workshop called "Deep Massage Relaxation," led by Eleanore Richardson. Participants had been taught various massage and relaxation techniques earlier in the week, and then on Friday, many had a once-in-a-lifetime "out of body" experience. After becoming deeply relaxed through multi-person massage, "six or eight people put their hands under you and lifted you very gently off the table," Toms says. "My eyes were closed, and there was no perception of where you were in space. I didn't know if I was four inches or four feet off the table! It was simply amazing."

Also in 1986:

- Donations were taken up for a Radford University student named Petie who was recovering from a heart transplant; the SUUSI community collectively gave hundreds of dollars to help with Petie's medical expenses.

- A petition seeking to designate SUUSI a "Nuclear Free Zone" was circulated and presented to the Board.

- A special workshop for people who had significant fears of the water and/or swimming was offered in the Peters Pool. Instructor Marjorie Gelbin proudly declared two brave souls graduates of the class and praised them for "discovering something in themselves for which they should be exceedingly proud." The following year, a total of seven people took part in Gelbin's empowering, life-altering workshop.

- Two childhood friends who had not been together at Summer Institute since 1962 at Blue Ridge – Carolyn Winstead (nee Atkinson) and Arthur Cannon – were reunited.

- Under the headline "Southeast Hell, We've Gone National!" the Wednesday NUUS reported that the twelve hundred participants had come to SUUSI from a total of 29 states. It was also reported that 18 people were able to attend thanks to the new scholarship program.

At the end of the week, Director Phil Sterner proudly announced that for the first time, Radford had offered SUUSI a two-year contract, and that the Institute would return to the Radford campus for its 13th and 14th years in 1987 *and* 1988. He also distributed – and later compiled – what was the most thorough SUUSI evaluation questionnaire yet. Detailed feedback was obtained about each program department and demographic group. The information obtained, complete with statistics and analysis, allowed SUUSI Staff to make specific plans for improvement in 1987. The evaluations were even analyzed for word frequency; the four most common descriptors of the 1986 experience were "loving," "supportive," "caring" and "fun."

The following year would go down in history as the Year of

the Balloon. When they received the catalog in the mail, past participants were greeted by a colorful depiction of a large hot air balloon with the words "SUUSI 87" emblazoned on it, lifting off toward rainbow-colored mountains and a rising sun. Just below, the still-traditional line of various-sized stick figures seemed to watch the balloon head off into the distance. The year's theme, "Horizons," was perfectly captured in the drawing, which proved to be a popular and nearly ubiquitous logo that year.

But there was a surprise waiting for participants when they arrived at Radford in July. Right there in the Commons was a real-life, multi-colored hot air balloon, which literally became the centerpiece and focal point of the 1987 SUUSI, beckoning one and all to see Radford, and SUUSI, from a new perspective by going "up, up and away" into the sky above campus. Vertical, tethered trips aloft were offered all afternoon during Sunday check-in. Adventurous participants were able to arrive at SUUSI, set their gear aside and hop into the basket of a hot air balloon for a unique, panoramic view of the SUUSI community.

Rides were also available Sunday night following Ingathering, and throughout the week. Lines quickly formed at the Intergenerational ("IG") Tent to purchase rides, which were a bargain at $2 per lift. For an extra $2, one could enter a drawing for a free, two-hour "fly away" balloon ride bright and early Monday morning. Bob Winchester of Largo, Fla., attending his tenth SUUSI, was one of the lucky winners, along with Karen Olson of Boca Raton, Fla., and Holly Francis of Sylvania, Ohio. Winchester wrote about the experience in the NUUS, saying:

> Silently, we ascended away from the campus. It was five after seven... The peace and tranquility is hard to describe, as we drifted along at 1000 feet... This is especially exciting when you realize that you cannot control where you are going... We brushed through the tip top of the trees. [Eventually,] Charley [Page, of Charlotte, the commercial balloon pilot, who was a registered participant at SUUSI

that year] pulled the cable that opened the parachute valve at the top of the balloon, so we would drop fast. We did... We hit the fresh mowed field and bounced, as the balloon dragged us. We hit again, tipped on our side, then tipped again. [Finally,] in orderly (and happy) fashion, we crawled out, top one first...

When we arrived back at [campus] we learned that we had flown nine miles. Then came the ritual of the returned balloonist... We had a champagne toast after kneeling together on the ground, with a bit of earth and champagne sprinkled on our heads. The champagne was good, even at 8:45 a.m.!"

One day later in the week, the balloon (and its occupants) became accidentally un-tethered and began floating gently away from the Commons. While reassuring the startled SUUSI participants that all would be well, Page calmly and quickly brought the balloon back down to the ground on the other side of campus.

Thanks to a significant reduction in the registration fee for children and youth (Director Phil Sterner's idea), more people than ever were able to expand their horizons in 1987, with memorable outdoor experiences not only in the air, but in the water, and on and under the ground. Bill Spurgin and Bonnie Sheppard's Nature Program

The hot air balloon begins to rise above the trees at Radford in 1987.

*A participant's eye view of the Radford campus
from the hot air balloon*

*This picture became one of the iconic
images of SUUSI in the 1980s after it
appeared in SUUSI promotional material.*

included 17 new nature trips and another innovation called "Post Theme Talk Specials" (trips that left after theme talk and returned in time for dinner). Workshop Coordinator Joan Lawson-Looney added 53 new general workshops to the previous year's offerings. With registration fees at just $111 for adults and $55 for those under 18, SUUSI remained an affordable family vacation.

From a well-received SUUSI slide show at Sunday night's Ingathering (put together by Kathee Williams), to the tearful singing of "Dear Friends" at Closing Circle on Saturday morning, the SUUSI community had become a round-the-clock happening. There was stargazing with Don Male, a concert by Windfall, and a "Sommerfest" German-themed Picnic – this time, on the Commons in front of Muse, complete with a root-beer garden and music. Of course, there were also old favorites like the tug-of-war, the earth ball and a softball game. With the Picnic on campus (and the heat bearing down), the Fun Run at Radford City Park was moved to the early morning and reduced to 1.5 miles. Runners were bused to the race.

The list of theme speakers in 1987 included two non-Americans. Kathleen Hunter, the Executive Director of the Canadian Unitarian Council, spoke and did a workshop on "The True North and the Horizon Beyond the 49th [Parallel]," adding a new flavor to the diversity of SUUSI with her wit, humor and – at times – simple truth-telling (pointing out that Canada had been known to Europeans for more than 500 years before Columbus came to the "New World," and reminding listeners that "There has never been a war of Canadian origin, nor for a Canadian cause.")

Her British counterpart, Christine Hayhurst, told participants about Unitarianism on the "other side of the pond," and brought greetings from the General Assembly of Unitarian and Free Christian Churches in Britain.

For the growing number of children on campus, old favorites like Dirty Day and Dixie Caverns were augmented by a trip to the Duck Pond at Virginia Tech. Floating Eagle Feather continued to delight with stories, songs and dance. At the end of the week, the youth produced a memory book complete with pictures, personal notes and comments – a copy of which was lovingly presented to outgoing Director Phil Sterner.

SUUSI's first true service project, another Sterner initiative, gave children and adults the opportunity to extend their horizons by working side by side to improve the lives of others. Volunteers created a playground for children at the Radford Women's Resource Center, which operated as a shelter for clients and their children from a four-county region. Local SUUSI community member Bobbie Littlefield, who worked during the year as the shelter's Domestic Violence Services Coordinator, and fellow SUUSI-ite Bud Evans (who supervised all construction) organized the project. Nearly three dozen people took time out from SUUSI to help.

The volunteers built and installed a sandbox, put in a hopscotch pad, painted, and otherwise helped spruce up the shelter. Other volunteers took some children on a field trip to give their mothers a break – and when they returned, the kids each had new shoes and a bag of takeout food from Hardees. SUUSI volunteers even constructed the parts of a three-level tree house throughout the week, using the scene shop at Porterfield – then took it to the shelter to assemble and install. One delighted boy, upon seeing the full tree house take shape, exclaimed, "When it rains, we can play in the bottom floor, and then when it stops raining, we can climb around on top!"

The Women's Resource Center was also the beneficiary of a new idea at the end of the SUUSI week. Participants were encouraged to leave behind any window fans that had "suddenly become an albatross for the trip home," to be donated to the shelter. In closing out the books for the year, the Board also voted to make a $500 donation on behalf of SUUSI.

There were many nightlife options in 1987, including not only Serendipity but Cabaret, Ballroom Dancing, CACHE and the Quiet Lounge. Meanwhile, 12-Step programs like Alcoholics Anonymous, Al-Anon, Narcotics Anonymous and Adult

Children of Alcoholics were meeting throughout the week. By this time there was also an on-call UU minister serving as SUUSI chaplain. SUUSI participants and leaders also organized a cancer support group and similar supportive sub-communities. AIDS was now a major concern, and Dr. H. Clay Smith of Richmond gave talks on "safer sex" to both adults and teens.

With the other half of the Governors Quad (Trinkle and Stuart) under renovation that summer, space was once again tight, though unlike in 1986, no registration limit had been set. In the end, total attendance was 1,230.

The teen community was delighted to return to its home base in the renovated Peery Hall. Teen programming – as well as the number of participants – expanded, adding new activities like a teen-only canoeing trip. There was an organized, outdoor, officially sanctioned pie fight on Wednesday, and a new welcoming ceremony was added on Friday afternoon in which 13-year-olds could get a glimpse of the legendary Teen Dorm and participate in a ceremonial "graduation" from the Youth Program. The week concluded with an all-night sleepover (though little sleep was had) on the roof of Peery Hall, where teens and their staff awaited the sunrise and the teary goodbyes of Closing Circle. Joel Finkelstein was elected by the teens as their first-ever representative to the SUUSI Board (though he would have to be non-voting, due to the laws of incorporation in the state of Florida).

But it was something that happened in the Highlander Room on Thursday night just before CACHE that forever changed the SUUSI experience, not only for teenagers, but for everyone. A cast of 16 teens and three adult teen staffers lip-synched their way through an adapted version of the musical "Hair" in the first ever "Teen Way Off Broadway." Written and co-directed by Teen Director Bill Gupton, the performance took the elements of traditional Way Off Broadway (adapting a Broadway musical to a SUUSI setting, with plenty of SUUSI in-jokes and humor), added music geared toward younger tastes, and highlighted the talents of the SUUSI teens.

Throughout the week, the teens had held midnight practices, largely in secret – then announced their performance in the Thursday NUUS:

> When the moon is in the seventh house, and Jupiter aligns with Mars, then peace will guide the planets, and love will steer the stars –
>
> You've heard of Way Off Broadway? Well this is so far off Broadway, it's brought to you directly from the teen dorm! The teens and the teen staff are bringing you a SUUSI-fied version of the musical "Hair"... Everyone is welcome to come experience the grooviness. Be there or be square!

A hundred or so people jammed into every nook and cranny of the hot, dark Highlander Room that night, utterly unaware that they were witness to the beginning of what would become one of SUUSI's longest-running traditions. As Clayt Lauter, who played an "Army Guy" in the show, says, "At the time I no more believed that TWOB would become a SUUSI icon, than I believed we would grow up." It is hard to remember that there was no choreography and no actual singing in the early Teen Way Off Broadways (performers mouthed the words of songs played by Radford's "Doug the DJ" over the CACHE sound system). But there was plenty of unlimited teenage energy, enthusiasm and emotion. Co-director Bruce Fiene shared his perspective on the first-ever TWOB in a memory book that commemorated the 20th Teen Way Off Broadway performance in 2006:

> I remember very distinctly the last scene... when Bill [Gupton, whose character had just died in the Vietnam War] was put into a body bag (in this case it was a sleeping bag). U2 was playing ["Bullet the Blue Sky"] and everyone was truly crying. No acting – these were real emotions, as if Bill had died. I was bawling like a damn baby, as

was everyone else. It was *so real*. I think a number of the audience were crying, too.

In fact, I am tearing up as I am writing this now. Weird but true. Nothing like really seeing someone you love put into a body bag. To this day, I hold this moment in my memory as a very special time.

The following night, Friday, brought another first for SUUSI, again involving the teens: an All-Ages Serendipity. Virginia had changed its drinking age to 21, effective at the beginning of July, so to accommodate those in the young adult age range who had anticipated being able to attend their first Serendipity but now would not be able to, SUUSI announced that no alcohol would be served or could be brought into the Heth Ballroom on Friday night until midnight. The result was to make the first two hours of Serendipity an all-ages dance event. A cover band, the Waller Family Band, provided the tunes, making the final night of SUUSI 1987 a memorable one indeed.

Robby Greenberg, however, most vividly recalls the following morning's Closing Circle. Phil Sterner, in his final act as Director, spoke to those gathered in the Commons – where the hot air balloon had held court all week. He said to them, "Each of you come to SUUSI *for* something. I challenge you to create that something ... *back home*. I challenge you to expand your SUUSI horizons to include your life at home." Greenberg says Sterner's challenge left her sobbing – and changed her life. She got in the car, drove home to Florida, and became a regular at a small folk music club there.

"That's where I met my husband-to-be, and I decided to get into the music business," she says. "I put together a venue of my own, and also started promoting music in my church [in Fort Lauderdale]. I quickly developed a lot of contacts in the folk music world. A couple of years after Kathee Williams had started Concert Hour at SUUSI, I took that over, and began bringing in some of the artists we now love as SUUSI musicians. There is an old saying: 'Be the change you wish to see in the world.' Phil Sterner challenged me to do that, and I am eternally grateful."

The SUUSI Board was also busy in the post-SUUSI glow of 1987. In years when the Institute had ended in the black, a practice had developed of making donations, on behalf of SUUSI, to other Unitarian Universalist organizations. The Mountain, in fact, was the recipient of a donation from SUUSI every year from its founding through 1989, including the purchase of a copier that year. At its meeting in October of 1987, the Board chose to be particularly generous, authorizing contributions of $3,000 to The Mountain, $1,500 to the Council of UU Camps and Conferences, $250 to the Continental UU Young Adult Network and another $250 to *Synapse* (the newspaper of the Young Religious Unitarian Universalists). It also set aside $5,000 for "computer needs" and another $5,000 "to reduce costs for 1988." The remaining surplus, after the books were closed, went to the SUUSI Scholarship Fund.

In addition, the Board created a task force to gather all previously approved policies and create a permanent Policy Book. Included were compensation policies for staff, workshop leaders, and theme and worship speakers, policies related to scholarships, and those designed to attract more ministers to SUUSI. As the result of one new policy, the following year's catalog contained this statement: "LIABILITY – SUUSI offers environments and experiences less familiar than at home. By enrolling in SUUSI, you acknowledge and accept these risks."

Other new policies that were passed and added to the compendium included the creation of a youth position on the Board, and a statement (which had been requested by participant petition the previous year) declaring SUUSI a nuclear free zone. It read: "We denounce the development, production, deployment and use or threatened use of nuclear weapons for any purpose. Accordingly, we declare to all our brothers and sisters throughout the world that we as individuals, and as the Community of SUUSI, are henceforth to be nuclear free zones."

SUUSI stood behind this action the next summer by inviting

former Minnesota Sen. Eugene McCarthy to be a theme speaker. McCarthy accepted the invitation and even came to SUUSI in return for the Institute covering his travel, room and board costs (no honorarium was offered; at the time, there was an ongoing debate within the Board about paying for top-level speakers). McCarthy had been a very popular liberal candidate for the Democratic Presidential nomination in 1968; twenty years later, on Tuesday morning, July 26,

Former Senator and Presidential candidate Eugene McCarthy addresses SUUSI at the Tuesday theme talk in 1988

he received a prolonged standing ovation from many hundred SUUSI-goers who had gathered in Preston Auditorium to hear and see the unrepentant anti-war activist. McCarthy's talk was moved from the smaller Porterfield Auditorium in order to accommodate what was most certainly the largest crowd ever to attend a SUUSI theme talk, before or since.

The former Senator delivered a scathing indictment of the American military-industrial complex, with particular emphasis on the nuclear arms race that was the cornerstone of the Reagan Administration's foreign policy. In addition to his often humor-laced attacks on the U.S. war machine, McCarthy offered a prescient commentary on big business, calling corporations "powerful, amoral institutions" motivated by only one principle – greed. The next day's *Radford News-Journal* published a front-page article on McCarthy's talk (which was attributed as being "Courtesy of RU Public Information"), describing the Southeast Unitarian Universalist Summer Institute as an "organization which supports McCarthy's anti-nuclear, anti-war liberal politics."

SUUSI was back on the front page of the *News-Journal* the following day, when staff writer Jay Conley wrote about the Unitarian Universalists' week of community service at the Against All Odds Clubhouse, a day care center serving mentally and emotionally challenged adults. The article spanned two pages and included three pictures of SUUSI participants painting, cleaning and working on the building's porch swing. The UU volunteers also built picnic tables and benches for the center. The 1988 SUUSI Service Project was again coordinated by Bobbie Littlefield, who was quoted extensively in the newspaper article.

Director Louis Bregger had chosen "Live Your Dream" as the theme for SUUSI 1988, and Denominational Coordinator Jake Haun brought in Jeremy Taylor, one of the world's preeminent authorities on dreams and dreaming, to give not one, but two theme talks – on Monday and Friday mornings. In addition, Taylor led an evening workshop, Monday through Thursday nights, titled "Dream Work." In all that year, nearly a dozen workshops had the word "dream" in their title. Now coordinated by Maureen McAndrews, the general workshops were arranged into categories – Arts/Skills/Leisure, Cognitive, Music/Dance/Movement, Personal Growth and Self Improvement, and Religion/Philosophy/Denominational.

Workshop subjects ranged from drawing to death and dying. There was a workshop called "Cosmic Consciousness" alongside one titled "Spirituality: A Bad Dream for Unitarian Universalists." The ever-popular gloria wright continued to offer well-attended workshops on relationships, while Chuck Larkin, who himself had quite a following, taught budding musicians to play the "musical saw, jaw harp, bones and spoons." Seldom had such an eclectic array of workshops appeared in the catalog. There was even one offered by Chris Foreman on "Programming the Pocket Computer," which promised hands-on experience with "a computer so small it fits in a shirt pocket!"

SUUSI, however, was still several years from becoming fully computerized. Jerry King remembers "running a cord out a second or third floor window in Muse, down the side of the building, and all the way to a Nature computer" that was outside under a tree. "Those were the low-tech days," he laughs.

That year Bob Hileman began his long tenure as the "Dean of Fun," overseeing Serendipity and Nightlife. Tuesday was "toga night" for both the adults at Serendipity and the teens at CACHE. Later in the week, the teens also enjoyed an "air band" competition and "prom night."

For the younger set, there was a renewed emphasis on bringing the heritage and principles of Unitarian Universalism to life. Melissa Matthews, an age-group leader in the Youth Program who would become Youth Director in 1990, emphasized a program balancing both structure and spirituality. Kit Howell, minister in Fort Lauderdale, was brought in as Youth Minister, and offered a fresh, age-appropriate perspective on the UU faith to each group. Meanwhile, the 1988 Youth Staff T-shirts were among the most popular ever, each having been individually tie-dyed by staff tie-dye artist Steve Anderson.

The teens were particularly awash in tie-dye that year, what with ongoing, daily tie-dying activities in the Governors Quad, and a groovy Friday night concert at CACHE by Atlanta hippie band

The 1988 Dirty Day King and Queen

Y.U.R. ("Your Universal Reality"). The second-annual Teen Way Off Broadway – which in 1988 had become an official workshop, complete with a listing in the catalog, required pre-registration for participants, and even *daytime* rehearsals – was The Who's rock opera "Tommy." Once again, there was one, very crowded Thursday night show in the Highlander Room.

Way Off Broadway wrapped up the week with two performances on Friday night. A total of 79 people comprised the cast, crew, orchestra and staff of "Oliver." Other musical memories from 1988 include Lee Knight's singing that set the mood on Tuesday morning for Sen. Eugene McCarthy's theme talk, and the SUUSI debut of Adele Abrahamse's "The Old Dominion," which had been selected as one of the finalists in a contest to become the official state song of Virginia. Windfall performed at the Picnic on Wednesday, providing entertainment for a meal that featured a return to "traditional food like fried chicken" after the previous year's German-themed fare.

The Young Adult Program extended its age range five more years, to include those aged 18-30, and had meetings on the 12th floor and the Penthouse of Muse. In addition to frequent tie-dyeing, they held a "Genesis" workshop, worship and discussion sessions, and began the practice of registering together for nature trips as a group.

As the SUUSI community grew ever larger (registration topped 1,300 for the first time in 1988), other affinity groups were forming as well. One such collective, the River Nymphs – or as they are officially known, the EEEEAOORNATSI (the "Eternal, Effervescent, Ethereal, Evanescent, Ancient Order of River Nymphs and Terrorist Society, International") – had originated at SWIM, where that camp's shared bathroom included a large round "fountain" used for washing feet, giving babies baths, and so on. One year, several women decided to "initiate" one another, using the fountain, into a semi-secret society they initially dubbed the "River Nymphs." They took their group to SUUSI the next summer, and each year since, they have requested shared housing space, becoming something of a SUUSI institution. As their rooms, suites, and sections of the dorm became ever more elaborate, the Nymphs decided they needed an "ambience coordinator," and welcomed their first man, Patric Leedom, to fill that role.

Acting on a suggestion made in the 1986 participant evaluations, Director Louis Bregger authorized renting a golf cart to help the physically challenged get around campus. Participants who needed transportation were required to obtain a "Star Car Pass" from SUUSI Services, which was now under the direction of Judy Newell. Apparently the able-bodied were eager to hop a ride to and from workshops or dorms, because the SUUSI NUUS printed repeated reminders that the service was intended "only for those needing special assistance." It would be several years before the Star Car became available to all, and only after SUUSI began renting multiple vehicles.

Other news of note in 1988:

- Thursday night's intergenerational program was called "The Dream of Peace." All ages gathered at the I.G. Tent to share personal dreams of peace, which were collected and later delivered to elected representatives in Washington, D.C.

- That same night, Dick Merritt and Barbara Green were married.

- The tradition of holding daily receptions for different constituencies continued, with a special event for the gay community on Monday, and parties hosted by the UU Service Committee, SWIM and The Mountain, respectively, on Tuesday, Wednesday and Thursday.

- Both registration fees and the average summer temperature continued to climb. The cost of registration went up $5 per participant, regardless of age, with room and board also following suit, while 1988 was remembered as "one of the hottest SUUSIs yet."

But easily the biggest news of the week – and the most disconcerting to attendees – was the announcement on Friday that Radford itself, which had long since become synonymous with SUUSI for most participants, soon would no longer be the site of SUUSI. Conference contracts now were typically signed two years in advance, and when contract discussion time had rolled around earlier that week, Radford's Conference Services staff regretfully informed the SUUSI leadership that the Institute would not be able to gather there in 1990. Rumors and anxiety quickly spread throughout the community, and on Friday it was made official with the publication of an article in the SUUSI NUUS:

SUUSI 1990

Guess what? We have the opportunity (and necessity) of finding a new home for SUUSI in 1990. We will enjoy SUUSI '89 here in Radford, but, quoth the raven, "Nevermore."

Two things have changed for Radford University:

(1) They have adopted a policy to promote and support only those summer programs that directly relate to the educational goals of Virginia, and

(2) R.U. feels that we are getting too big, and they can no longer serve us and our needs as they once could.

This discussion is final and negotiations with them have borne no fruit. We maintain good relations with R.U., and will continue to do so. We, the Board and Staff, accept this as a great opportunity and challenge, and we're up to it!

Want to help in this process? Answer the appropriate question on the evaluation form.

Louis Bregger
SUUSI Dreams Director

At its regular end-of-SUUSI meeting on Saturday, the Board appointed a sub-committee to find a new location for SUUSI by July 1990. The Site Selection Committee was to be chaired by Jim Littlefield, a Virginia Tech professor and resident of nearby Blacksburg. Lynn Wheal, Bonnie Sheppard and Bill Spurgin would also serve on the committee, and Reid Swanson, who had just been chosen Director-Elect, was to be an ex-officio member. The group immediately began work.

Meanwhile, at the same time the Board was meeting, many other SUUSI participants were taking part in a long-standing and cherished post-SUUSI Saturday ritual at Sal's Italian Restaurant in Radford, where those who were not yet quite ready to make the transition back into the "real world" would gather each year to enjoy one final meal together before saying goodbye and going their separate ways. With the news of SUUSI's impending departure from Radford fresh in their minds – and for many, heavy on their hearts – the dear friends wondered if their traditional Saturday lunch the following summer would be their last at Sal's.

The period between SUUSIs that year was a very busy one for the Board. Quickly, the Site Selection Committee laid some groundwork, so that on the first weekend in November, 1988, the full Board was able to meet on the campus of Virginia Tech in Blacksburg. Following a video presentation by Tech representatives and a tour of the campus and facilities (and assurances from the university that, although they could not give SUUSI exact contract costs for a couple more months, Tech would strive to be "competitive" with Radford in their pricing), the Board voted to move SUUSI to Virginia Tech in 1990, asking for a three-year letter of intent from the university. The 1989 SUUSI at Radford was to be a farewell.

Before that bittersweet week could occur, however, there was much more business for the Board to conduct. A contingency fund of $20,000 was established from SUUSI reserves "to facilitate the move from Radford to Virginia Tech." Littlefield moved that a SUUSI Endowment Fund also be established, to provide for the long-term viability and financial security of the Summer Institute (the motion did not pass, and it would not be until 2010 that the SUUSI Endowment Fund was finally created). The Board appointed Linda Sterner as treasurer to replace the retiring Bob Sax, who had held that role for nearly a decade. It was a change that necessitated making a full transfer of SUUSI's financial assets from Miami to Atlanta.

Dealing with two sites at once – Radford for 1989 and Tech for 1990 – posed a significant challenge for the SUUSI leadership. Board minutes stated that "Radford is [now] less cooperative" in terms of space availability and financial decisions. At the same time, once the commitment to Virginia Tech had been made, it proved to be very difficult to get a firm, contracted agreement from the larger university on what its charges would be. Tech had originally promised a detailed cost breakdown to SUUSI by

January 1989, but that was soon changed to December 1989. In the end, it wasn't until the spring of 1990 that firm costs were provided. This would prove to be an ongoing issue.

On the other hand, a SUUSI Vision Committee that had been appointed by the Board, and was working closely with Director-Elect Reid Swanson, was very enthusiastic about the possibilities for growth that a move to Virginia Tech could engender. It reported that the change to a larger venue created the potential of SUUSI "becoming 2,000 participants, more public, pulling in / fostering special interest groups... [even] sponsoring, splitting off [or] setting up a second SUUSI."

Concerns were raised at roughly the same time about institutional insurance. SUUSI's carrier had stopped offering coverage for conventions and conferences. Wink Lucas was recruited to locate a new insurance carrier, and the Board voted to set aside $10,000 "for uninsured losses" to allow the purchase of a policy with a higher deductible. The entire discussion was made more poignant by the fact that the beloved Lodge at The Mountain had recently been destroyed by fire.

Some controversies were also consuming the Board's energy during the days leading up to the 1989 farewell SUUSI at Radford. The Board had put in place a new code of behavior for all SUUSI leaders (staff, Board and workshop leaders). However, some leaders, including most publicly and visibly Rel Davis, the fiercely independent south Florida minister, refused on principle to sign any "code of behavior," forcing the Board's hand. The Board responded by creating a category for individual "exceptions" to the requirement, a policy that remained in effect for several more years.

Another minor firestorm was brewing after one SUUSI participant made ill-advised use of the mugbook to send promotional material about nudist events to hundreds of past SUUSI attendees. The result was a passionate discussion at the Board level about the advisability of SUUSI offering clothing-optional programming. In the end, it was decided not to ban clothing-optional activities (it would be a few more years before such a ban was enacted). Instead, a new policy was put in place for 1989 – and prominently printed in the catalog – stating that "photography of participants on clothing optional hikes will not be permitted." Another, more forward-thinking policy required that all workshops directed toward "couples" now be explicitly inclusive of same-sex couples.

After this unusually active off-season for the SUUSI leadership, the entire SUUSI family reunited in Radford on Sunday, July 23, 1989. The Wednesday NUUS reported the largest attendance ever at Radford – or anywhere – despite problems with the post office that had caused many regular attendees not to receive their catalogs. Apparently, congregations picked up the promotional slack, distributing catalogs to a wide audience eager to register for the last SUUSI at Radford.

Every minister who was present – nearly two dozen – came onto the Preston stage to take part in the Ingathering chalice lighting, setting the tone for a SUUSI filled with ritual and ceremony, transition and emotion. With SUUSI once again about to change venues, one of those ministers in particular, Don Male, was honored by the Board for his unfailing dedication to the community. Male, who was now attending his 31st consecutive Summer Institute (and 29th as a workshop leader) had

Don Male speaks to participants at Radford

been instrumental in helping guide the Institute through the so-called "Nomad Years" of the late 1960s and early 1970s. All week long, donations were collected to help name a room in Male's honor at the UUA Pickett and Eliot House bed and breakfast in Boston. More than $15,000 was raised, and a plaque was placed in a private room at the bed and breakfast in Male's honor as a memorial to one of SUUSI's brightest lights.

"Share Your Light" was the 1989 theme, chosen by Director Louis Bregger to inspire participants to offer their gifts to the world. Attendees were asked to consider "the pattern of light through tree leaves on a mountain trail, the warm glow of friendships new and old ... the sparkling laughter of children at play, the light of self-discovery in a workshop, sunlight playing on a waterfall ... [and the] inspirational light of knowledge from a theme talk."

The week's first theme talk was given by perhaps the world's most prominent pagan, National Public Radio correspondent and best-selling author Margot Adler. In her talk, titled "Sharing Our Gods: Diversity, Polytheism and the Experience of Pagan Spirituality," Adler told an overflow crowd:

> Just as the health of a forest or meadow is measured by the number of different insects and plants and creatures that make it their home, so diversity in the spiritual world will mark the health of the human community. The polytheistic vision doesn't preclude monotheism as an appropriate *individual* path, but it does insist that the larger vision is multiple – that the universe is too rich and large and varied to be captured so easily by a single prophet, system or holy book.

As if in response to Adler's theme talk, there was a particularly wide variety of worship experiences during SUUSI 1989. That same night, long-time SUUSI participant Michael McGee returned South (he had been called as minister of a church in Cleveland) to lead a service titled "T-Shirt Theology," which he invited everyone to attend while wearing a T-shirt that expressed their personal theology. The following evening, Alexis Jones did a service featuring the poetry and music of UU troubadour minister Ric Masten. On Thursday night, there were two worship services; at Moffett Quad, an outdoor pagan service titled "Women, Witches and Power" drew more than 300 participants, while indoors at Porterfield, Kit Howell, who was once again SUUSI Youth Minister in 1989, led a service dedicated to change and transitions in the lives of both the young and the no longer young. Such a service has continued to the present day.

The SUUSI NUUS had several articles during the week memorializing members of the SUUSI community who had passed away during the prior 12 months. Joe Watkins, Sharon Jones and Henry Wah were remembered. The Friday NUUS included a poem from a "purposely anonymous" writer titled "Notes on Attending SUUSI at a Riper Age":

> Oh, had I discovered SUUSI
> In my younger days of life!
> What a blast it would have been.
> The trust, the love, the care we share
> Sends goose bumps up my skin!
> Oh well. It never pays to yearn
> For a thing that could never go...
> My present joys at SUUSI
> Bring my heart an inner glow.

Workshops in 1989 included – literally – a "Nap Workshop," and others ranging from "Past Life Regression" to "Introduction to Clowning." Lee Knight brought back memories of the Summer Institutes of the 1950s with a workshop on "Social Justice and Labor Songs." Dan Aldridge, an African-American UU minister from Atlanta who was in the process of trying to start a new congregation there, spoke on "Color or Culture." (Aldridge made two trips to Radford that summer, having mistakenly driven up to

Virginia the previous week.)

The Nature Program continued to offer whitewater rafting, though parachuting had been discontinued a few years prior. There were three options of "Triple Waterfall Slog" – one that clearly stated in the catalog "NOT a skinny-dipping trip," and two others that said "Numerous falls and two deep pools. Skinny-dipping and clothing optional between the pools. Minimum age 18." One popular new Nature offering was a Thursday trek to the Mountain Lake Hotel, where just three years earlier the hit movie *Dirty Dancing* with Patrick Swayze and Jennifer Grey had been filmed. There, SUUSI participants hiked around the lake, took souvenir photos at iconic spots from the movie, and ate lunch at the famous restaurant.

Young adults, still meeting on the Muse Penthouse, turned that outdoor area into a nightly dance floor for SUUSI's last year at Radford. The beat of the music could be heard all over campus. FSLD ("For Sure Let's Dance") was promoted as "a dance alternative" to Serendipity and CACHE "for high-energy, freestyle dancing to modern rock and roll." Also new to the 1989 agenda was the first organized effort to collect SUUSI participants' aluminum cans for recycling.

A generational shift – and great progress in SUUSI's open affirmation of its gay and lesbian members – was heralded by a notice in the NUUS from "Us and Our Friends," a group which for many years had been a safe place for SUUSI's gay and lesbian community to gather and share alongside what today would be called their straight allies. Us and Our Friends wrote joyfully of their "special thanks to the young people who are sharing with us this year. How wonderful to see our dreams from the time of Stonewall flower in your beautiful hearts and minds, as you grow up in the freer environment which we fought for. In many ways, you are the role models we never had in our [own] youth."

A significant (some would even say cosmically significant) event occurred on Wednesday night, July 26, 1989. While some participants were attending a tenth anniversary party for Mary

Ann Somervill and Scotty MacDiarmid, who had been married at SUUSI 1979, and others were at the Board candidates' forum, a powerful storm rolled through Radford. Lightning struck and felled the Wisdom Tree, to many the symbolic heart of SUUSI on the Radford campus. For more than a decade, participants had gathered daily under the stately old white oak to discuss philosophy, religion and whatever else may have come to mind. Couples had been married there. For SUUSI, it was a sacred place of life-changing insights, life-altering decisions and countless simple moments of profound peace.

The next morning, as SUUSI early risers made their way to breakfast, they saw (and heard) workers with chainsaws cutting the remaining pieces of the tree, to be hauled away. Word quickly spread throughout the SUUSI community, and scores of participants flocked to the Memorial Garden to take a section of the tree, as a keepsake both of SUUSI, and of Radford. Many people still have their own "piece of the Wisdom Tree." The poetic symbolism of the tree's demise coinciding with SUUSI's departure from Radford could not be overlooked.

*The remnants of the Wisdom Tree the morning
after the lightning storm*

Norm Peterson was moved to write an obituary for the tree in the Friday NUUS:

THE WISDOM TREE
SUCCUMBS TO LIGHTNING

After 350 years of providing strength and peace and shelter and inner ease, the great oak east of the Library was fatally wounded by lightning during Wednesday night's storm. The giant oak dominated the Alumni Memorial Garden, and was the site of 15 years worth of Wisdom Tree workshops. Nearly a whole generation of SUUSI-ites have viewed her majestic boughs while absorbing great thoughts...

My introduction to the garden was Monday when I went to get some info for Rev. Mike Young about the space as a possible site for his morning meditations. I was much taken with the grand sense of peace I felt in the shelter of this matriarch, centuries older than these United States. The Wisdom Tree had grace. I hugged her goodbye last night.

Indeed it seemed as if the final few days of SUUSI 1989 were one prolonged hug goodbye. Thursday evening, the Board held an open forum to discuss the move to Virginia Tech, answer participants' questions and allow a space for people to share their feelings. Later that night, in the basement cafeteria of Muse (where there was space for a considerably larger audience than in the Highlander Room at Heth), Teen Way Off Broadway offered "a loving tribute and fond farewell to Radford" in the form of its third annual production, "Alice in SUUSI Land." Alice was played by Amy Davis.

It was the first Teen Way Off Broadway with an exclusively teen cast, and also the first to feature live singing, when Shannon Evans and Nicole Sage performed "Time Is on My Side." The memorable finale, a dance number to the tune of R.E.M.'s

"It's the End of the World As We Know It (And I Feel Fine)," summed up the SUUSI community's mixed emotions as the week was drawing to a close.

Then on Friday night, "Way Off Broadway Revisited" provided "musical memories of our years at Radford." Beaupre Preston had replaced long-time Director Millicent Simmons, who did not come to SUUSI in 1989. Along with choreographer Mary Nell McLauchlin, Preston helped cast and crew live up to the adage "the show must go on," dedicating her week to putting on one last memorable Way Off Broadway show at Radford with the "greatest hits" from a decade of SUUSI Broadway musicals.

The SUUSI Cantatori got in on the action too, with a "non-concert" on Friday afternoon as a culmination of their last week at Radford. In the Youth Program, every age group's Friday Closing Circle reflected the mood of departure; there was an "On the Road to Blacksburg" party for the 4-5 year-olds, while the 8-9 year-olds participated in a "Farewell to Radford" ritual.

The Board even paid for the following quarter-page advertisement on the community page of the *Radford News-Journal* on Friday, July 28, complete with the 1989 "Share Your Light" logo:

THANKS AND FAREWELL TO RADFORD

For the past 16 [*sic*] years, the Southeast Unitarian Universalist Summer Institute (SUUSI) has called Radford home during the last week of July. Radford University can no longer accommodate our growing numbers, so we are moving to Virginia Tech in Blacksburg.

We have thoroughly enjoyed our time in Radford and will miss this wonderful community and its friendly citizens.

Thanks for your hospitality.

Board of Directors,
SUUSI

Also on Friday, the Board issued this press release:

The Southeast Unitarian Universalist Summer Institute (SUUSI) announced today that its 1990 meeting will be held on the Virginia Polytechnic Institute (V.P.I.) campus in Blacksburg, Va.

The decision to hold the Institute on the V.P.I. campus came after several months of searching for a suitable location by the SUUSI Board of Trustees. Betty Green, SUUSI Board President, states that "the facilities in Blacksburg will allow us to continue the high quality of programming for which SUUSI is noted in Unitarian Universalist circles throughout the United States."

Moving is not a new phenomenon for SUUSI, which was first established in 1950 at Lake Waccamaw, N.C., as the "Southern Family Institute." ... The last 14 years have been marked by significant growth in attendance for SUUSI, with approximately 1,400 participants attending this year's session. This phenomenal growth has made SUUSI one of the largest gatherings of Unitarian Universalists in the world – exceeded only by the denomination's annual meeting...

According to Director-Elect Reid Swanson, "Leaving Radford will not be an easy move. For many, Radford is the only place they've ever experienced SUUSI, and we have enjoyed a good working relationship with both the University and the community. Still and all, the move presents many exciting opportunities and possibilities for future SUUSIs!"

On Saturday morning, July 29, what was certainly the largest Closing Circle in SUUSI history assembled on the Commons at Radford University for what was dubbed simply "The Farewell." Emotions and tears flowed freely as young and old said goodbye not only to one another for a year, but to an era at Radford. Each person was given a candle, and asked to make a commitment to "share their light" with the world, before at last blowing out the flame and symbolically bringing to an end SUUSI's 15-year relationship with Radford University.

Chapter 5:
All Roads Lead to SUUSI

S taff and Board members began wearing special T-shirts that proclaimed "All Roads Lead to Blacksburg – SUUSI 1990." The shirts featured a road map of the New River Valley with Blacksburg as the central point. Yet the road to Blacksburg was anything but smooth for the Southeast Unitarian Universalist Summer Institute, which had grown quite comfortable (some would say complacent) with "the way things always were" at Radford. The adjustment to new surroundings, combined with some significant initial challenges working out SUUSI's relationship with a new and much more complexly layered university institution, made the transition to Virginia Tech a difficult one for all concerned.

Making the Move to Blacksburg (1990)

A s soon as the emotional goodbyes to Radford were complete, the planning began in earnest for the first-ever SUUSI at Virginia Tech. Director Reid Swanson chose as the theme for 1990 "Roots and Wings," a particularly apropos phrase from Carolyn McDade's popular hymn "Spirit of Life." The theme perfectly captured a year in which the Summer Institute would turn 40 and – mindful of the strength of deep roots that extended back to Radford and beyond – spread its wings to fly into a new and exciting future in Blacksburg.

In anticipation of the move, the catalog was completely revamped. Swanson chose a striking 8½ by 11 horizontal layout (the catalog would remain in that format through 1996) peppered with new icons to designate different sections and provide a completely fresh look. The cover drawing, which also appeared on T-shirts that year, was a beautiful, soft-toned scene of a green tree (the Wisdom Tree?) gradually transforming into a lovely white bird, about to take flight.

With the move to Virginia Tech came major turnover in most key staff positions. In addition to a new Director, there was a new Treasurer (Maureen McAndrews had replaced Linda Sterner), a new Enrollment Coordinator (Bonnie Weathers had taken over from Reid Swanson), a new Teen Director (Colleen Murphy had succeeded Bill Gupton), and a new Youth Director (Marlene Walker had replaced Trudy Atkin).

Meanwhile, communication with Virginia Tech – notwithstanding the valiant efforts of SUUSI's local "man on the scene," Jim Littlefield – proved particularly frustrating. From the start, accurate budgeting for 1990 proved nearly impossible, as officials at Tech were unable to give consistent cost estimates even for such basics as room rates and meal charges. SUUSI, which had been accustomed to being the largest and most important conference on campus each summer at Radford, had difficulty adjusting to the fact that it was "just another big conference" in Blacksburg. For their part, Virginia Tech's conference services staff had never hosted a group that was as logistically autonomous (or attitudinally independent) as SUUSI. "They haven't run across anybody who does as much of the work *themselves* as we do," Swanson reported to the Board in September 1989. By this point in its organizational development, SUUSI was itself a well-oiled institutional machine – as, of course, was VPI. SUUSI staff expected to handle their own registration, key and meal card distribution and collection, and many of the other arrangements that typically are provided by the host institution at a conference.

Thus, late in 1989, when Virginia Tech surprised the Board with a $30 per participant "activity fee" designed to cover its costs for services that SUUSI did not want or expect Tech to provide, it took Swanson months of judicious negotiation to resolve the issue. In fact, negotiations about various costs and fees, from meal rates to off-duty security guards, continued right up to, and even during, SUUSI week in 1990. At one point the Board feared it had drastically under-budgeted, given several unanticipated fees (and state sales tax, which proved to be another bone of contention) – but when all was said and done, a higher-than-expected turnout made up the difference. Still, concerns about working with Virginia Tech were so strong among the leadership that the minutes of the Saturday Board meeting held the day *before* SUUSI officially started in Blacksburg indicate that the Board was being urged to "consider looking into the possibility of another site for future SUUSIs."

All of this behind-the-scenes drama was unknown to participants – 1,425 of whom (a record that still stands today) arrived at Virginia Tech on Sunday, July 22, 1990, to begin a new era in SUUSI's history. For those coming to SUUSI, it literally did seem as if all roads led to Blacksburg. As registrants drove toward Virginia Tech, coming from 35 different states, Canada and the Virgin Islands, many reported seeing signs directing them to the new location of SUUSI "all the way from I-64 right to Donaldson Brown." Certainly all around the sleepy college town of Blacksburg, and all over the campus itself, the bright yellow, professionally produced, realtor-type yard signs with a large arrow pointing to "SUUSI Registration" helped everyone find the Donaldson Brown Center. A large, modern conference center complete with auditorium, meeting and banquet rooms, and comfortable hotel accommodations, it embodied the difference between Radford and Virginia Tech.

Long lines at Sunday check-in, which reminded some old-timers of the year at Fontana, also reflected the change. SUUSI enrollment staff and their Virginia Tech counterparts had not yet worked out a way to coordinate their different systems for distributing keys, maps, meal cards and other necessary information. Since participants had no idea where anything was located – dorms, meals, workshops – every participant was, in some way, a "newcomer." Even for veterans, the joy of the annual Summer Institute reunion was tempered by what for many became an extremely frustrating first few hours in Blacksburg.

The SUUSI NUUS described the scene:

> We're here! The hellos echo. Newcomers look lost, and the many-timers can't help much 'cause they haven't been to Tech before. Hugs are shared because familiar faces are so welcome in a strange place, and because new faces just look like they could *use* a hug.

Eventually, of course, participants found their way to their rooms. Some people had chosen to take rooms in the relative luxury of the Donaldson Brown Center (for $45 a night), while most had opted for an area known as the Slusher Quad, well on the other side of Tech's quite large campus. There, participants lived in one of four dormitories (actually just two buildings) – Slusher Tower, Slusher Wing, East Campbell and Campbell Main – for $60 per bed for the week.

Following a hasty, and by most accounts unsatisfying, Sunday dinner at Dietrick Cafeteria, the community assembled in the Slusher Quad to begin the banner parade to Ingathering. Some folks were wearing specially made congregational T-shirts; others sported the requisite "All Roads Lead to Blacksburg" shirt. Many were adorned with wacky hats as part of a SUUSI "40th Anniversary Party Hat Contest" (Pat Hunter was the contest winner, in a hat festooned with dangling carrots – "roots" – and lightweight wooden wings). With drums beating and church banners flying, the mass of colorful characters processed past dormitories – where curious summer students hung out the windows cheering them on – and across the expansive Drill Field that lies at the heart of the Virginia Tech campus. Then, climbing a small hill and some steps, they at last entered the stately stone walls of Burruss Hall, marching into a cavernous and noisy auditorium, where they were officially welcomed by VPI President Dr. James

D. McComas. Pete Leary performed a song specially written for the occasion titled "Roots and Wings." The traditional honoring of those who have attended Summer Institute the longest took on new meaning in the strange venue, and an air of excitement and optimism spread throughout the crowd. SUUSI had proven, once again, that it was a *community*, not a *place*.

The first banner parade at Virginia Tech

But when Ingathering ended, the throng dispersed in what seemed to be a thousand different directions, and the sheer size of this particular SUUSI, and this particular campus, began to sink in. Gone were the days when most of the evening events could be held in a single central building, as they were at Heth in Radford. On SUUSI's first night at Virginia Tech, Serendipity took place in Owens Cafeteria, Cabaret and Quiet Serendipity in Donaldson Brown, Late Serendipity in the Slusher Lounge, Ballroom Dancing in the Wesley Student Center, and CACHE in the Baptist Student Union (the latter was moved, after a couple of days, to Donaldson Brown when the Baptists abruptly "cancelled our contract with them after a state officer reviewed the [SUUSI] brochure and was uncomfortable with some of our offerings").

On Monday morning, Rev. John Buehrens (by now co-minister

of All Souls Church in New York City) returned to SUUSI after an absence of several years to offer the first theme talk at Tech, in the Donaldson Brown Auditorium. It was titled "The Roots of Responsibility." The reassurance of the familiar – theme talks and worship services, youth programming and athletics, but most particularly, nature trips (the vast majority of which remained unchanged, due to Blacksburg's proximity to Radford) – helped participants settle into the SUUSI rhythm as the week progressed. But some of the changes to routine were so jarring that they quickly became the stuff of legend.

The bathroom situation was perhaps the number one topic of conversation throughout the week. Although those staying in the hotel accommodations at Donaldson Brown were unaffected, the majority of SUUSI participants that first year at Tech were housed in dorms that did not have private or even semi-private bathrooms. Instead, each floor in the Slusher Quad shared one large bathroom, with toilets and showers. If the residents of a particular floor that housed only adults agreed – unanimously – to make their floor's bathroom unisex, it was designated as such. Otherwise, men's and women's bathrooms were alternated by floor, and participants not only had to leave their *room* for a toilet or shower, but often their *floor* as well. The newsletter frequently reminded people to "wear robes" on bathroom trips, and NUUS "advice" columnist Ms. Demeanor (Suki Nickerson) dispensed humor-laced etiquette tips.

Another significant change in amenities from those at Radford, however, was no joking matter. While Radford had been a flat, relatively compact campus, Virginia Tech was neither. Anyone with mobility challenges was profoundly affected, but the campus' overall lack of accessibility proved particularly difficult for SUUSI to swallow. Those in wheelchairs had to go around to the back loading dock of Dietrick Dining Hall and take the service elevator up to the cafeteria at each meal. Certain dorms were no better, with split-level floors, zigzagging hallways, and no direct access to elevators. As a musical protest, Vonnie Hicks performed a very well-received version of Fred Small's "Talkin' Wheelchair Blues" at Cabaret on Thursday night. By the end of the week, SUUSI participants had collected hundreds of signatures on a petition requesting improved accessibility, which Director Reid Swanson delivered to the university's President.

Of course, there were plenty of positives about the new location as well. Virginia Tech proved to be quite progressive when it came to recycling, providing recycling receptacles on each floor of the dorms, as well as in the lobbies of every building. Workshop spaces – though in constant flux throughout the week as Tech struggled to accommodate SUUSI's huge volume of space needs – were deemed much more comfortable and spacious than those at Radford. The facilities at the Donaldson Brown Center drew rave reviews from the adults (but the Youth Program, which also took place there, sorely missed Radford's old Governors Quad, and particularly the McGuffey nursery). Tech's outdoor spaces, such as those for sand volleyball, proved very popular (the well-rested team from Donaldson Brown won the annual dorm volleyball tournament, though the other teams remarked that it "really wasn't a dorm" and decried the group's "home bathroom advantage").

Some adults were immediately enamored with Blacksburg's golf course, while the children were downright delighted with the Duck Pond. Nearly everyone eventually found their way to the Duck Pond, for reasons ranging from the Road Race (men's winner, Joel Finkelstein; women's winner, Maureen McAndrews) to meditation workshops to bird watching. And in the middle of the week, Wonderful Wednesday at the Duck Pond replaced the traditional Picnic (Food Services did not offer takeout or catered meals on campus). Participants were invited to gather before or after their evening meal for familiar events like the tug-of-war (now called the "tug-of-peace"), the watermelon-seed spitting contest (Vonnie Hicks was the winner with a distance of 23 feet), and an old-fashioned sing-along.

Befitting both the theme and the year of transition, there were many other instances of the old and the new at SUUSI 1990. Noralee Traylor put together a nightly film festival, with movies such as *The Atomic Cafe*. An evening "Denominational Hour" was coordinated in Donaldson Brown by Roger Comstock. On Thursday night, SUUSI's first alternative worship service on the Drill Field celebrated women's spirituality and attracted a huge crowd.

Meanwhile, a Teen Adventure Program blended the Nature and Teen programs. Jake Haun III led the self-selecting group on daily outdoor challenges like rock climbing, whitewater rafting, rappelling, caving and a ropes course. Topics for adult workshops that year included animal rights, alternative families and "A Hero's Journey." The Service Project successfully transitioned to Blacksburg, as SUUSI volunteers helped to build a storage shed, paint, plant flowers and generally beautify the Children's Shelter Home of Blacksburg.

On a lighter note, on Thursday night at Cabaret, according to the NUUS, "300-plus Unitarians yodeled their way into the Guinness Book of World Records," led by the irrepressible Pete Leary. (There is no way to know if the claim of a world record is true, or mere hyperbole, but today the world record for the largest simultaneous yodel stands at 1,795 people.) That same night, just past Donaldson Brown in downtown Blacksburg, young adults and the young at heart enjoyed a concert, arranged for SUUSI, at Buddy's Bar, where Athens, Ga., rock band the La Brea Stompers rocked the house.

The move to Blacksburg also helped to move SUUSI into the modern age. A rudimentary network of a few computers was being created under the direction of Jerry King, who was now serving as coordinator of a Computer Services Staff. And the days of having to walk all over campus in search of someone you needed to talk to were numbered; Director Reid Swanson actually carried a beeper in 1990. Apparently the technology was sufficiently new and intimidating that the NUUS felt a need to print instructions to participants:

HOW TO DIAL THE BEEPER:

Dial the beeper number, then dial the number of the phone from which you are calling, then the asterisk, and wait for the mechanical "Thank You"... Then hang up and wait for a return call.

The first week at Virginia Tech was a difficult one in the Youth Program. Donaldson Brown was hardly an ideal setting for children's activities – much less for a program serving more than 150 children aged a couple of months through 13 years. There were heavily traveled streets both in front and in back of Donaldson Brown, as well as between youth programming and most any destination the children might be headed (which included some new outings like tours of an insect museum and a dairy farm). In addition, there was no appropriate outdoor area for large-group activities, no playground and no adequate nursery space. The bedraggled Youth Staff even had to deal with a "watermelon explosion" early in the week.

Meanwhile, Tech declined to offer discounted meal rates for children under the age of 4, as Youth Staff had come to expect at Radford. The result was that many Youth Staffers ended up missing lunch themselves, as they were otherwise occupied, feeding and supervising SUUSI's youngest members. Adding to the congestion and chaos at Donaldson Brown, some parents of kindergarten and younger elementary age children also chose to meet their kids there for a brown bag lunch, rather than pay the full rate at Dietrick Dining Hall.

Everything came to a head when, in the middle of the week, the new Youth Director, Marlene Walker, suddenly resigned, leaving Assistant Youth Director Melissa Matthews – who had two children of her own under the age of 4 – to guide the program to the end of the week. By Friday, everyone involved was glad when that first week of youth programming at Virginia Tech was over. The Board publicly expressed its gratitude to Matthews for stepping in, and she was invited to officially become Youth

Director. She served for two more years.

A change in the SUUSI Bylaws meant that youth age 6-17 were now allowed to vote only for the teen (youth) representative to the Board. A rotating system was set up in which there would be two such youth representatives, each serving two-year terms, with one elected every year. The person serving their second year (presumably by then 18 years old) would hold the one voting position on the Board representing the interests of all the youth. Jessica Alcorn of Atlanta won the first election in 1990.

The first week at Blacksburg culminated with Teen Way Off Broadway on the main stage in Donaldson Brown Auditorium (there was no Way Off Broadway that year). Before the show, four teens – one of them in costume, as he was about to be in the show – came out from the wings to sing a song that instantly became part of the SUUSI vernacular. "The SUUSI Blacksburg Blues," written and performed by Yancey Clayton, Doug Grigsby, Steve Johnson and Brad Taylor, offered a commentary on SUUSI 1990, through the eyes of some SUUSI teens:

> I woke up this mornin', got into my car.
> I was headed to Blacksburg, ya know it was far.
> Eight truck stops later, and a Stuckey's too,
> I was pretty darn tired before I was through.
> I got the SUUSI ... Blacksburg ... blues!
>
> I hit registration, at half past two,
> It took me three hours, before I was through.
> I headed for my dorm – five miles away,
> Up three flights of steps, to where I would stay.
> I got the SUUSI ... Blacksburg ... blues!
>
> I opened my door; room was kinda small.
> Had to use the bathroom – it was down the hall.
> I was feelin' kinda hungry, so I went for some food.

I didn't eat much – man that stuff was crude!
I got the SUUSI ... Blacksburg ... blues!

After dinner, we saw some guys in pads.
Those steroids with legs, they thought they was bad.
Then we danced the night away
At this funky fresh place we call CACHE.
I got the SUUSI ... Blacksburg ... blues!

After worship, we started to think:
"Hey everybody, why don't we play wink!"
We got in the van the very next day,
It took us two hours, just to find some hay.
I got the SUUSI ... Blacksburg ... blues!

As the audience was still roaring its approval, the curtain rose on "The Wizard of Blacksburg." The first line brought the house

*Dorothy (Kim Edmonds) and the Cowardly Lion (Michael Ivey)
in "The Wizard of Blacksburg"*

down, and seemed to sum up the experience of those who had attended that largest SUUSI of all time: "Toto, I don't think we're in Radford anymore!" The performance featured solos by Kim Edmonds (now Gordon) as Dorothy, singing "Over the Rainbow," and Michael Ivey, as the Cowardly Lion, singing "If I Were King of the Forest." Walden Lechner played the "Wizard of Blacksburg," who just happened to look – and sound – a lot like SUUSI Director Reid Swanson.

The show was a smash, and cemented the reputation of Teen Way Off Broadway as one of the annual highlights of the SUUSI week. And the moral of the story – that regardless of its location, the magic of SUUSI will always touch the hearts of young and old alike – helped many participants begin to let go of Radford, and embrace Virginia Tech.

Making the Adjustment to Virginia Tech (1991-1993)

According to the Board minutes of Saturday, July 28, 1990, the final morning of that first year in Blacksburg, the week ended with "no firm commitment from Virginia Tech for next year." Yet SUUSI did return in the summer of 1991 – and things went a lot smoother the second time around.

Housing continued to include the four dorms of the Slusher Quad, but Cochrane Hall was added as well, since fewer participants chose to stay in the Donaldson Brown hotel rooms (where rates had increased by more than 10%). Parents and children alike hailed the move of the Youth Program from Donaldson Brown to Campbell Main, where the kids quickly made a comfortable home for themselves, taking full advantage of the green spaces in Slusher Quad during what was an unusually hot SUUSI week.

Ingathering on Sunday night was followed by the first-ever "Opening Circle." Marti Toms conceived of and coordinated turning a thousand-plus Unitarian Universalists into "the world's largest UU." After leaving Ingathering, participants were asked to make two huge, concentric circles on the Drill Field outside Burruss, with the lines of people facing one another. At a designated spot, the two circles were joined, and people began moving sideways, creating a giant, snaking pair of concentric "U" shapes – and allowing each person, in just a few minutes, to greet everyone else who had come to SUUSI. The Opening Circle tradition, later refined with amusing video instructions that were shown during Ingathering, continues to this day, serving as the only time during the SUUSI week that all, or virtually all, of the community is joined together in one place.

With that auspicious beginning, SUUSI 1991 was officially underway. The theme that year was "We Believe," with a wide array of workshops available for participants to explore their own and others' beliefs. Titles included "Spirituality for Atheists," "Introduction to Thomas Merton," "Understanding the Bible," "Explorations in Spirituality" and "WomanSpirit Rising." There were two different sessions of "A Course in Miracles." Unitarian Universalist beliefs were also reflected in the offering, for the first time, of the "Welcoming Congregation" workshop.

The Youth Program gave SUUSI's younger participants structured games, crafts, activities and age-appropriate discussions that were designed to help them explore Unitarian Universalism, the Seven Principles and the diversity of faiths included within UUism. Evening programming for children ages 8-13 supplemented the curriculum. There were the usual youth favorites like Dirty Day and the Pandapas Pond hike, as well as a new favorite – the Duck Pond.

At the Duck Pond, participants christened a large, shady tree "The Singing Tree," and – reminiscent of the Wisdom Tree at Radford – it quickly became a gathering spot where musicians performed, sing-alongs took place and storytellers held court. Bright and early Tuesday morning, 150 (surely a record) SUUSI-ites gathered at the Duck Pond for the annual Fun Run.

Theme speakers and worship service leaders made good use of the "We Believe" theme. Monday's theme talk was given by Rep. Jim Olin, a member of the nearby Roanoke church who was serving his fifth term in the U.S. House of Representatives. Olin was also known as the author of the Virginia Wilderness Protection Act, which brought under government protection 81,000 acres of forests and streams.

Natalie Gulbrandsen, the Moderator of the Unitarian Universalist Association, also spoke, as did John Buehrens, who two years hence would be elected UUA President. Tom Warth, the new Director of The Mountain, was welcomed on Thursday, which was designated "Mountain Day at SUUSI." That night, the WomanSpirit group led a well-attended outdoor worship ritual under the full moon on the Drill Field.

During the days, however, it was oppressively hot in 1991. At least one SUUSI computer fell prey to the heat, and Ballroom Dancing was cancelled after just two nights when the location (the lobby of Cochrane Hall) could not be sufficiently cooled by the multiple fans that had been commandeered for the occasion. SUUSI volunteers sweltered but persevered to complete the Service Project, building an outdoor play set and completing gardening tasks at the Children's Shelter Home.

Meanwhile, indoors, volunteer stitchers labored (without air conditioning), to piece together quilts from squares that had been brought from congregations all over the country. The project was the brainchild of Cheryl Davis, and was led by master quilters Regina Liske and Christine Hudgins. By week's end two large, beautiful quilts were displayed in glass cases in the lobby of Donaldson Brown; one was to be donated to the Women's Shelter in Radford, while the other was raffled off as a fundraiser for future SUUSI Service Projects. Three smaller, child-size quilts that had been made from pieces provided by SUUSI youth were donated to the Children's Shelter Home.

The spirit of service – which, after all, is a major part of what "we believe" – extended to the Nature Program as well. "Service Hikes" were arranged, allowing hikers to take part in trail maintenance and cleanup programs while hiking trails in the Jefferson National Forest. "Since SUUSI participants have enjoyed the trails over the past dozen years, we thought it was a wonderful idea to give a gift of trail maintenance back, to show our appreciation and set an example," said Director-Elect and Nature Co-Director Dawn Kenny.

Morning and evening editions of the newsletter were produced by editor Norm Peterson using recycled paper. The "SUUSI A.M. Times" was primarily a schedule of the day's events, while the evening "SUUSI NUUS" had the usual mix of information and humor. The popular column by "Ms. Demeanor" returned, and an ongoing debate about the environmental impact of "slogging" through creeks kept things lively. A daily report was provided for eating enthusiasts, updating readers on the latest exploits of the dynamic duo of power eaters from Florida, Gary Fields and Paul Langrock (who was also conducting a campaign to be elected to the Board). The pair offered inspiration and instruction on how to get the most – literally – out of the all-you-can-eat meal plan at

"Tie-Dye Steve" Anderson and his wares

The SUUSI Cantatori, directed by Eleanor Sableski

Dietrick Dining Hall.

Unlike the previous year, the food in 1991 received positive reviews from meat eaters and vegetarians alike. It turned out that the year before, a new food services director had begun his position at Virginia Tech the very same week that SUUSI – with its insistent, copious and often conflicting demands – had arrived on campus for the first time. It was not a good scenario. But in 1991, the Dietrick staff proved to be very helpful and responsive (even using some recipes offered by SUUSI participants), earning the following blurb in the Thursday NUUS:

> Cafeteria? Bravo! Bravo! Bravo!
> Let's thank Food Services for a job well done. Food is great and presentation super. John E., Brent and his merry band are superb!

In the Teen Dorm (once again, a section of Campbell), a

teen magazine was produced featuring poetry, literature, art and commentary. Teens – now numbering 130 – had a variety of program options, including a more flexible Teen Adventure Program that allowed teen participants to pick and choose which day trips they wanted to take, as an alternative to signing up for the full week. Teen Way Off Broadway capped the week with two performances of "Hair 1991," an update of the classic Vietnam War era musical set in the recent Gulf War. So many teens wanted to be in the play that except for a couple of central characters, there were different casts for the first and second shows. Sienna Baskin, who played Jennie in the second performance, recalls a midnight cast trip that took place Thursday night, less than 24 hours before the performance:

> The Waffle House! ... We all sat in a circle in the grass and got in character, and then we were in character all night at the Waffle House – full hippie costumes and face paint and everything. It was method acting for 14-year-olds. I think that night was formative for me. I truly believed I was born in the wrong decade!
>
> I also still get shivers when I think about doing "Orange Crush" [by R.E.M., chillingly choreographed by Dana Taylor]. We stormed in through the back of the theater in fatigues and guns and freaked everyone out. It all seemed so big and professional. That show introduced me to a lot of great music.

On Friday night, lines stretched outside and around the block as people waited to get into the cramped, non-airconditioned theater at the Methodist Wesley Center just off campus to see one of the Teen Way Off Broadway shows. Just down the street at Donaldson Brown, Way Off Broadway returned to the SUUSI stage with two performances of its own. "Oklahoma," under the direction of Fricka Raycroft, featured choreography by Mary Nell McLauchlin. Both versions of SUUSI "Broadway" were timed so that theater fans did not have to choose between them, but rather could move easily from one to the other and catch both shows. That year's "Oklahoma," it turned out, would be the last Way Off Broadway.

One new performance program was added in 1991, and it proved to be very popular. "Concert Hour" was created and coordinated by Kathee Williams, and featured a nightly concert spotlighting different styles of music. The week's performers were Last Rights, Carole and Bren, Will Tuttle, and the SUUSI Chamber Music Ensemble. Meanwhile, Cabaret continued to "offer professional quality volunteer entertainers an opportunity to improve their skills in front of a supportive and appreciative audience." Among the performers was Nancy Bartlett, who returned to SUUSI as well as the Cabaret stage after a nine-year absence.

The SUUSI experience also proved to be rewarding for newcomer Verna Safran, who shared some of the things she did and learned at her first SUUSI in the Thursday NUUS:

Things I never did before (for adventure): Sang in public. Did the La Bamba. Learned to tango. Went on an early-morning bird walk. Asked a man to dance.

Things I have done before (for anchoring): Attended worship services. Hugged old friends. Got a backrub. Gave a backrub.

Learned something about prioritizing. Totally overwhelmed on my first day, I dropped two courses and had time to sit on the grass and leave room for the unexpected. Also scrapped the notion that the good stuff is happening someplace else, and realized that "wherever I am now is where I'm meant to be."

Got in touch with the kid in me. Made an ice cream sundae at the Fair. Enjoyed a delightful moment when a three-year-old girl came up to me and asked, "Have you seen Christy?" Thought it was great that kids think everybody in the world knows everybody else, and keeps track of them.

Talked about church business with John Buehrens. Talked about poetry with David Moore. Talked about ageism with Pal Palmore. Talked about courage with gloria wright. Talked and talked and talked.

Stayed up later than I have since college. This accepting environment is such a great place to learn to trust others, and dare to be ... myself!

At the end of the week, the SUUSI Vision Committee completed two years of work that had begun just as the Institute was leaving Radford by presenting its recommendations to the Board. The Vision Committee was composed of John Frandsen (chair), Jim Littlefield, Jill Menadier, Pete Tolleson, Paula Heusinkveld, Don Male and Phil Sterner. Their report, titled "The Future of SUUSI," included this abstract:

> The mission of SUUSI is to allow participants to experience in one week what Unitarian Universalism can be at its best. The size of the Institute should not be limited. Outreach should be emphasized and expanded. Programming should continue to be primarily created by its leaders, but additional diversity can be developed...
>
> Attention should be paid to developing programming for groups with special needs. Workshops should generally be open to all ages. Adjunct meetings at SUUSI should be encouraged. Some changes are desirable in dormitory arrangements. The Institute should establish and build an endowment. A salaried Executive Coordinator should be appointed. Measures are suggested to develop increased participation by professional religious leaders.

A few months later at The Mountain, at a momentous winter meeting in December, 1991, the Board initiated some changes that would shape SUUSI for years to come. It began by affirming the intent of the Vision recommendations, and officially adopting the mission the committee had proposed: "The mission of SUUSI is to allow participants to experience in one week what Unitarian Universalism can be at its best." To that end, the Board took several steps designed to assure the long-term stability and viability of the Institute.

Perhaps the most controversial of these was a short, simple policy declaration stating that "SUUSI will not sponsor any nude activities." In the often impassioned discussion leading up to that decision, one Board member noted that "these events [clothing-optional nature trips] and their publicity have an impact on SUUSI – and affect its reputation – in a way that is far out of proportion to their rather minor part in the overall SUUSI program." It was pointed out that in 1990 – a year when nearly 10 percent of all nature trips listed in the catalog were clothing optional – many trips had to be rerouted after an official from the National Forest Service contacted SUUSI to inform the Nature Staff that nudity in national forests is against the law. Another Board member shared the experience of having overheard SUUSI being referred to back home as "the nudist camp." Still another expressed concern over the sad fact that many "outsiders," upon looking through a catalog consisting of 50 or more pages and literally hundreds of different workshops and activities, often focused their attention only on the words "clothing optional."

Ironically, soon after the Board's decision – and a few months prior to the next SUUSI – Board President Bonnie Sheppard received a copy of a newsletter from a group called the "Blue Ridge Naturists" that cited SUUSI as a large conference which was friendly to nudist hiking. Sheppard quickly wrote to the Naturists, and also to the National Park Service, outlining SUUSI's change in policy.

That winter the Board also discussed – and passed – a new policy that affected all parents and their minor children. Concerns had been raised about "out of control" young people, and Virginia Tech had levied significant charges to SUUSI for damages to spaces in both the teen and YA dorms the previous year. The new policy, which along with the others was communicated to the SUUSI community in a special winter edition of the NUUS, read: "The SUUSI Board affirms the need for a safe and nurturing environment for our youth. SUUSI and the parents and guardians of youth at SUUSI need to recognize their responsibility and partnership in creating such an environment. SUUSI must continue to take all reasonable steps to assure the safety of youth participants, and to that end, insure that facilities, staffing and programming are adequate. Parents and guardians of youth must recognize and accept their role in caring for their children while at SUUSI. They must realize that SUUSI is not a "sleep-away" camp, and that they must be responsible for their children outside of youth programming time."

When teens registered for SUUSI 1992, they were required to sign a revised covenant that reflected the new policies. Again, note the similarities – and the differences – with previous teen covenants:

RULES FOR TEENS (14-17)

1. Local and state laws with regard to alcoholic beverage consumption must be adhered to – i.e., NO UNDER 21 DRINKING.

2. Federal and state laws with regard to illicit drug use must be adhered to – i.e., NO SMOKING OF POT.

3. Youth must be in rooms of the Youth Dorm at CURFEW – 15 minutes after the last evening program.

4. Parent/guardian will be responsible for damages done to an individual teen's room.

5. No smoking by teens under 18 years of age as mandated by Virginia State Law.

6. Parent/guardian and teen agree to meet at least once a day for a check-in.

7. With the exception of programmed activities, leaving campus without the express permission of the teen's parent/guardian is prohibited.

Bed checks will not be made by Youth Staff. However, after curfew Security Personnel will patrol the Youth Dorm and Quad area.

Parents and/or guardians will need to establish ground rules and room curfews with their teens during non-programmed time. Youth Staff is responsible only for those teens who attend scheduled programming. Teens and parents are urged to use the sign-out schedules posted on the Teen Dorm doors.

I, ___(youth)_____, understand that violation of any of these rules will result in my immediate removal from SUUSI.

I, ___(parent)_____, understand that if my child or I fail to comply with any of these rules, I will have to take my child home.

In addition, every person staying in the teen or young adult dorms – regardless of age – was required to include a $25 damage deposit with their registration.

Each of the Board's new policies, in one way or another, proved to be controversial. Some saw them as evidence of a growing conservatism in the broader culture, or as encroaching on the kind of personal freedoms that had made the SUUSI community so unique. SUUSI Board and Staff, however, cited their role as stewards of the overall (and long-term) well being of that community. Freedom, they pointed out, must always be balanced with *responsibility*, as the fourth UU Principle reminds us. Many of the policy changes, they continued, reflected the advice and counsel both of SUUSI's liability insurance carrier, and of its Risk Manager. Ready or not, happily or not, SUUSI was entering the modern era.

Director Dawn Kenny wrote eloquently about the need for a heightened awareness of our mutual responsibilities in an open letter to the 1,255 participants who arrived in Blacksburg for

SUUSI 1992. Here is the text of that letter, which appeared in the Sunday NUUS:

> Welcome! I know that you are as happy as all of the 300 volunteers are, that SUUSI is finally here! We are all here to learn, have fun, and share in the sense of community that has always been SUUSI.
>
> As SUUSI has grown, however, we feel we have lost some of the feeling of connectedness. This year, we all need to realize that as individuals, we have a responsibility to contribute to SUUSI's continuing success. There are many ways each of us can help.
>
> We are only here on the VPI campus for one week. Many of the people who are here year-round get their only impression of Unitarian Universalists from their contacts with us during this week. We owe it to ourselves to demonstrate to the people of this community – from the people in the town to the people who work in Dietrick Dining Hall – our respect for all people, their beliefs, and, as Jim Scott says in his song, "the oneness of everything." We should assure that our actions indicate that responsible and supportive behavior is what is expected.
>
> We demonstrate our caring for one another by speaking out if we see someone about to do something which could be destructive to her or himself, someone else, someone's property or the environment... In particular, we need to help our SUUSI children remember that they are guests on this campus.
>
> The young adults have decided to take a positive leadership role by volunteering to inspect all teen and young adult rooms after check-out [on] Saturday, and to clean up any mess that is found. If all of us would make sure they do not have anything to clean up, I know they would appreciate it...
>
> This year, we come to SUUSI to reawaken in ourselves

the essence of SUUSI. In doing so, we acknowledge our responsibility to each other, and to the world as a whole. Each of us is responsible for keeping the spirit alive. To do that, I call upon each of you to enjoy your time here, and to make sure you RENEW THE SPIRIT!

Indeed, in addition to the emphasis on personal and collective responsibility, 1992 was characterized by a renewed focus on the spirit at – and of – SUUSI. Both candidates for UUA President, John Buehrens and Carolyn Owen-Towle, addressed the theme of "Renew the Spirit" in theme talks. Former SUUSI Director and current UUA Executive Vice President Kay Montgomery also returned to offer a theme talk. Workshops throughout the week included "Spirituality and Aging," "The Path of Mindfulness," "Prayerwheel" and "Music, Spirituality and the Body."

The youth, meanwhile, under the direction of Youth Director Melissa Matthews, each day explored, in age-appropriate ways, famous Unitarian Universalists. Monday was devoted to scientists, Tuesday to artists, Wednesday to ministers, Thursday to U.S. Presidents and world leaders, and Friday to literary figures. A motivated, dedicated Teen Staff – which had now grown to 15 from just two a decade earlier – helped the teen program continue to evolve, deepening both its spirituality and community, under the leadership of Teen Director Colleen Murphy. Teen Way Off Broadway (which was beginning to be known affectionately as "TWOB") had a new Director, Devin Gordon, and was now SUUSI's only "Broadway." Friday night's performance of "The SUUSI Brothers" was again held at the Wesley Center.

An impressive total of 196 young adults, who were now for the first time grouped together in an age range of 18 to 35, were housed in Vawter Hall (dubbed "Vawterville"), and themselves created programming both spiritual and fun at all hours of the day and night. Nature helped by providing, for the first time, four dedicated YA-only nature trips – canoeing, kayaking, tubing and hiking.

Tech's new Squires Student Center had opened, and offered participants the opportunity to bowl, play pool or grab a quick snack, though no SUUSI activities were held there that year. Heavy equipment and the sounds of construction were ubiquitous all over campus, causing more than one disruption. A springtime flash flood that had damaged Donaldson Brown (as well as Memorial Gym) a couple of months earlier created havoc with many SUUSI plans. Theme talks and worship services were moved to Owens Ballroom, while the Owens Food Court was the site of CACHE.

The flood forced check-in to be relocated to Shultz Dining Hall. Located on the opposite end of the very large Virginia Tech campus from all SUUSI housing, Shultz also was where Serendipity and Cabaret would be held. Shuttle vans ran back and forth across campus throughout the week, well into the wee hours of the night. Midweek, in a very creative response to the situation, CACHE and Serendipity were combined into an all-ages, alcohol and smoke free (but air conditioned!) dance space for two nights. The newsletter promised that both DJs, who were naturally inclined to play very different music for very different audiences, "will cooperate closely ... for a great blend of music on our common ground – the dance floor!"

Some of the week's musical highlights included a performance by Jim Scott at Concert Hour, and the debut of the commissioned theme song for the week, "Renew the Spirit," by the duo Carole and Bren, at Ingathering. The pair also led the banner parade, playing "Trumpet Tune."

By necessity, participant fees had been raised somewhat significantly in 1992. Virginia Tech had increased per-registrant charges by nearly 20 percent in just two years, and SUUSI was taking a financial hit. Even the Forest Service was charging a user fee for nature trips. Total SUUSI costs for room, meals and registration went up $15 for all adults, $55 for teens, $20 for 13 year olds, $5 for ages 4-12, and $30 for those under 4. A cap was also placed on enrollment in certain age groups, including a limit of no more than 15 children in the nursery.

The higher cost of SUUSI, combined with what some saw as newly restrictive policies, inevitably created a certain amount of tension. An ongoing dialogue in the newsletter – much like the previous year's debate about the environmental impact of nature trips – focused on the pros and cons of "individuality" versus "community" in Unitarian Universalism. The "clothing optional" controversy continued, with a group of "Natural UUs" posting flyers around camp promoting events later in the year. The Board quickly pointed out that neither the flyers, nor the trips, were "authorized by SUUSI." Adding to the edgy air, Monday night's sermon by Tampa minister Mike Young was titled "Clothing Optional." (Though Young never mentioned nudity, and did not use the words "clothing optional" until his final sentence, the sermon spoke about integrity, and the dangers both of fundamentalism, and of "trying to achieve legitimacy in the eyes of the 'downtown' church.")

Service to the broader world continued to expand in 1992. Nature offered free Jefferson National Forest trail cleanup trips each day of the week. Both the Quilt Cooperative and the Service Project continued their work. Speakers and workshop leaders reiterated the connection between "doing service" and "renewing the spirit." Responding to a newsletter "want ad" seeking an "experienced RN ... to work in the First Aid Office and on-call during the week of SUUSI," registered nurse Shirley Gordon of Sterling, Va., began a SUUSI first-aid ministry that would span nearly two decades. In the course of her time as SUUSI's nurse, both unofficially and later officially, Gordon dealt with close to a thousand medical incidents ranging from stubbed toes to broken bones.

Once again, there was a SUUSI wedding. Marty McNulty and Lindsay Stroh, who had met at SUUSI in 1985, were married on Monday afternoon among their friends at the University Chapel. Roger Cowan, the minister of their church in Palm Beach, Fla., did the honors.

Wednesday night's poignant worship service, attended by several hundred people of all ages, has become one of the signature moments in SUUSI history. Us and Our Friends, the group of gay and lesbian SUUSI participants and their allies, had requested the opportunity to "lead a service that would be a patchwork quilt of people's experiences of being gay and having gay loved ones," according to Bonnie Crouse. The service featured music from Carole and Bren, Kathee Williams and Will Tuttle. Speakers shared personal stories about the devastating effects of homophobia, about friends who had AIDS, and about being a lesbian in a Unitarian Universalist church and not being allowed to teach Sunday School.

Among the participants was a group of young people who learned, just before the service, by reading it in the program, that Floating Eagle Feather – who had given many of them some of their fondest SUUSI childhood memories during his many years on Youth Staff – had recently died from AIDS. The immediacy and power of the night's emotions are etched in the minds of all who were there.

"Some of the kids were on the floor crying, holding tight to one another," says Crouse. "But they wanted to go on with their part of the service. It was a pretty powerful moment. They were doing a recitation of why gay people need a church, and why straight people need a church, and how the reasons are the same for all of us."

Crouse dedicated her sermon that night – titled "The Pride, The Rage: A New Understanding of the Gay Rights Movement" – to her friend Jerry Taylor, the former president of her congregation in Winston-Salem, N.C., who had been murdered just the previous week, a victim of homophobic gay-bashing. She concluded her remarks with a powerful challenge to SUUSI, and to Unitarian Universalism:

We come into your sanctuaries literally *seeking sanctuary*, from a world in which we hear ourselves described as degraded, immoral, sick, damaged, and incomplete. We hear Jesse Helms announce his campaign kick-off by calling homosexuals "disgusting people;" we hear judges declaring us unfit to parent, and presidential advisors calling us a threat to the family. What we *want* to hear, are the voices of Unitarian Universalists, telling them they are wrong.

After a brief hesitation, the packed house in Owens Ballroom erupted in applause. Pat Berry, who was in the audience, wrote in the next day's SUUSI NUUS, describing her experience of that remarkable worship service:

> I listened to the words of Bonnie Crouse, and when she finished I stood as I clapped. And never before did I feel totally channeled and true as I did when I stood there, the only person in my vision standing. It felt like minutes, and I still stood. We all were still clapping, until slowly a few others stood also, and then a few more.
>
> Then it looked like everyone stood, clapping loudly. Those minutes standing alone were not awkward or self-conscious. I was doing the right thing, and I now know my truest, deepest calling, just as I knew I wanted to be a mother, and just as I knew teaching was my calling also. Thank you, Bonnie, for awakening me to another fulfilling direction I need to put my energies into... Work I will, for UU to be truly inclusive.

Potent seeds had been planted that would, indeed, renew SUUSI's spirit.

A year later, SUUSI gathered once again to "Maintain the Vision." A loveable new icon caught the fancy of the SUUSI community – a pictograph of the Native American deity Kokopelli. Director Dawn Kenny selected Kokopelli as the logo for 1993, describing him, and what he represented, in the catalog:

The flute player ... carries in the hump on his back the seeds of plants and flowers, and with the music of his flute he creates warmth. As the Indians [of the Southwest] migrated, signs of Kokopelli were left on rocks to indicate the revitalization of the earth, the spreading of seeds, and the nurturing of growth to provide sustenance for future generations. [Kokopelli is] a symbol of recycling life.

The joyous little symbol appeared everywhere at SUUSI in 1993 (and beyond). There were of course the annual logo T-shirts, which that year were a distinctive organic oatmeal color and were manufactured by Clothes for Consciousness, a socially and environmentally responsible company. There were Kokopelli earrings and jewelry, temporary tattoos and sidewalk drawings. The Native American theme carried over to workshops, where offerings included "The Religion of Native Americans," "Earth Circle" and "Spirit Drum Circle." The now-traditional Thursday night alternative worship service focused on the theme, and the Youth Program included activities like rain sticks and mask-making.

New Youth Director Elizabeth (Thompson) Drake gave the Youth Program its own theme, "Embracing the World," and shared her vision for the week: "It is my hope that the children will leave SUUSI with a greater understanding of global community, and a desire for a peaceful, fair and free world in which we accept all peoples." To that end, each day the age groups explored the cultures of a different continent; Monday was North America, Tuesday was Asia, Wednesday was Europe, Thursday was Africa and Friday was South America. From their new home in the Slusher Wing, the kids made African gourds and collected materials to package and send to children in another country in a SUUSI "exchange program." Old and unsold SUUSI T-shirts were gathered up and sent to natives in a Nicaraguan village.

Ric Masten, a Unitarian Universalist poet, singer and

"troubadour minister" whose song "Let It Be a Dance" was already popular in the SUUSI community, came from California to offer the Tuesday morning theme talk, and appeared at an informal daily workshop titled "Dialogue with a Poet" – in which he explored, with a large crowd of eager participants, different themes in his poetry. A dozen of Masten's poems, with accompanying pen and ink drawings, appeared in the Theme Book, and there was, of course, a book signing at the end of the week (both the Theme Book, and the poet's own books, flew off the shelf at

Ric Masten (right) with Alexis Jones singing "Let It Be a Dance" in 1993

the SUUSI Bookstore). Most importantly for posterity, Masten also performed a memorable duet of "Let It Be a Dance" with Alexis Jones, offering his blessing on a new SUUSI tradition that would last more than two decades – the poignant Friday morning singing, by Jones, of the signature song.

Jones himself added a new workshop to the SUUSI offerings in 1993. He called it "SUUSIBOYZ." The description in the catalog read, "One of the most powerful sounds in music is that of a male chorus. Attend one or both short daily practice sessions [scheduled before and after the normal afternoon workshop slot], split for your SUUSI convenience. Join in this brotherhood of joyful noise." The $15 workshop fee included the first of what would become annually coveted BOYZ T-shirts, as well as music for the week.

Robby Greenberg, who was now in charge of Concert Hour and

recruiting musicians to bring their gifts to the SUUSI community, convinced Relative Viewpoint to make the journey from Florida to Blacksburg in 1993; Gary Gonzalez and his family have been coming ever since. Relative Viewpoint consisted of Gonzalez on guitar and vocals, along with his brother-in-law Rick Groom and his niece Chris Groom on vocals and harmonies. They wrote and performed the year's theme song, "Maintain the Vision," at Ingathering on Sunday, and later in the week sang at Concert Hour. Other 1993 Concert Hour performers included Aztec Two Step and Carole Eagleheart.

On Thursday night, the SUUSI Cantatori, with Eleanor Sableski and Reid Swanson, led a musical worship service that celebrated the release of the new UUA hymnal *Singing the Living Tradition*. The service also provided a space for participants to lift up the memories of those loved ones who had died during the previous 12 months, as well as those who had been prevented from attending SUUSI because of poor health. Prior to the worship service, a distinguished panel held what was billed as a "UU Theological Forum." Speakers included Ric Masten, Leon Spencer, Ann Marsh, Wade Wheelock and Stephen Shick.

Wednesday night's worship was a collaboration between the teens and young adults. That year the teens were working on the Welcoming Congregation program, leading late-night Teen Dorm worship, and playing ultimate frisbee and euchre. Friday night's Teen Way Off Broadway performance debuted an original song by Devin Gordon, "Looking for the Dawn," sung by Sienna Baskin.

SUUSI participants experienced yet another logistical challenge in 1993, the result of ongoing construction at Virginia Tech. Dietrick Dining Hall was closed, so hungry diners had to trek all the way to Shultz – a cavernous, unwelcoming space on the extreme far corner of campus, next to downtown Blacksburg – for lunch and dinner. This twice-daily exodus was aided by continuously running shuttle buses, and became both the bane of many participants' existence, and the source of an endless supply of jokes and wisecracks. Breakfast, on the other hand, was served at the Owens Food Court, and generally received positive reviews. Thankfully, Donaldson Brown was back in operation, and was the site of Serendipity, several workshops, Teen Way Off Broadway and, once again, Sunday check-in.

One other major disruption occurred, at the end of the week, when approximately 4,000 RVs arrived on campus for a weekend camping conference – requiring SUUSI vehicles to be moved from the Litton-Reeves parking lot on Friday afternoon, and making for a very chaotic load-out on Saturday morning.

As always, workshops in 1993 ran the gamut, from "Chocolate" to "Experiencing Existential Psychology." One workshop in particular, "How to Notice, Recognize and Enjoy Feelings and Emotions," facilitated by the self-described "relentlessly encouraging" Howard Smith, had a profound impact on Ames Guyton. "The work involved experiential exercises to enhance our skills on listening intensely," says Guyton, "and expressing [the] feelings of the moment, as one sought to live each moment to the fullest." Guyton was inspired to go home and write a narrative about the "emotional power" of the workshop, and of his experience in it.

Though dedicated SUUSI-goers had grown accustomed to the vagaries of the Virginia Tech experience, overall attendance continued to fall precipitously (down in 1993 to 1,095 from a high of 1,425 just three years earlier). The SUUSI Staff was expressing its frustration about facilities and services not only to the SUUSI Board, but also directly to Virginia Tech employees – who, in fairness, were only able to do as much as their superiors authorized. The bureaucratic structure of the VPI service delivery system was beginning to run counter to the expressed needs and desires of a very large group of open-minded, but at times less than flexible, Unitarian Universalists. To make matters worse, SUUSI had begun running an annual operating deficit, which it blamed primarily on "hidden fees and costs" that would appear each year in the final bill from Virginia Tech – costs that apparently had not previously been discussed or agreed to.

Bill Spurgin, who had been authorized by the Board the previous year "to check with Radford to determine if it would be possible for us to go back there in the future," reported at the end of 1993 that a return would not be possible "now," but that Radford had indicated an openness to being contacted again the following year. A subgroup of the Board – outgoing Director Dawn Kenny, incoming Director Maureen McAndrews, Jill Menadier, Ken Schmidt, gloria wright, Mark Harris and Tonya Ridings – was appointed to become a new, more active Site Selection Committee, and began aggressively pursuing options. Kenny and Ridings were the co-chairs.

Of the 11 universities approached during the next off-season, only three responded positively: Radford, James Madison (in Harrisonburg, Va.), and North Georgia College (in Dahlonega, Ga.). Radford was in the process of building both new facilities and its conference service infrastructure, and thus would still not be available for a couple more years. SUUSI would remain at Virginia Tech until Radford was ready to welcome it back.

1994-1995

Ironically, life at Virginia Tech was about to become much more comfortable and accommodating. In 1994, SUUSI was moved to a different part of campus, with dorms that surrounded a very large – and flat – open field (originally known as the "Prairie Quad," but in later years more commonly referred to as "Lee Quad"). It offered sand volleyball courts and ample space for outdoor community activities. Most SUUSI participants were housed in Pritchard, O'Shaughnessy and Johnson halls, but some lucky souls were assigned to Payne Hall – a new dorm that boasted the twin luxuries of bathroom suites and air conditioning. From the moment on Sunday evening when the community gathered there to begin the banner parade, the Prairie Quad became SUUSI "home base."

That banner parade featured the largest-ever SUUSI contingent from one church. By now participants had come to expect a "sea of Clearwater blue" T-shirts to dominate the parade each year, but in 1994, there were a record 94 attendees from the Clearwater church ("94 in '94!" was the rallying cry).

Director Maureen McAndrews' theme was "World Healing." Workshops – which were coordinated by Karen Chandler and Sharon Mayes – received their highest overall evaluation in years, and many of them addressed the theme directly. There was "Achieving a Greener Lifestyle," "Healing from Violence," "The Healing Power of Creativity," "Eating the Vegetarian Way," "Chemicals Everywhere" and more. One workshop, "The Heart of Healing" by Lois Winter, addressed the noetic sciences and dealt "with nature and [the] potential of mind and spirit as they apply to health and well-being." Long-time SUUSI favorite gloria wright led a drop-in discussion in the 3rd floor lounge at Payne on "Caring for and Nurturing Our Souls and Soulful Relationships."

Nature, now under the direction of Bill Bestpitch and Dee Medley, offered new aquatic trips like a "Rubber Duckie" adventure, in which participants bounced through whitewater rapids in West Virginia in a small, inflatable, one-person rubber craft called a "funyak." There were also photography trips that focused on the visual detail of nature's beauty, as well as a young adult "mystery night hike." Closer to campus, participants were invited to take a short walk to a nearby grove for an old-fashioned campfire sing-along under the stars, featuring several beloved SUUSI singers and musicians.

Will Tuttle's "Earth Healing" workshop promised "a musical and meditative approach to compassionate living." Popular Concert Hour shows included Fred Small's first appearance at SUUSI. Even the kids got in on the musical fun, enjoying a children's song swap.

Folks loved that the new housing locations were much closer to Donaldson Brown (home to theme talks, the quieter parts of nightlife and TWOB), Owens (breakfast, Serendipity) and Shultz

The infamous "Sea of Clearwater Blue"

(still lunch and dinner). Community time seemed tailor made for the Lee Quad. And the Artists' Co-Op became a popular destination, located as it was on the first floor of Payne, where participants could shop in air conditioned comfort.

One first-timer had a particularly good time that week. Meg Riley from the Unitarian Universalist Association's Office of Gay, Lesbian and Bi-Sexual Concerns, was a new SUUSI attendee in 1994, and wrote, "It has been a wonderful time here. The generosity and helpfulness of the staff and attendees has been AWESOME. The teens are inspiring. The playfulness is delightful. As a UUA staff member, I felt sought out and respected but still able to play, relax and goof off without worrying 'what people thought.' Clearly, people are too busy having fun themselves to judge my idiosyncrasies. This is [a] very unusual [experience] for UUA staff. I will recommend SUUSI to my colleagues – often we lose the chance to enjoy UU community." Riley returned the following year to lead both a theme talk and a worship service.

Another denominational leader, Denny Davidoff, kicked off the theme talks on Monday morning, and also led two

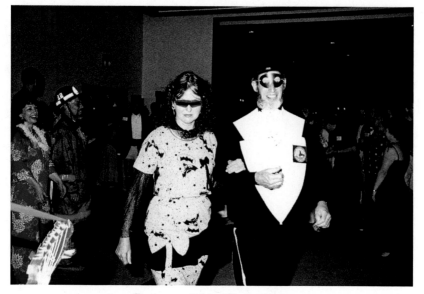

Costume night at Serendipity

workshops during the week on the Association and its operation. As Moderator of the UUA, Davidoff was now working closely in Boston with President and long-time SUUSI friend John Buehrens.

Eight different support groups, including Overeaters Anonymous and Co-Dependents Anonymous, had sprung up within the SUUSI community, reflecting a growing awareness of the challenges of freedom within human relationships. As the Board often told participants, "We have an abundance of freedom at SUUSI. With that freedom comes full responsibility."

There was another SUUSI wedding in 1994. Bill Gupton and Jennifer Sanders were married on Thursday afternoon, under the gazebo at Claytor Lake State Park, with Morris Hudgins officiating. Nearly a hundred people made the half-hour drive to Claytor Lake for the ceremony, blew soap bubbles at the couple as they walked down the aisle together, and then enjoyed a cruise-boat reception on the lake. Youth Director Elizabeth (Thompson)

Drake rearranged staff schedules and programming to allow as many Youth Staffers as possible to attend.

The following night, Teen Way Off Broadway returned to the Donaldson Brown stage with its first-ever fully original script, written by TWOB Director Devin Gordon. "The Miracle of Summer"was described as "an exploration of the magic of SUUSI."

While most agreed that there was, in fact, something very special about the ongoing community that is SUUSI, life in any community of a thousand people is not without its problems. Complaints ranged from a decided lack of hot water for showering in Pritchard to ongoing issues with both the quality of food at Shultz Dining Hall, and with its location. The most common gripe in post-SUUSI evaluations, however, centered around excessive nighttime noise, especially in the corner of the Quad where teens and young adults were housed. Increased access to (and egress from) the Teen Dorm, which now had more than twice the number of external doors as previously, created other headaches. A new rule for the teens indicated "there will be no leaving the teen dorm between 1 a.m. and 6 a.m., unless accompanied by your parent or guardian, or for a preapproved, scheduled activity."

Meanwhile, the Board was dealing with a number of institutional challenges. SUUSI ended in the red once again in 1994, largely the result of unexpected charges from Virginia Tech. In addition, of the 1,050 registrants, a record 62 received some kind of scholarship aid. (It should also be noted, however, that just prior to the 1994 gathering, SUUSI unexpectedly received a small but very thoughtful donation from the Low Country UU Fellowship in Charleston, S.C., which was in the process of dissolving.)

In response to several unfortunate incidents – and in recognition of an increasing awareness within the broader culture about the issue of sexual harassment – the Board put a harassment policy into place just prior to SUUSI 1994. The policy, which was widely publicized in the catalog and SUUSI NUUS, read:

> SUUSI affirms its commitment to maintain an environment free of discrimination, harassment, and violence based on sex, race, color, ethnicity, religion, national origin, age, physical challenges, gender or affectional orientation. SUUSI expects its Board, staff and participants to conduct themselves in a professional manner, with concern and respect for their colleagues, participants and surrounding community.

As is often the case with new behavioral policies, this one was quickly tested. Over the course of the next two summers, one adult had to be asked to leave SUUSI altogether, while two others were prohibited from leading future workshops or holding a leadership role in the community. During that same time span, four teens were asked to leave the Teen Dorm for various violations of teen rules.

One other policy decision created its own minor stir. The Board determined that "No programs or activities are to be promoted or advertised at SUUSI other than those that are approved or sponsored by the SUUSI Staff or the SUUSI Board." Ever since the banning of nudity at SUUSI events, there had been an ongoing controversy about the unauthorized public promotion of clothing optional activities that were to take place offsite and/or beyond the SUUSI week. Most people in the surrounding community – and many in the SUUSI community – saw these, and other, flyers taped up around campus and presumed the activities they promoted were sanctioned by SUUSI. By 1994, the Board had had enough, and placed strict limitations on the use of SUUSI's name. Initial discussions about trademarking or copyrighting the Institute's name occurred at this time as well.

Yet the biggest issue on the Board's plate remained the question of SUUSI's long-term location. Many veteran participants nostalgically longed for what they remembered as simpler times at the more intimate campus in Radford. Meanwhile, costs at Virginia Tech continued to climb, and complaints about the sprawling Blacksburg campus continued unabated. Most alarmingly, attendance had fallen for the fourth straight year.

At its meeting on May 5, 1995, the Board chose to actively pursue a venue change. A month later, on the first weekend in June, two staff members – Director-Elect Sharon Mayes and Nature Co-Director Bill Bestpitch – made official visits on behalf of the Board to both Radford and James Madison universities. The latter had also been deemed to be a potential site for SUUSI, but there were several concerns (related primarily to the layout of the campus and its inability to offer firm commitments regarding space and amenities). In addition, JMU indicated it would not be available until at least 1997.

Radford, on the other hand, as Mayes excitedly wrote to the Board, "WANTS US BACK!" The news was received with enthusiasm, and so when the community gathered once again in Blacksburg on July 23 for SUUSI 1995, it was all but a done deal that the week would be the last at Virginia Tech.

The theme for 1995 was a popular one – "Building Community." The logo featured a large, steaming soup bowl, and a "recipe for community":

> Combine generous amounts of all these ingredients; stir gently and let simmer for a long, long time: acceptance, commitment, contributions, gentleness, honesty, humor, individuality, respect, responsibility [and] trust.

The year's T-shirt, which included the recipe on the back, was a popular seller in the Bookstore.

With rumors running rampant about an imminent return to Radford (in fact, a deal had not yet been signed), the mood around campus was noticeably more upbeat. Participants were delighted to learn that Dietrick Dining Hall was available once again. Newcomer Meg Barnhouse energized the community with workshops like "Dancing with Your Dreams" and "Inner Warrior for Women." Though the tree itself was long gone, John Burciaga offered, in his words, "a resurrection of the Wisdom Tree" workshop, sparking memories and whetting appetites for Radford.

Other workshops reflected the changing times. Workshop leader Nina Lee Braden asked participants in the catalog, "Haven't a clue what a computer on-line service is? Wondering what your friends are talking about when they mention logging onto the 'net'?" Those who were intrigued could sign up for her workshop, titled "An Introduction to On-Line Services." There was even a workshop on "Reading and Writing Erotica" and another on "Choosing a College."

More than 20 hours of performances at Cabaret were taped in order to produce a CD featuring SUUSI performers. The cover of the CD, which came out the following year, showed the steaming soup bowl of community against a bright yellow background – the 1995 SUUSI logo. Past SUUSI theme songs like "Creating Community" by Sharon Robles and "Roots and Wings" by Pete Leary were included, as was "Only After Searching" by Carole Eagleheart, "Reach Out" by Cyndi Craven, "Come to My Window" (a Melissa Etheridge cover sung by Mina Greenfield) and "Fixing a Hole (a Beatles cover performed by pianist Philip Fryberger). Sadly, the CD gained some notoriety more than a decade later when David Adkisson, who also played and sang on it, shot and killed two people and wounded eight others at the Tennessee Valley UU Church in Knoxville.

In addition to recording music at Cabaret for future CD release, SUUSI Nightlife Coordinator and musical impresario Robby Greenberg in 1994 received permission to begin selling musicians' tapes, CDs and merchandise at Cabaret and Concert Hour. Sales were robust, with part of the profits going to SUUSI, and musicians enjoyed the extra exposure.

Teen Way Off Broadway presented "Jesus Christ SUUSI Star" on Friday night at Donaldson Brown. In true Unitarian

Universalist fashion, Jesus was a woman ("Jesie"), played by Corinne Martin. She remembers the week well:

> I had never sung in front of so many people, nor do I think I ever would have if TWOB never existed. I still love everything about that show: getting ready for the week, the auditions, the rehearsals, the late nights of practice and merriment with fellow TWOB'ers in the dorm and on the fields, the performances, the aftermath of it all, being called "Jesie" at Closing Circle the next morning. It remains one of the happiest and most rewarding experiences I have ever had.

Two pieces in the newsletter that year also captured the special spirit of SUUSI 1995. The first appeared on Wednesday under the headline "The SUUSI Canal":

> "What *happened* to the volleyball court?" you might wonder. Well, some kids were playing in the sand Monday night, and discovered that if they dug deep enough, they hit water. Conflict arose when some "moved in on" others' ponds.
>
> At first the kids used force and guerilla tactics to attack and defend, until they decided, at some point, to form a partnership and connect their ponds. The suspicion and paranoia dissolved with the boundaries (and canal banks), the kids became creative and encouraging, and they shared their few tools.
>
> A lesson in community building, by the kids. I feel proud and renewed.

Then on Friday, under the headline "Dirty Day Revisited," the NUUS recounted the return of one of the original participants in Dirty Day:

[In] 1974, when SUUSI was at Fontana Village, [some] five-year-olds were left in a small cottage with a group of indoor games for a few hours during a Thursday afternoon rainstorm. They soon decided that they could have more fun outdoors, in spite of the rain.

They found that a footpath down to the cabin from the parking area made a great slide during a rainstorm. Unfortunately, it stopped at the back side of the cabin. So they opened the window at the back of the cabin, removed the screen, and spent the afternoon sliding down the walkway, entering the window, crossing a bed, then the carpet, to the front of the cabin, out the door and up the steps back to the parking area. This was the etiology of what was later to become known as Dirty Day at SUUSI.

On Wednesday, one of those five-year-olds, Rene Cline [now in her mid-20s], joined the Youth Staffers and SUUSI Youth who attended Dirty Day. Rene was a full participant in the activities of the day, and left the mine as dirty as any of the kids. Photos of the activity revealed that this year's 'Dirty Dozen' were among the dirtiest ever! The tradition continues...

Other highlights of that final (at least for a while) year at Blacksburg:

- For the first time in two decades, whitewater rafting no longer appeared among the nature listings. Nature did provide a new hike, up Kelly Knob, to a rocky cliff with a stunning view all the way back to Blacksburg, and even into West Virginia.

- The SUUSI Service Project, with guidance from Special Events coordinator Marti Toms, connected with the New River Valley chapter of Habitat for Humanity. Volunteers logged 175 hours of service on a local house that would become the home for a single mother and her four children. Habitat was very pleased with SUUSI's efforts, and invited the group back to work on another house the following summer.

- UU minister Jeremy Taylor, then serving as president of the Association for the Study of Dreams, returned to SUUSI for a theme talk and a workshop, titled "The Magic Mirror."

- In an experiment that would last only one year, those 18-year-olds who wished to live in the Teen Dorm for one final, transitional year before moving into Young Adult housing were allowed to do so – provided they adhered to all teen rules. Four persons chose that option, one of whom moved on midweek.

- Community Time was moved to the terrace and grassy area just outside Dietrick, and featured a "first-ever street festival" to kick off the week.

- Contra dancing, led by Warren Pollans and Gayle Binge, attracted 120 participants on Monday and Tuesday night.

- Members of the New River Valley UU Fellowship in Blacksburg were invited to spend all day Wednesday at SUUSI. The idea was that, for a minimal $15 fee, they could "see for themselves what SUUSI is all about," hopefully improving the Institute's reputation in the community (which had been damaged by the ongoing issues of nudity, alleged promiscuity, and drug and alcohol use).

- Partially in response to the SUUSI Vision suggestions from a few years prior, a new staff position was added – Assistant to the Director. Like other Core Staff roles, it offered free SUUSI registration and fees, but *not* a part-time, year-round salary as had been suggested by the Vision Committee. The first Assistant to the Director was Holly Francis.

- The Young Adult Dorm, which was still growing, offered its own Childcare Co-Op for the first time. YA's were divided into "tribes" to better connect participants to a smaller group within the community.

Though the younger group of adults was growing, overall SUUSI attendance was down once again. Many elderly participants had given up on the hills, steps and long walking distances of the Blacksburg campus. For the first time since 1979, attendance was below 1,000. Meanwhile, fees continued to climb. If SUUSI were to remain viable, something needed to change.

Imagine: SUUSI Returns to Radford (1996)

When the Board met on the closing Saturday in 1995, no firm commitment had been made about the following year's location. The Summer Institute – which many times had found itself without a home – was suddenly in an unprecedented position. Never before had two locations been vying for SUUSI's business, yet that is exactly what was happening; Virginia Tech hoped SUUSI would stay, while Radford wanted SUUSI to return.

During SUUSI week the Site Selection Committee had met with representatives of both universities. Peter Mullen, Tech's Conference Coordinator had, according to the Board minutes, been "very good about trying to meet our needs" that year. "They want us to stay here," the Committee reported. Meanwhile Radford, they said, "wants us, and they are excited about getting us back." RU's Conference Coordinator – a brand new position designed to bring more summer business to Radford – was Christi Leftwich, who made a strong case to the Committee for SUUSI to move.

Without making a decision between the two offers, the Board tabled the issue and headed home. Board members reconvened via telephone conference call on August 20, weighing the pros and cons of each site. Complicating a decision was the fact that the Summer Olympics were to be held in Atlanta from July 19-August 4, 1996 – and the Board feared conflicting with the Olympics would cost SUUSI many participants at a time when attendance was falling steadily. Virginia Tech had offered SUUSI its traditional fourth week in July, which would be right in the middle of the Olympics. Radford, on the other hand, had been more flexible about dates, since SUUSI would be the "only conference on campus."

Other factors were in Radford's favor as well. Their costs were estimated at $5,000 to $10,000 lower than Tech's, and their flat, compact campus was in stark contrast to the hills and distances that participants had complained about ever since the move to Blacksburg. And, there was the intangible of nostalgia; Radford was remembered almost reverently by those who had attended there.

Virginia Tech offered virtually unlimited space, a fact that was seriously considered. SUUSI's size had been one of the main contributing factors to its departure from Radford after 1989, and this time around, Radford was setting a numerical limit, up front. For 1996, they could accommodate no more than 1,000 beds, and would issue no more than 1,200 meal tickets. The Board discussed the possibility of some attendees camping offsite, but it was also pointed out that only 991 people had registered for SUUSI in 1995.

After much discussion, the Board's vote was unanimous. SUUSI would return to Radford for 1996. And though the idea of changing weeks clearly pained the SUUSI traditionalists on the Board, in the final analysis, the desire to avoid overlap with the Atlanta Olympics prevailed. SUUSI was scheduled to begin on July 14, 1996, and end on July 20. Postcards were mailed to all prior-year registrants announcing the change of venue and date.

The theme would be "Imagine." In the catalog, new Director Sharon Mayes wrote:

> John Lennon wrote the song "Imagine" 25 years ago. Since then, its call to our humanity and compelling melody have become part of our collective consciousness. His song appeals to our idealism, our most heartfelt values, and our knowledge about the potential of our minds. Just to hear the tune is to feel a desire to dream, to reflect, to feel respect and awe for our human potential. It also carries us beyond our limitations, into the realm of our expectations.
>
> Power. Liberation. Personal expression. Play. Exploration of potential. These are what we find at SUUSI, and when we imagine. This summer, let's come together and respond to John's / our yearnings – to imagine a better world for ourselves as individuals, and as a society.

When those who had answered the call to "imagine" arrived on campus on Sunday, July 14, the marquee at BT's Restaurant proclaimed "BT's Welcomes SUUSI." Long-time attendees were giddy with excitement. Some even bent down to kiss the Radford ground. Many took notice of readily apparent improvements around campus. Where the tennis courts had been, adjacent to the Governors Quad, a brand new student center (Dalton) now stood. Heth was no longer the student center, but it would remain the center of SUUSI life for the week. There was a new "clock plaza" in front of Heth, which served as a meeting point for participants. A few dorms had been air conditioned, relieving at least a couple hundred members of the SUUSI community of the need for the bulky window fans that had long been synonymous with Radford. Much ado was made about the fact that all rooms now had telephone jacks, and that participants could bring their phones from home and not only call out, but also call one another! (However, two different telephone outages occurred, in two different parts of the campus, during the week.)

Several different dorms and program configurations gave the familiar Radford surroundings an air of newness, even for SUUSI veterans. Families and the Co-Op were assigned to Moffett.

The SUUSI BOYZ sing in 1996

Teens were in Bolling – and were delighted to have a building all to themselves for the first time since the heyday of LRY at Blue Ridge. Young adults were housed in Floyd, and other adults were in Ingles, Tyler, Jefferson, Norwood and Madison. Muse would be used only for meals, while the new Dalton would host CACHE each night. Youth programming, including the nursery, was in Pocahontas (McGuffey was no longer a nursery). Though SUUSI was spread out all over the Radford campus, compared to Virginia Tech it still felt warm and intimate.

Check-in, as it always seemed to do when there is a site change, proved to be a challenge for the SUUSI Staff, but participants were so glad to be back at Radford that they hardly cared about any time spent in line. They were guided through the check-in maze by color-coded pieces of yarn, and then were welcomed by a computer staff which was implementing an all-new computer system (the software programs in use since the early 1980s had finally been replaced). Former Computer Services Coordinator Mark Gramlich and his successor, Rob Martin, had been working on the system for the better part of two years. Though there were a few glitches throughout the day, by sunset 950 participants had arrived and been processed. SUUSI '96 had begun!

Sunday night's Ingathering was steeped in all the emotion of a homecoming. As participants entered Preston Auditorium, they were handed a program printed on sky blue paper complete with fluffy white clouds. The chalice was lit – a "special exception to Radford's policy of no open flame on campus" – and Bill Bestpitch performed Boomslang Meade's "When I Die I Want to Go to Radford." A youth chorus, under the direction of Kathee Williams, sang "Pure Imagination." Rev. Jaco ten Hove sang his song "Right Here, Right Now." Kim Edmonds made a cameo appearance as Dorothy from the 1990 TWOB, reversing her opening line from "The Wizard of Blacksburg" by saying "Toto, I don't think we're in Blacksburg anymore..." And of course, John Lennon's "Imagine" was played.

Later that night, a new era opened at Serendipity as young adult DJ Elizabeth Drake brought a fresh approach, and music more likely to appeal to a younger crowd of dancers. Attendance at the venerable late-night Summer Institute dance party had begun to wane in recent years, and evaluations routinely expressed dissatisfaction with "the mix of music and the atmosphere" at Serendipity. By bringing in Drake, Nightlife Coordinator Robby Greenberg was acknowledging the beginning of a subtle generational shift in the SUUSI community.

SUUSI worship life was experiencing a similar evolution. Newly ordained minister Bill Gupton, whom Mayes had tabbed to be Denominational Coordinator, saw SUUSI as a congregation (albeit a unique one that only worships together one week a year). Linda Ferguson created new and inspiring rituals for the Young Adult Program. The Tuesday night worship service centered around children and religious education. For the first time, SUUSI made an explicit, covenantal commitment to the next generation by dedicating babies into the community. Kirk Ballin, minister of the nearby Roanoke church, officiated at SUUSI's inaugural baby dedication ceremony, dedicating 10 of the community's newest members – Niall Donegan, Zakiya Jacob, Summit Jaffe, Robyn Lipkowitz, Samantha Olmert, Patrick Sanders, Dante Taylor, Sophia Taylor, Bryce Timberlake and Sage Timberlake. Several years later, some of those babies would bridge into young adulthood, in a ceremony that also began in 1996.

During Thursday night's worship service, Rev. Barbara Wells of Woodinville, Wash., a denominational leader in the young adult movement and an early advocate of rites of passage for UU teenagers, led SUUSI's first-ever bridging ceremony. Holly Acebo, Rachel Babb, Rachel Barker, Jenny Burger, Katie Clark, Jon Craig, Kirsten deFur, Abram Diamond, Jess Evans, Nan Gould, Rachel Hoefgren-Harvey, Royal Hooper, Corinne Martin, Harmony Poire, Mary-Anne Primack and David Russell bridged into the SUUSI young adult community.

A worship service on Wednesday night called "Movement of the Spirit" centered around liturgical dance. It was coordinated by Dana Taylor, founder of the Dance Choir at UUCA in Atlanta. Then on Friday night, following Teen Way Off Broadway, the annual earth-centered service (led by Dick Merritt and Barbara Green) moved from "alternative worship" into the SUUSI mainstream. The UUA's "Sixth Source" – a respect for the interdependent web of existence – had become part of the Purposes and Principles the previous summer, so the recognition of this aspect of SUUSI's spirituality had special significance for participants at Radford in 1996.

Change seemed to be everywhere that year. Instead of a cumbersome 15-passenger van called the "Star Car," a cute golf cart named the "Star Cart" took over as the preferred mode of transportation for the physically challenged. Thanks to the work of Roanoke resident Linda Wallis, all 19 Core Staffers had the free use of pagers for the week, courtesy of Prime Time Rental, and many staff members also enjoyed free cell phone usage, from Blue Ridge Cellular. The minutes of the spring Board meeting noted that "email is great," and that more than half the members of the Core Staff were now using it. For the first time, the mugbook included email addresses (though only a few). The Summer Institute was slowly moving into the modern era.

Leaders recognized the need for effective publicity and communication, especially with a program that was still – overall – suffering from falling attendance. The Board began a lively discussion about creating an "internet presence" for SUUSI. Bright green-and-white bumper stickers (which read simply "Imagine ... SUUSI") were mailed in the spring to all pre-registrants, who were encouraged to display them on their drive to Radford. Embroidered "Imagine" baseball caps and attractive canvas tote bags bearing the 1996 logo were hot sellers in the Bookstore. That year's T-shirt proved to be one of the most popular yet; an amazing 262 shirts sold out quickly. Sales of the "Creating Community" CD, recorded the prior year at Cabaret, were also brisk, and gave participants a great opportunity to promote SUUSI upon their return home.

The Teen Program went 24/7 in 1996, with a large Teen Staff (working under Teen Director Catharine Murray and her assistant R.J. Edwards) helping provide workshops and activities around the clock – something that was far easier to accomplish in a space no longer shared with other SUUSI participants.

The rules for teens had changed dramatically from just four years earlier:

1. No weapons, violence or destructive behavior.

2. No use or possession or alcohol or drugs.

3. There will be no leaving the teen dorm between 1 a.m. and 6 a.m. unless accompanied by your parent or guardian, or for a pre-approved, scheduled activity. A pre-approved, scheduled activity is one that appears in the SUUSI brochure and/or confirmation newsletter and/or Sunday newsletter.

4. No smoking in the teen dorm.

5. Parent/guardian will be responsible for damages done to an individual teen's room.

6. Parents/guardians will establish their own expectations for their teen, and will maintain daily communication. Also, they will inform Teen Staff prior to removal of their teen from the campus.

7. The SUUSI Director shall provide information to encourage and empower teens to decline sexual intimacy of any kind, and further, that education shall be provided about sexual identity, violence, and safe sex.

8. The Board recommends that parents/guardians of SUUSI teens discuss sexuality with their teen prior to SUUSI.

Teen workshops in 1996 included body image and homophobia, as well as drumming, tie-dye, "god/goddess," massage, ultimate frisbee, euchre, beading and thrifting. Meanwhile, in the Young Adult Dorm, the popular Alternative Baby Co-Op ("ABC") was continued for the second year, and quiet and loud housing options were offered. There was a daytime YA tubing trip, and a late-night canoe outing.

Bonnie Crouse helped create one of the most memorable and emotional moments of the week on Friday afternoon. "It began pretty much as a guerilla action," she recalls. "Since the AIDS quilt couldn't come to SUUSI, we made our own." Colored chalk was provided as people passed between Jefferson and Madison, on their way to workshops or dinner. They were asked to draw their own "quilt" squares on the sidewalk, memorializing those who had lost their lives to AIDS. "It was an opportunity to touch people in a way I think many had not been touched before," says Crouse. Among the names written on the sidewalk that day was that of Floating Eagle Feather.

The President of the UUA, John Buehrens, returned to SUUSI to give a theme talk and offer an informal, one-day, drop-in workshop he called "Conversations with the President." Minister appreciation was lifted up with the introduction of "Hug a Minister" day. There were nearly two dozen UU ministers among the 950 registrants in 1996.

SUUSI celebrated the Olympics in Atlanta by holding its own "SUUSI Olympics" in the Moffett Quad throughout the week. Events like the Fun Run and the Inter-Dorm Volleyball Tournament took on new significance, and the kids' "Wacky Olympics" was transformed into a friendly Olympic competition for all ages. Then, on Friday night, many participants huddled around small television sets in dormitory lounges – between Teen Way Off Broadway performances and worship services and nightlife – to catch a few minutes of the Opening Ceremonies from Atlanta. Try as they might, SUUSI planners had been unable to avoid at least a slight overlap with the Centennial Olympics.

The giant "Double U" had been moved to the Closing Circle on Saturday – where it was announced that Radford had invited SUUSI back, and had promised that the fourth week of July would be available the following year. Though they would have to wait for the mugbooks to be mailed to their homes (it seems the new computer system was not cooperating) – and despite the fact that electricity was turned off all over campus just before noon that day, forcing many to use the stairs to get the final portion of their belongings loaded out of the dorms – it was a happy group of campers who were already imagining returning to Radford and returning to the traditional week for SUUSI in 1997.

Three More Years at Radford (1997-1999)

The unusual 53-week gap between SUUSIs was nothing if not eventful. The November Board meeting in Atlanta opened with the good news that total costs at Radford had proven to be $30,000 less than the previous year at Virginia Tech. Combined with an increase in fees for 1996 (by $30 for adults living in non-air-conditioned space, and by even more than that for children), this meant that SUUSI was back in the black. Treasurer Dawn Kenny reported to the Board that "We are about where we want to be with our reserves."

Later in the meeting, there were several important policy decisions affecting the younger members of the SUUSI community. It was agreed that beginning in 1997, proof of age (a notarized copy of one's birth certificate or, in the case of a teen who was of driving age, a copy of one's drivers' license) would be required for all minors registering for SUUSI. Next the Board took up a request from the Core Staff to change the age range for the Young Adult Program from 18-35 to 18-25. Though the Core Staff earlier in the fall had, according to the minutes, "unanimously recommended" this policy change, there was vigorous debate within the Board about the ramifications of such a move. After what the meeting minutes call a very "lively discussion" that lasted "for a considerable time," a vote was taken, and by an 8 to 3 margin, the upper age limit for the SUUSI Young Adult Program was lowered to 25. Immediately a second motion was introduced to "reconsider" and lower the age range in stages, going only as far as 18-30 for the coming year. That motion failed by the same 8 to 3 vote.

When word got out about the policy – which it did more quickly than ever before, through SUUSI's brand-new "internet home page" – a furor ensued within the YA community. Several young adults boycotted the next SUUSI and have never returned.

Adding to the drama of the tumultuous off-season was the unexpected resignation of Director Sharon Mayes. Nancy Massel

– who had only been appointed Director-Elect on Thursday of the previous SUUSI, and who was not yet even officially approved by the Board – was immediately elevated to Director. Massel went on to serve in that capacity for three straight summers (a SUUSI first), and later returned for another year as Director in 2002 (another first) – making her the only person in the history of SUUSI to serve as Director four times.

When the SUUSI community reconvened in Radford on the last week of July, 1997, the fallout from the Young Adult decision continued. Sienna Baskin, a Hampshire College student who had been an active teen leader at SUUSI earlier in the decade, was selected as Young Adult Coordinator. Those in the YA Program that year had an excellent mix of community and personal growth experiences and opportunities designed for and by their peers, but resentment lingered in the older group of former young adults, who were angered that they had not been consulted about the impending decision, charging the Board with acting without transparency. A Sunday night "transition ceremony" for 26-35 year olds was offered at the beginning of the week, "to give you a sense of closure on one part of your lives, and open the door to the next," but was neither well-received nor well-attended.

On Wednesday night, disaffected older young adults aired their grievances directly to the Board at a town hall meeting. On Friday, the following appeared in the SUUSI NUUS:

AN OPEN LETTER TO THE SUUSI COMMUNITY

As you may already be aware, a well-intentioned but dramatic change was made this year to the structure of SUUSI's young adult community. The age range of the young adult program was changed from 18-35 to 18-25. Following the SUUSI Board candidates' forum Wednesday evening, SUUSI's Board members heard the views of many people affected by the age range change at the town hall meeting.

Board members expressed the rationale and reasoning

behind the decision, while engaging in a constructive discussion with young adults who were expressing their displeasure at not being involved in the decision-making process. Due to time constraints at Porterfield Hall, a continuing dialogue followed. Among the concerned parties who were present, a consensus was reached on the following points:

- The age range of 18-35 of the young adult program was, for many participants, too broad; therefore, the SUUSI community should support the young adult program (including both housing and programming) for ages 18-25 as it currently exists.
- A strong suggestion is made to provide a common housing and community area (i.e., 24-hour lounge) for adults 21 years old and over who choose to establish a focal point for creating community. This area would be age-centered, but not age-specific, to include 21 to 30-something SUUSI participants, many of whom enjoy a late-night lifestyle. Such a housing and community area would provide the opportunity for participants to make connections with people of similar interests.
- In the spirit of creating an intergenerational community, we encourage the creation of a 24-hour space as a common meeting and information center for the entire SUUSI community.
- We encourage the SUUSI Board to communicate to members of any group or program if major changes affecting said group or program are being considered. We would further encourage the Board to request feedback from the affected group or program before rendering decisions.
- These points will be presented to the Board at the next meeting for its consideration. A continued

dialogue including the entire SUUSI community is strongly encouraged.

Signed,
Concerned members of the SUUSI
Young Adult community

Other age groups also experienced disorienting changes in routine in 1997. The Youth Program's longest standing tradition, which even predated SUUSI's presence in Virginia – Dirty Day – was morphed into "Squeaky Clean Day," much to the dismay of many children (and parents, some of whom had participated in Dirty Day themselves). Further, each morning for the youth was to begin with a brief "Daily Ingathering" at Theme Talk (similar to the "children's time" that is common at the beginning of Sunday worship in many Unitarian Universalist churches). Following the Daily Ingathering, children met their age groups in the lobby outside the Porterfield Auditorium.

Adults had to make several adjustments as well. Radford's new alcohol policy restricted the possession of alcohol to only Heth (Serendipity, Cabaret, nightlife) and individual dorm rooms (not lounges, common areas or refrigerators). Radford University also had banned all indoor smoking (including in dorm rooms), so groups of smokers gathered outside entrances to buildings, necessitating notices in the newsletter requesting a "buffer zone" between the smokers and all building doors.

Even the mugbook was different, adopting a spiral-bound format with digital images that were not yet of sufficiently high resolution to turn out well in print. But one change was almost universally appreciated: Dalton Cafeteria was now open to the SUUSI dining community. When it had met the previous year during the second week of July, SUUSI had shared the campus with another group (as well as with summer students), but in 1997 – as the only group on campus – SUUSI attendees could enjoy the many diverse offerings and excellent food at Dalton.

Relative Viewpoint performing in 1997

*The Nature Tent, open for business
rain or shine*

Muse, however, was undergoing renovation and was not open for housing. Adults roomed in a variety of dorms – some of them now air conditioned (AC rooms came with a slightly higher price tag for participants). The full Governors Quad was back in use. All over campus, special "night owl keys" were issued to participants who needed access to their dorms after 2 a.m., when all exterior doors were locked (swipe cards had not yet become a part of the campus culture).

Nearly two dozen nature trips were cancelled prior to SUUSI that year due to low enrollment, and notices in the newsletter throughout the week indicated ongoing participant confusion about everything from whether or not a trip was taking place, to what exactly constituted a "tied immersible shoe." But as the week wore on, the "Nature Tree" – located between Pocahontas Hall and Peters Gym – became an informal gathering place for the community, while also serving as the starting point for nature outings, which were billed in 1997 as "Bambi! Bugs! Beavers! Butterflies! Biodiversity!"

Of the 151 workshops, almost half were new. Topics ranged from theater games to Zydeco dancing, from improving your handwriting to publishing your book, from the I Ching to ceremonial rattles. Evaluations indicated that participants responded well to the revitalized lineup of workshops, which that year were coordinated by Mary Dahm.

On Thursday night, a "Cycle of Life" service brought together elements that had begun as parts of separate worship services in earlier years. A baby dedication, a bridging ceremony and a memorial ritual were all integrated into one service of transition. Bill Gupton told the overflow crowd in Porterfield, "Tonight, we will mourn the passing of the dead, we will honor the passages of the living and we will dedicate ourselves to those just born. For many of us, SUUSI itself is a holy place – the sacred ground of our lives. There are those among us who mark the passing of each year not on January 1st, or at Christmas, or on a birthday, but with our holy week together during July, in the mountains of Virginia, when once again our extended family gathers in reunion at SUUSI. Tonight, we are here to celebrate the generations that make this extended family what it is."

Following the service, those who chose to stick around in Porterfield were treated to a special live recording of a radio show, in the style of Garrison Keillor, informally dubbed "A SUUSI Home Companion" but officially known as "Neighborhood Voices." Barry Smith-McCauley put together the vintage-style variety show, which featured SUUSI musicians, storytellers, poets and comedians.

Teen Way Off Broadway entered its second decade the following night, with Mina Greenfield as its new Director. A glimpse inside life in the Teen Dorm appeared in the Wednesday NUUS:

The sign says "Welcome to Teenland!" ... The first greeting is the sound. Teenland citizens sit on the steps of Jefferson, drumming for people who pass by. It is a happy sound, the sound of youth celebrating life...

The rhythm of Teenland takes hold as soon as you walk though the door. There is always music – often from drums and guitars. Classical music being played on a piano drifts into the lobby from another room. A nose-whistle chorus is planned for later in the week.

A row of festive mailbags hangs on one side. The image of the bags mirrors that of the banners above the stage in Porterfield – every one of these has a unique story to tell.

A teen returns from a group outing. It has been raining. Water on the floor marks this passage, and the leader of Teenland [Teen Director Catharine Messamore] takes note. The teens call her "Czarina" – more a term of affection than a name for a leader. They are happy to see her, and they are also happy to do the jobs she sometimes gives them. The Czarina hands a mop to one of her flock, who dances down the hall with a smile on her face as she takes up the task.

"Where's your nametag?" The Czarina sees someone without identification. She is happy to see that the tag is merely covered by the teen's shirt. Making sure everyone wears a nametag is one way the Czarina expresses her concern for security and for the safety of her people. She keeps a close watch on this space – no one is allowed upstairs without an escort.

Down the hall, signs hang above doorways: "Puzzle Room," "Tattoo Place," "Beauty Parlor," "Chat Room," "Teens Under Construction." In the beauty parlor, tie-dyeing is underway... Voices echo through the halls – just two of many voices that tell many stories.

When you hear the drumming at the gates of Teenland, take a few minutes to stop in and hear some of Teenland's stories. These people are happy to be alive, and happy to be in this moment.

That sentiment was shared by many adults who were 1997 newcomers to the SUUSI community and its magic. At the end of the week, a compilation of comments by SUUSI first-timers was printed in the NUUS. Some examples were:

"I should have gone into training for all this relaxation."
"I'm glad it rained. We cancelled a nature trip in favor of a nap."
"It's like G.A. [the UUA General Assembly], but without the plenary sessions. All the fun and none of the business!"
"A wonderful atmosphere. There's peace, love and friendship you don't find at a college reunion."
"You have to be careful you don't wear yourself out here!"
"The ingatherings and worship services build a lot of community."
"I'm surprised it took me so long to get here. I'm especially grateful to my daughter, whose interest in Native American rituals sparked my enthusiasm to attend 'Making Ceremonial Rattles'."
"It's an enriching experience. The classes have made me more self-aware."
"I finally have a name for what I am... I am a noetic scientist – someone who is connected to the inner self, others and the Earth."
"I'm putting in for vacation time next year when I get back to work on Monday. And I'm bringing someone with me!"

Several others must have done the same thing, because

attendance in 1998 was up from the previous year – for the first time in a decade. Registration rose to 930 people, many of whom were encouraged by a new early-bird registration policy that allowed participants to assure themselves of priority housing assignments and, most importantly, simply a place at SUUSI '98. (Radford was still limiting the number of registrants it would accept, though SUUSI had not come close to reaching that limit since its return.) Those who paid a $25 non-refundable registration deposit ($50 for a family) prior to the mailing of the catalog and the opening of registration were guaranteed a spot and given their choice of dorms. The effect was to create a sense of demand, particularly for air conditioned rooms (which that year cost each adult registrant an extra $70). Overall, total adult fees had risen to $360 per person (without air conditioning).

In keeping with the year's theme of "Circles," Sunday's banner parade marched not to Preston, where participants would have sat in rows in an auditorium, but rather to the Moffett Quad, where they could hold Ingathering in a circle on the lawn. In a poignant moment, one of the service leaders read a letter to the SUUSI community from a young man who had grown up at SUUSI, Clayt Lauter – who was now a Marine stationed in the Middle East.

Another writer, a first-timer known only as "Jonathan," vividly described the impact of that first day at SUUSI 1998:

> An old friend, met here unexpected, gifts me with a hug. "We all hug at SUUSI," he explains, unnecessarily. "Of course we do," I think, and note with surprise that I have already become *we*.
>
> Later, at Ingathering, I will become even more we. We all will. Laughter, stories, songs, announcements, welcome. SUUSI has begun! After the opening, people stand around talking, hugging, touching, getting reacquainted. Kids throw frisbees; two circle the field on in-line skates.
>
> My friend sees me and smiles again. I walk over and say

hello. We sit and talk, a long time, building friendship. Just like that, the process has begun. The fabled SUUSI circles are opening. What will I find inside? Who will I be when I emerge?

Highlights of the week included, once again, a moving Thursday night Transitions Service led by Meg Barnhouse, titled "Gateways on the Circle." Evening worship the preceding night featured "A Celebration of Jazz." There was an air of simple, spiritual beauty to all the services and theme talks, thanks in part to the tone set by Phyllis McCafferty. McCafferty, the new Denominational Coordinator, provided altar cloths to enhance the SUUSI chalice, and a decorative "pulpit quilt" she had bought at the 1990 SUUSI Artists' Co-Op. The quilt, made by Regina Liske, was titled "Flaming Chalice XII," and included the words "Time is the flame in which we live."

There was a poets' coffeehouse in 1998, organized by Jennifer Bosveld. David Roth performed at Concert Hour and also led two workshops, "Making Joyful Noise" and "Songwriting." Rev. Chester McCall facilitated an untitled, drop-in workshop at the end of the week that asked participants to "examine the dynamics of oppression, discuss the UUA's anti-racism initiative, and explore ways of ending oppression in our lives."

On a less serious note, the following workshop was announced in the Tuesday NUUS:

How to Avoid Sleep Deprivation at SUUSI   Limit 360
SUUSItarians are renowned for planning dozens of activities without down time. Tired as you are, do you find yourself tossing and turning, unable to sleep? You need this somnambulant technique for quickly transporting yourself to dreamland, awakening at will, totally refreshed and ready to go. Required: Bed, PJ's, teddy bear, alarm

clock. No stimulants 40 hours prior. 10% lecture, 90% snooze. [Optional followup: Dream Work.]

Thurs. 2 pm – Fri. 1 p.m.   Drop-Off

In response to feedback asking for more "dry Cabaret" so that teens, in particular, could share their musical talents and enjoy those of the adults, Nightlife Coordinator Robby Greenberg arranged not one, but two completely alcohol-free, all-ages nights at Cabaret, as well as one "hybrid" night in which the first half of the evening was dry. Responding to an ongoing "formal vs. informal dance" debate from the previous year, she also calculated

The 1998 Bridging Ceremony

– and reported in the Confirmation NUUS – that there were "about 20 hours of Serendipity at SUUSI. This year we have 38 hours of dance workshops... Jazz in the morning, belly dance and East Coast swing in the afternoon, and folk dance, contra and more belly dance in the late afternoon/early evening." Thus, she concluded, Serendipity's style would remain primarily informal, open dance.

Nature offered two special "post theme talk trips" in 1998 – a strenuous hike for adults along the ridge top of John's Creek

Mountain, and a Ravens' Cliff family hike and picnic that included exploring Cripple Creek with an afternoon swim in a nearby pond. For water enthusiasts, there was a new trip called "Yakitty Yak," featuring instruction and then experience with one-person "sit on top" kayaks. Teens were able to enjoy a similar "Teen Yak" trip, while the 9-10 year olds got to go caving.

Youth Director Kathleen Murphy arranged for other special programs for the children, including an age-appropriate opportunity to "focus on peaceful conflict resolution and valuing individual differences." The practice of a Daily Ingathering at Porterfield continued to build intergenerational connections. On Friday afternoon, the kids gave a special performance for the parents as they were being picked up from programming for the final time.

Folks in the family dorm faced a health scare when a 3-year-old girl contracted meningitis and was hospitalized. The experience brought out the best in SUUSI, as later recalled by her family:

> To add to this devastating [diagnosis], we were 400 miles from home, on vacation at SUUSI! Our panic and concern at that time is indescribable. The meningitis was eventually diagnosed as viral and not serious, but the 36 hours we spent waiting for that news was a time we never want to relive.
>
> One of the blessings from that experience is that we learned again, and in a different way, what a caring community SUUSI is, and how many dear friends we have there. During our crisis, the forces of the SUUSI community were at our disposal – facilities, medical people at SUUSI on vacation, lots of hugs, tissues for tears, friends to lend support with the other children in the family, contacts in the Radford and Roanoke area, Health Department resources to explain the illness to others at SUUSI, offers of homes to stay in if we couldn't go home right away. I could go on and on.

For seven years, I've considered SUUSI the best week of the year. Now, SUUSI has a special new place in the hearts of our family.

(Signed),
Linda and Jessica Sanders, and
Sheri, Joe, PJ, Jason, Steven and Katie Gebbia

That special SUUSI spirit also came together on Tuesday afternoon, in an informal memorial service for long-time SUUSI leader Wink Lucas. Under a tree not far from the site of the old Wisdom Tree – and fittingly, in front of Lucas Hall – friends, family and the SUUSI BOYZ gathered to remember Lucas, who had died suddenly in his sleep at the age of 55, less than a month earlier. Among his many SUUSI roles, he had been Nature Director, Risk Manager, Director's spouse and a proud member of the BOYZ. For many of those at the memorial, he also had been the person who had recruited them to come to SUUSI in the first place.

Other items of note from 1998:

- The Used Book Sale began, offering participants the chance to get rid of some old books, purchase new reads for the summer, and raise money for the SUUSI Scholarship Fund. The sale replaced the "Jail and Bail" fundraiser, in which bidders at Serendipity had "jailed," then "bailed out" various SUUSI celebrities.

- "Rant and Rave," a comment box seeking feedback from participants during the week, was introduced. The idea was to gather, and be able to respond to, people's comments before the following year, "so feelings won't fester."

- Sienna Baskin had taken a job at the Unitarian Universalist Association in Boston, and Jay Camp took over the reins as Young Adult Coordinator.

- Teen Way Off Broadway's production of "The UU Files" (a takeoff on The "X-Files" television show, suggested by Jim Blowers) featured a very large tinfoil spaceship that lifted off and landed amid dry ice stage-effect smoke (courtesy of Radford theatre technician Carl Lefko).

- A change to the SUUSI Bylaws made it possible, for the first time, for persons living outside the three-district region to serve on the Board.

- A steady stream of participants made use of a new amenity – a pair of publicly available computers in Heth – to check email and remain connected to news and events from the "outside world."

Unbeknownst to most SUUSI participants, as the end of the millennium drew closer, there was trouble on the horizon. For some time the Core Staff had been frustrated with what they perceived as less than supportive service from Radford, while the Board was experiencing its own issues with Radford's Residential Life Department – which each year would present a final bill with thousands of dollars in unexpected fees and charges. In fairness, the long-standing SUUSI tradition of "personalizing" individual dorm rooms by moving furniture around in (and among) rooms created unnecessary work for RU housing personnel. Many participants appeared unwilling to put items back as they had found them before leaving.

When SUUSI had been charged $2,731.72 in damages to rooms in 1997, the Board had disputed the charges, and Radford had agreed to drop them. But a year later, when that same charge reappeared on the 1998 bill as overdue, SUUSI's relationship with Radford suddenly soured. Following a concerted campaign by

Board and Staff to educate participants about the cost to SUUSI –
and ultimately, to each participant – of leaving rooms in anything
less than pristine condition upon checkout, damage charges to
SUUSI dropped to $465 in 1998. However, the outstanding
$2,731.72 from the previous year remained a bone of contention
– as was a new charge for $11,213 for one "extra night" of room
rentals.

Director Nancy Massel reported the situation to the Board
at its April 1999 meeting in Jacksonville. The minutes of that
meeting summarize the issues:

> Radford is taking a hard line on damages. We are being
> held responsible for damages in rooms we did not have
> keys to. Residential Life is charging us for 7 nights. They
> claim that everyone arrived on Saturday, not Sunday. In
> '97 we disputed some damages. At the time, they dropped
> the charges. Radford is again requesting payment.
> Radford mentioned that some of these amounts may/will
> be turned over to collection and/or they will contact the
> State Attorney General.

Massel was asked to take the concern higher up the Radford
hierarchy, and also to contact SUUSI's legal counsel. Dawn
Kenny was instructed to immediately contact Virginia Tech about
its availability as a site, and steps were taken to resurrect a Site
Search Committee.

As this cloud hung over their heads that spring, the Core Staff
made preparations for SUUSI 1999. For the first time, the catalog
was posted on the internet (on a link off the Council of Unitarian
Universalist Camps and Conferences' website; SUUSI Computer
Services was still in the process of buying the rights to SUUSI's
own, current domain name). By now there was also a SUUSI
listserv, where information could be quickly disseminated.

A total of 839 participants (the lowest figure since 1977)
arrived at Radford the last week of July in 1999 to find only

Participants in the 1999 Service Project

one air conditioned dormitory available in what proved to be a particularly hot year. One registrant – Clayt Lauter – came all the way from Cairo, Egypt, where he was serving in the military. Those who made the pilgrimage from south of Radford, using I-77, overcame their own set of obstacles in order to get there; construction on the interstate highway left hundreds of SUUSI-ites grumpy – and very late for check-in.

The popular Dalton Dining Hall was no longer available, and meals were once again back in the basement at Muse. The Childcare Co-Op was in transition, having been dropped as an official SUUSI-sponsored program. Parents were left to their own devices, and quickly pieced together a "baby-sitting network" through signup sheets posted on the walls of the family dorm. A new curfew for all children younger than teens was set at midnight.

A new tradition was started on Sunday evening as the Teen Program led the banner parade, which for the second straight year marched to an outdoor Ingathering, this time on the Muse Quad.

There was a lot happening for young people at SUUSI 1999. New Youth Director Kathee Williams sought to bring back some old favorites, while also creating a meaningful year of transition for the 13-year-olds. With their own staff of five, that group spent the week engaged in a full-blown Coming of Age program much like those offered in UU congregations. They participated in the SUUSI Service Project, learned about Unitarian Universalist and SUUSI traditions, explored their own and their family's belief systems, had a scavenger hunt and a "mystery trip," and even did some activities with the teens they would be joining the following year. The program culminated on Friday with a rite of passage into the Teen Program, in which each young person was given a "spirit name" by the staff that had worked with them all week, while parents ceremonially placed masks that the young people had made and decorated on their children's faces. The new teens then were led away to a welcoming ceremony by emissaries from the Teen Dorm, attended their first CACHE (held this particular year in the recently air conditioned Peters Gym). They finished the night with a farewell sleepover at the Youth Dorm.

Young adults had some similar programming. The week kicked off with a pajama party and sleepover in the YA Dorm. Throughout the week, conversation groups tackled subjects like homophobia, careers, and "homogeneity" (discussion revolved around the lack of diversity in the YA program, at SUUSI in general, and their home lives). They threw their own "Millennium Dance Party" concurrently with Serendipity's "End of the Millennium Costume Party," which itself turned out to be one of the wackiest Serendipity Costume Nights ever.

Serendipity also began experimenting in 1999 with guest DJs, offering different volunteers the chance to select and spin tunes in half-hour and hour-long spots. The innovation proved to be wildly successful, and helped draw new people into Serendipity who had never attended before.

Teen Way Off Broadway got in on the millennial fun with "Return of the UUs," based on *The Return of the Jedi* and the *Star*

Wars franchise (that summer, the first prequel to the *Star Wars* trilogy was in movie theaters). Written and directed by Mina Greenfield and Kimmer Cecci, the show featured characters like "The Dorm Troopers" and "Darth Y'all" (Kristen Hall, a diminutive teen who had been acting on stage since age 6). Hall recalls:

> As an impish but eager-for-acceptance kid who had only been 14 for two weeks, I didn't really know much about SUUSI or what to expect from it. I signed up for TWOB because I ... thought that a theatre-related class was the only thing I could be certain that I would enjoy. I got the script in the mail and I couldn't believe my luck. I loved *Star Wars*, I already loved most of the songs, and I loved the silly script.
>
> I was then cast in the only role I had specifically said I was NOT auditioning for, with a song I didn't even really know [The Beatles' "Revolution"]. I had sung it in a Southern drawl [during auditions] just to be a goofball.
>
> As it turns out, a pint-sized Dark Lord of the Sith is one of my favorite roles I've ever played... [And] "Return of the UUs" is still the most fun I've ever had in a show, before or since.

That year's Teen Way Off Broadway also marked the first appearance of the now-legendary TWOB Cow (which had been created as a joke by cast member Steven Groom). The Cow's cameo consisted of flying through space (carried by a crew member) against a black curtain backdrop, chasing the "Millennium Chicken." The Cow – with occasional touch-up paint jobs and later sturdy, quarter-inch thick backing and handles – has appeared in every Teen Way Off Broadway since, and is cherished by the teenage cast and crew, who each year vote to designate one of their own as "keeper of the Cow" for the 51 weeks until the next SUUSI.

"Return of the UUs" was dedicated to the memory of Roberta Price – the mother of TWOB cast member Caty Price and former TWOB'er Robin Price – who had passed away at the age of 51 just prior to SUUSI. An empty seat near the front of the auditorium, marked by a single red rose, was left open in Roberta's honor – as has been done every year since.

SUUSI nightlife was transformed in 1999 with the creation of the Common Ground Cafe, which quickly became, as the newsletter put it, "the place to go to get away from it all, get snack food and desserts, and have some peaceful encounters during [otherwise] hectic nightlife." Held that first year in the Peery Basement, Common Ground was the brainchild of coffee impresario Arpie Maros, the new Nightlife Coordinator.

A newcomer from Miami, professional musician Amy Carol Webb, was recruited to perform at SUUSI that year. She was an instant hit, developing a following both young and old while appearing at Family Concert Hour, onstage at Porterfield in services, and at nightlife. Webb also led an "Empowering Your Voice" workshop that has become an annual SUUSI favorite.

There was even water polo at SUUSI 1999. More than two dozen people participated in a two-day water polo workshop and mini-tournament in the pool at Peters Gym, led and coached by Mark Rauterkus of Pittsburgh, who had worked with the U.S. Olympic water polo team.

By the end of the week, SUUSI's status at Radford was uncertain, but there was every indication another move was imminent. The 1999 participant evaluation forms included an open-ended question: "What are your three most important criteria for the location of SUUSI?" Among the things most commonly mentioned, across all ages, was air conditioning. The same feedback had already come to the Board, again and again during the week.

The Board held a meeting on Friday evening, with Director Nancy Massel and Director-Elect Dee Medley reporting on a visit they had made to Virginia Tech earlier in the week. There was good news, as recorded in the minutes of that meeting:

- The VT administration has reorganized, and set up Conferences as a separate area [in the university's flow chart].
- VT is very interested in having us come back.
- Two new A/C dorms are available, with over 600 A/C [beds].
- Meals are much improved.
- Handicap accessibility is much better.
- Prices include linens and pillows [linens had long been a sore spot at Radford, where they had originally been provided only if the participant was willing to pay an extra $20 fee; in the previous two years linens had not been available at all].
- Preliminary cost comparisons look favorable.

But the Board remained hesitant, and was not ready to make a final decision on the location for 2000 – instead setting for itself a deadline of Sept.15 to make a choice between returning to Radford for another year, or going back to Virginia Tech. A telephone conference call in early September sealed the deal, however; Virginia Tech was the unanimous choice of the Board for SUUSI 2000. The Core Staff held its fall meeting in Blacksburg, and reported that they were very pleased with all the changes that had been made there over the past four years.

As the clock ticked down to Y2K, SUUSI said goodbye once again to its sentimental home in Radford, and prepared to make a fresh start in Blacksburg.

A New Beginning (Virginia Tech 2000)

SUUSI was welcomed to Blacksburg a day early when the local UU Fellowship of the New River Valley hosted 68 SUUSI attendees for dinner on Saturday night, July 22, 2000. Of those, 35

Sunrise on a new era at Virginia Tech

people also chose to stay overnight with church members as part of a home hospitality program organized by Rosemary Bazuzi. The congregation also ran a shuttle service – six shuttles in all ran that weekend – for SUUSI participants flying into Roanoke airport.

When at last everyone had gathered at Virginia Tech the following day, they numbered nearly 150 more people than had attended the previous year at Radford. Registration, in the lobby of Slusher Hall, was congested and confusing, but the reward for successfully checking in made most participants forget any arrival difficulties: about two-thirds of the SUUSI community was housed in brand new, air conditioned dorm rooms arranged in suites of usually three rooms, with a shared living room / lounge and (compared to Radford) spacious bathroom.

After a banner parade – again, led by the SUUSI Teens – across the Drill Field and up the hill to Burruss, Ingathering was a celebration of Virginia Tech and of the 50th anniversary of the Summer Institute. A brief history of the five decades of SUUSI, written by Alexis Jones, was printed in the Ingathering program, and everything about the evening, from Paul Langrock's traditional "How Long Have You Been Coming?" to the music of SUUSI newcomer David Nachmanoff reflected an awareness of the historic nature of the occasion.

Many things about the return to Tech felt fresh and new: dorms such as New Residence Hall ("New Res"); vastly improved accessibility with curb cuts and ramps; permission to have burning candles, flaming chalices, and alcohol in residence hall rooms, lounges and common spaces (which would only last for that one year); Food Services cheerfully providing box lunches for nature trips, youth meetings and other activities; children being allowed to sleep on the floors of their parents' rooms – free!; the availability of a computer room with printers; ethernet connections and telephones in all the newer, air conditioned dorm rooms. In short, SUUSI arrived at Virginia Tech in the year 2000 with the sense of a community moving joyously together into a bright new future.

The theme was "Neighbors: Ancient Civilizations," providing fertile ground for speakers and programmers alike. Perhaps the most diverse array of theme speakers and worship leaders in SUUSI history, including three persons of color (Kristen Harper, Abhi Janamanchi and Chester McCall), challenged participants to consider what is meant by "neighbor."

SUUSI neighbors chipped in to help one another throughout the week. Volunteer leadership revitalized the Childcare Co-Op. An enthusiastic Youth Staff helped children explore a different ancient civilization each day and relate them to life in the year Y2K. Youth now went straight to morning programming instead of beginning the day at theme talk. Later in the week, the kids enjoyed what was billed as the "return of Dirty Day" – this time a sandy romp in the volleyball pit in front of Lee Hall.

Meanwhile, the teens – who had adopted as their symbol the Native American depiction of the god Kokopelli that had been so ubiquitous at SUUSI 1993 – took many long walks to the 7-Eleven, and rejoiced that real candles were permitted at late night worship. Games of teen vs. young adult capture the flag enlivened Lee Quad, and Friday night's hilarious single performance of "The SUUSI Bunch" (a takeoff on the '70s TV series "The Brady Bunch") in cavernous Burruss Auditorium left all of SUUSI laughing.

The year also marked the release of a new Amy Carol Webb CD – released at SUUSI – titled "These Are My Own."

Once again, many of SUUSI's main community activities were scattered throughout the campus. Serendipity (and dinner each night) was held in Owens, at the Hokie Grill. Breakfast and lunch were at Dietrick. Cabaret, theme talks and indoor worship services were also in Owens, in the Ballroom. Common Ground was located in the Slusher Lounge, and CACHE was at Deet's Place, on the first floor of Dietrick.

An effort to provide more new workshops, many of them intentionally just one- or two-day programs, gave participants more choices and greater scheduling flexibility. They ranged from a workshop on the culture and etymology of words ("Alligators to Vermicelli") to "A Thousand Years of Church Architecture." With the return to Blacksburg, the Nature Program revived some old hikes, including Audie Murphy's Hike and Bear Cliffs. There was also a new outing called "Deep Forest Novice Meditation."

The Mugbook Staff could have used some Zen techniques in 2000 to help it endure what has gone down as the most challenging mugbook year ever. By now digital photography and electronic communication had turned the production of the mugbook into a long-distance affair. The previous year, SUUSI had enjoyed its first truly high-quality mugbook. Photographed in Radford (by mugbook originator and returning staffer Vonnie Hicks), the 1999 edition had been digitally finalized and laid out in the mountains of North Carolina by Pepi Acebo, then sent through cyberspace to Colonial Printing in Richmond and ultimately shipped via courier to SUUSI – all in time to be distributed as usual on Thursday night.

In 2000, however, when the Mugbook Staff (which now included Rick and Kevin Hallmark) was ready to send all the electronic files to Acebo, it was discovered that SUUSI's new FTP site had insufficient capacity for the job. The staff tried SWIM's FTP site, but it was also not up to the task. Eventually a connection was made with a Kinko's in Asheville (ironically, Hicks was unaware that the Kinko's in downtown Blacksburg had the necessary technology and could have done the job quite inexpensively).

Then on Thursday, when he picked up the mugbooks at the Asheville Kinko's, Acebo noticed printing errors. Kinko's had to redo the work overnight. A courier service then took the shipment to the Asheville airport (rather than simply driving it to Blacksburg). Cancelled flights and missed connections in Atlanta meant that the mugbooks did not arrive at the Roanoke airport until late Saturday, hours after SUUSI participants had left for home.

The next weekend in Raleigh, a team of volunteers led by Chuck Davis and Kathy Kochevar helped Hicks mail the mugbooks to all SUUSI 2000 registrants.

Unfortunately, a few incidents of "townies" harassing young SUUSI women put another damper on the week's experience for some. Every SUUSI Staff member, Board member and volunteer had been required to take sexual harassment awareness training at the beginning of the week, and so the leadership was eager and able to address the issue. The Board entered into dialogue with campus police, and eventually more security patrols were put in place.

When the Board met at the end of the week in 2000, several guests made a presentation proposing the creation of a dedicated housing space and lounge – and targeted programming – for those in the 26-35 year-old range for the following year. The Board thanked the participants for their suggestions and took the request under advisement.

Later in the same meeting, Director Dee Medley reported that "the Tech staff has been wonderful – very welcoming and incredibly helpful and cooperative." She singled out Virginia Tech Conference Services employees Tom Deutsch and Julie Kamienski as a delight to work with, both during the transition period leading up to SUUSI and throughout the week. Medley was sad to announce that Deutsch had received a job promotion and would not be back the next year – but things had gone so well in Blacksburg in 2000 that there was no doubt SUUSI itself would be back the following July.

As Board member Priscilla Phillips remembers, "The moving back and forth was hard on us. Some folks liked Tech better, some preferred the nostalgia of Radford – but all of us were tired of the bouncing back and forth. Many people had come to the Board begging us just to *stay somewhere*."

That SUUSI would do – at least for the next seven years.

Into the 21st Century (2001-2006)

From the moment New Last Rights sang John Denver's "Back Home Again" at the 2001 Ingathering, SUUSI participants indeed seemed delighted to be back at Virginia Tech for a second straight year. The number of air conditioned rooms had increased once again. The request for programming geared toward the "older young adults" who had been disaffected by the YA age range controversy had been honored, and a new group called the Medians ("age-centered but not age-exclusive") was created. Its first coordinator was Pinkie Bergmann.

There was a new and improved computer system, thanks largely to the work of Devin Gordon. Sunday check-in introduced the "Fast Trak" option for those who needed no changes to their pre-registration – significantly speeding up the arrival process for everyone. Check-in was held in Owens Food Court, a vast improvement from the previous year's chaos at Slusher.

SUUSI even had a new mission statement. As a result of the

SUUSI Vision process, which included a survey conducted by Board member Mike Plummer, in March 2001 the Board adopted the following statement of SUUSI's purpose:

> The mission of SUUSI is to provide a one-week experience evoking the best within us, in concert with Unitarian Universalist principles. SUUSI offers the opportunity to share an intergenerational environment of love, personal freedom, ethics and joy in an intentional, non-judgmental community.

The statement began to appear in SUUSI promotional material, on the masthead of the SUUSI NUUS, and in the catalog. This 21st century mission, of course, reflected a significant change in emphasis from that of the Summer Institute of a half century earlier, which focused on skills and training for congregational leaders and on growing and strengthening the Unitarian movement in the South.

Another way the modern Summer Institute differed from its early predecessors was the sheer abundance of live music, performed by musicians with a wide diversity of experience and professionalism. From the Cantatori to the BOYZ, from Cabaret to Concert Hour, from Teen Way Off Broadway to Common Ground, by 2001 SUUSI was awash in virtually round-the-clock music. Mindy Simmons and the children collaborated in creating a musical version of the "Rainbow Principles." The duo of Kim and Reggie Harris won hearts with their singing at Ingathering, and later in the week wowed the crowd at Concert Hour. Multi-instrumentalist Bonnie Whitehurst (harp and hammered dulcimer, to name two) kicked off the week's Concert Hours on Monday, and Carla Ulbrich – who, ironically, had studied music at Brevard College – offered her distinctive brand of musical humor to an appreciative audience on Tuesday. One of the highlights of Friday's Teen Way Off Broadway ("Scooby DUU," directed by Kimmer Cecci) was a duet by Bing Putney and Becca Hamil as Sonny and Cher, singing "I Got You Babe."

SUUSI's evolution was also evident in participants' modes and methods of communication. Many remember 2001 as the year that cell phones permanently altered the SUUSI experience. Upon returning to Blacksburg the previous year, those who were using cell phones – still a minority within the community – found the Virginia Tech campus, with its preponderance of "Hokie Stone" (the thick, gray, dolomite limestone that composes the majority of

Amy Carol Webb

buildings on campus) rendered cell phones virtually useless. But improved technology coupled with more widespread cell phone usage by participants made 2001 a transformative year.

"All of a sudden it seemed everyone had a cell phone," recalls one SUUSI regular. "The way we interacted, the way we communicated – everything was affected." Plans could be made and changed. Meeting places could be arranged. Information could be instantly exchanged, and decisions more quickly reached. In the blink of an eye, the SUUSI experience had been radically changed, and in no time it was hard to imagine how the Institute had ever run without the assistance of cell phones.

As technology became more and more a part of SUUSI, participants sought balance in the experiences of the natural world. One of the most significant – and cherished – aspects of the modern Summer Institute had long been its wide range of outdoor activities and adventures. In 2001, the Nature Staff provided opportunities to do "Yoga on the Trail," "Drum Down

A leisurely afternoon at the Duck Pond for the SUUSI Youth

the Sun" or learn the "Ecology of SUUSI." Nature Co-Director Jen Lucas taught folks how to backpack. Teens went caving – at night. There was even an unplanned encounter with a black bear on one hike.

Also in 2001, the Nature Program added a series of workshops in which participants who wanted, for whatever reason, to avoid "the sweat and effort" (as the catalog put it) of more traditional nature trips could vicariously "explore the history and ecology of SUUSI rivers, caves, birds and ancient rock formations" – all in the comfort of a Virginia Tech dormitory lounge. Trip leaders shared information, images and personal knowledge of "some of SUUSI's favorite trips."

In the SUUSI NUUS, Nina West recounted a more first-hand experience from an introductory rappelling trip:

THOUGHTS ON DANGLING IN THE SAFETY OF MY BED

Awake at five in the morning and lying in bed, I am safe and relaxed – thinking about rappelling. Attempting to drop my hips lower than my feet, stepping backwards off the solidness of the rock defied every bit of instinct for self-preservation. Dangling from a rope 45 feet or so above the ground, I was a spider on a strand of web. Not an elegant or skillful spider, but arachnid nonetheless.

My world for those brief minutes became an intricate interplay of dependence – on rope, properties of friction, two pieces of aluminum, a tree, a nylon web into which I was strapped, and reassuring voices from a void below. In rock, earth, woods and insects – in sight, sound, touch, taste and smell. My few minutes of rappelling was yet another way of experiencing how deeply connected to, and dependent on, others I am.

The ministers who spoke in 2001 were superb. Gary Kowalski, of Burlington, Vt., gave a touching theme talk Monday morning titled "The Souls of Animals." That night, South Carolina ministers Meg Barnhouse and Jennifer Slade reminded worshippers that we are "Connected to the Earth and One Another." The next day, Mel Hoover roused the flock with stirring commentary on the way all human beings, regardless of "race," are quite literally related. Mary Katherine Morn continued the theme that evening, saying, "If we share 99.9 percent of the same genes, how different are we from each other? Why, then, is there separation and oppression?"

The SUUSI community was reminded of its connection with the residents of the New River Valley when it was learned that the Children's Shelter Home of Blacksburg – where many participants had volunteered as part of the SUUSI Service Project a decade earlier – had recently closed. Among other things it had done for the Home, SUUSI had built a large, wooden outdoor play set and had donated children's quilts (created from pieces made by SUUSI youth). In the spirit of service and interconnection, 2001 SUUSI participants arranged for both the quilts and the play set to be salvaged and given to a new Blacksburg homeless shelter called The Haven. Local resident Bob Underhill made the move of the play set possible by disassembling and reassembling it himself!

The 2001 Youth Program added afternoon workshop choices for youth aged 7-13. Selections ranged from card and board games to sports, tie-dyeing, yoga, drumming and songwriting. Kids (and parents) were delighted that options were available, and that youth empowerment and decision-making were being encouraged.

For some each year, the intensity of the SUUSI community can sometimes be too much to bear. A workshop billed as the Introverts' Alliance was offered in 2001, "born [the previous year] in a bathroom at SUUSI [when] two introverts came together to identify the stress of living in an extroverts' environment, [namely] SUUSI." Introspection was also available, any time of day or night, in the form of an outdoor labyrinth, made of tiny illuminated lights, in the grass outside Slusher Tower. Two formal workshops – "Walking a Sacred Path" and "Journey through the Labyrinth of Emotion" – added depth and meaning to the experience.

On the other end of the spectrum, another dance style was added to SUUSI's already remarkably diverse mixture of dancing opportunities. Irish ceili dancing, described as "like contra dancing in high gear," was new on the list of workshops. New ideas were afoot in Serendipity as well, which offered a pajama party and a trivia night. But it was also the end of an era at Serendipity in 2001, as "La Bamba," with its traditional midnight conga line, took place for the last time. Much to the dismay of many long-time Serendipity dancers, a younger crowd was making its musical demands heard, and "La Bamba" had begun sharing the midnight song spot, on alternating nights, with the B-52's' "Rock Lobster." One participant ruefully offered the "Serendipity Weather Forecast" in 2001, saying there was a "50 percent chance of La Bamba."

Though the SUUSI community now seemed well-settled back in Blacksburg, the year was not without its problems. A couple of streaking incidents resulted in this notice in the NUUS: "SUUSI is a place to be yourself and to drop some of the restrictions of everyday life – but ... not your clothes! Public nudity (even streaking) is forbidden at SUUSI." Another controversy revolved around the 7-Eleven, which in both Blacksburg and Radford had long been tantamount to holy ground for SUUSI Teens, and the destination of many a late-night pilgrimage. But in 2001, after a 7-Eleven clerk directed several rude and disrespectful comments toward some teenage SUUSI customers, the teens actually organized a boycott of the establishment for the remainder of the week and wrote a letter of protest to the company's CEO.

There were other issues as well. One adult participant had to be asked to leave SUUSI after engaging in ongoing sexual harassment. Saturday's Closing Circle had to be cancelled because of torrential rains. And an ongoing dispute about medical bills created a huge headache for the Board. During the week, a participant had broken his ankle when he slipped on some ice cream. Though the participant was able to return to SUUSI following treatment at a local emergency room, his medical bills mounted over the next few months. SUUSI and Virginia Tech – and eventually even the Commonwealth of Virginia – exchanged letters about potential liability (the participant was uninsured). To resolve the issue, SUUSI ended up filing its first insurance claim as an incorporated institution. The experience highlighted the need for a Risk Manager, and also led the Board to make arrangements for having legal counsel on permanent retainer.

The unexpected resignation of Director-Elect Catharine Messamore that same fall left the Board looking for a new Director. They turned to someone they knew well – Nancy Massel, who graciously agreed to fill in on short notice, just as she had in 1997. Given that this was her fourth time as Director in the past six years, Massel was already up to speed, but even she had to adjust to a few new wrinkles that had been put in place before the faithful gathered once again in Blacksburg in July 2002. SUUSI's very own website, hosted in-house by Youth Co-Director Michael Ivey, was now up and running, as was the "suusi-friends" email list. In fact, participants could apply for SUUSIships online, though full online registration was still several years in the future.

For the first SUUSI after 9/11, Massel chose the theme of "Blessings." The logo showed the word "blessings" in many different languages and religious traditions. Ingathering that year, which many evaluations deemed "the best ever," was led by Meg Barnhouse, and concluded with the revival, after a two-year absence, of the giant Opening Circle on the Drill Field. Near the end of the ritual, several jubilant teens broke free from the circle and went to the middle, surrounding the drummers and bringing them into the circle – which quickly morphed into a spontaneous celebratory dance. SUUSI 2002 was off to a great start.

The next morning, a special section in Dietrick Cafeteria was adorned with balloons and set aside to welcome first-timers. Board members and other SUUSI leaders ate with them and helped orient the newcomers to the week ahead. That morning's theme talk, titled "To Give and to Receive," was delivered by UUA President William Sinkford.

Nancy Massel had asked her staff to focus on strengthening the sense of community at SUUSI; an unofficial mission was adopted which reminded volunteers, and the community, "We strive to create an environment in which who we are can be freely and fully expressed in a community we trust to hold safe space." For the first time, Cabaret was fully alcohol-free, and opened to all ages all of the time. The Lee Quad was transformed each afternoon into a vibrant community space where hair-dyeing and henna tattoos, toenail painting and face painting, bubbles and drums, Twister and checkers gave everyone a way to get engaged.

But the return of the beloved SUUSI Picnic was easily the most popular gathering of the week. Virginia Tech agreed to serve dinner outdoors on Friday evening, and participants thronged to the Eggleston Quad for hot dogs and burgers (meat and veggie) and all the fixin's. There was sand volleyball and tug-of-war. People relaxed in lawn chairs and reveled in the sound of laughing children. All that was missing was Claytor Lake.

The Nature Program had many new offerings in 2002. There was a new hike to Tinker Cliffs and a new cave – Pig Hole. There was canoe fishing ("catch and release; bring your own rod and reel") and a beer-tasting hike called "Hooch in the Holler" ("total consumption 16 oz."). "Mud Wallow" and "Teens' Where the Hell Are We Going" were also on the docket.

Of course, not everything went smoothly during the week. On Tuesday night, a couple of canoes capsized in the dark, and for an anxious period of time, the whereabouts of some participants was unknown. The report of the incident indicates that the Nature Staff handled the situation superbly – and with the help of the Giles County Search and Rescue Squad, eventually everyone was located and returned safely to campus. To show the community's appreciation for their help, SUUSI made a donation to the Rescue Squad.

Workshop Coordinator Mark Evans placed an emphasis on congregational leadership development in workshop choices. Martha Shore and Wendell Putney, UUA Compensation Consultants, offered "Pay What's Right, Not What's Left." Thomas Jefferson District Executive Qiyamah Rahman did a leadership training titled "Don't Sweat the Small Stuff: Facilitating Meetings, Groups and Discussions." Phil Sterner led "Financially Healthy Congregations." There was even a workshop on how to make a congregational banner.

On Thursday night a record number of teens – 52 – bridged into young adulthood. A special collection was taken during the service to help support the UUA's new teen/young adult initiative, "Mind the Gap." The next night, Teen Way Off Broadway, with new Director Chris Groom, went Shakespearean, performing "A Mid-SUUSI Night's Dream." Julia Rigby played "Helen" (Helena) and sang a solo – "Escape," by Enrique Iglesias.

Four years later Rigby, then a Theatre Performance major at Virginia Commonwealth University, recalled her moment in the TWOB spotlight:

> A play is always a bonding experience. It throws a bunch of strangers together with nothing but passion in common, and asks them to give each other their complete trust. TWOB takes that bonding to the extreme because of the added layers: a short, intense rehearsal period, total lack of sleep, shared living quarters and the unique Unitarian Universalist atmosphere...
>
> [And] the crowd always roars! I will never forget the applause, shrieking and laughing that accompanied the mere act of my pulling a microphone out of my backpack in "A Mid-SUUSI Night's Dream." People are not that generous in a typical ... production.
>
> It had always been my dream to play Helena, [but] being as she's tall and blonde, and I'm a short brunette, I thought I was doomed to play Hermia forever. TWOB gives people a way to live out their dreams!

Rigby continues to act on stage to this day.

Throughout the week in 2002, SUUSI participants were encouraged to consider – and share – the blessings in their lives. A large poster near the Info Office gave people a place to answer the question "How has SUUSI blessed your life?" The newsletter invited submissions about SUUSI blessings. One writer thanked Dave Salman and Nancy Mayer for their years of service to the SUUSI community coordinating (and often driving) the Star Car. Another thanked Massel for stepping in once again when SUUSI needed an experienced Director. Yet another celebrated the dedication of Massel's mother, Roz Massel, who was "retiring" after several years on the Enrollment Staff, the most recent three as Registrar.

Staci Shore expressed her gratitude for the gifts of friendship and drumming:

> After facing some financial difficulty in the past couple of months, I was able to squeak out coming to SUUSI with my daughter for the fourth year in a row. My wonderful friends Amy Carol Webb and Brooke Bell insisted on my taking the drum-making class with Hugh Teller. Having been my friends, they knew how much I wanted a drum, and would not take no for an answer. Not only did they take care of the cost, but I have had the great pleasure of making my drums with love and passion with my friends. What a true SUUSI blessing!

Another participant wrote:

> My SUUSI blessing is getting to spend lots of time with my amazing daughter... Yesterday when we went to the SUUSI Bookstore, all she wanted was "The Kids' Guide to Social Action." She's been spending her extra time reading it and coming up with ideas to bring back to our congregation. What a blessing to share space with such a lovely 13-year-old!

At Family Concert Hour on Tuesday, when Peter Mayer sang that "everything's a miracle ... everything's holy now," he captured the mood of the week. Another song that proved to be extremely popular that first post-9/11 summer was "I Pledge Allegiance," which Relative Viewpoint sang during Ingathering and again the next night at Cabaret. T-shirts with the lyrics ("I pledge allegiance to the people of this country, and of all the world, and to the republic that lends a hand. One planet under peace, with liberty and justice for all") were hot sellers in the Bookstore.

Only 886 people attended SUUSI 2002, well down from the 1,038 of the previous year. A letter was sent to each 2001 participant who did not come in 2002, asking for their reasons, telling them they were missed, and inviting them to come back the following year. Among the reasons given for not attending, only 15% reported that they had not had a good experience in 2001; most of those cited a concern that SUUSI was "too big" for their taste. Fully 81% of respondents indicated they did plan to return in the future.

The Board made other intentional efforts at outreach prior to 2003. Registration discounts were offered to first-time attendees from Virginia and North Carolina. Promotional material asked, "Will you create good memories with your family this summer – ones that will last for years, not just moments? Will you go to a place that's exciting and supportive, so you're comfortable enough to try something new? Come to SUUSI. It works – and it lasts."

SUUSI 2003 also got a boost when it was listed in *Frommer's Budget Travel* as a good value and "low cost family summer camp." All the promotion must have helped – and many of those who promised to return must have kept their word – because registration shot back up to nearly 1,000.

Karyn Machler – the first person to have grown up as a child at SUUSI and later become Director – chose as her theme "Simple Gifts." As she wrote in her Director's Welcome in the catalog, "One of the greatest (and most simple) gifts my parents ever gave me is SUUSI."

Indeed, the generational torch was being passed at SUUSI. At Ingathering it was announced that Don Male, who perennially held the honor of being SUUSI's longest-attending participant, was ill and could not attend. In fact, Male had missed two of the past three Summer Institutes, and had recently had a pacemaker installed. Some of his friends, later in the week, placed a phone call to Male and his wife, Sue, to reach out to the Male family from SUUSI – learning, in that call, that Don would likely never be able to return to SUUSI. In fact, he did not. Male passed away from complications of Alzheimer's in 2008.

Other changes awaited those arriving at SUUSI in 2003. The previous three years, Tech had looked the other way as participants drove and parked on the sidewalks near dorms to load and unload their vehicles. Now the university was enforcing long-standing regulations against the practice, creating both a challenge and a blessing for SUUSI-ites. The challenge, of course, was that of hauling a week's worth of gear to and from approved parking areas; the opportunity – the simple gift – was the sense of community that experience created. Participants helped one another, monitored temporarily parked vehicles, shared carts and dollies, held elevator doors, and generally became more connected, right from the start, on Sunday afternoon. The feeling remained throughout the week.

As registrants sat for their mugbook portraits during check-in, for the first time they held name cards at their chest, making for easy identification during the (now fully digital and local) production process. Rick Hallmark, the "chief mugger" for the past few years, had moved on to become Communications Coordinator, and once again Vonnie Hicks stepped in to keep the mugbook going, remarking that he was "still amazed it all works" and noting things had come "a long way from the 35mm film camera and homemade batch processing tanks that occupied my first nights of SUUSI" in the early 1980s. Hicks dubbed the 2003 mugbook a "Hitchhiker's Guide and Mugbook," and the name has stuck.

Another name change that year involved one of SUUSI's main dormitories at Tech. The erstwhile New Residence Hall West had been christened "Peddrew-Yates" during the school year. Irving Peddrew III had been Virginia Tech's first African-American student, and Charlie Yates had been the first African-American to receive a bachelor's degree from a traditionally all-white public university in the South. SUUSI participants happily embraced the change – though strangely, the companion dorm to Peddrew-Yates, New Residence Hall East, retained its generic-sounding name.

A popular (if controversial) speaker made his SUUSI debut in 2003. When Davidson Loehr, minister of the UU church in Austin, Texas, stepped to the podium on Wednesday morning, he was following presentations earlier in the week by two of the denomination's most visible spokespersons – former UUA President John Buehrens and Meg Riley, the current UUA Director of Advocacy and Witness. Ever the iconoclast, Loehr began his theme talk (which was titled "The Simple Gifts of Liberal Religion and How 'UUism' Has Betrayed Them") by stating, categorically, that although he served as the minister of a UU church, he was not a Unitarian Universalist. He proceeded to explain why he considered the Seven UU Principles to be "seven banalities" that actually distract moderns from engaging in the deep spiritual work of true "liberal religion."

Loehr concluded by saying, "I believe we will be judged by whether we had the vision and courage to say 'No more shallowness. No more vacuous principles sitting on the altar, where deep and sometimes scary religious insights belong! We come for that – and will not settle for less'." Those who were present left Owens Ballroom buzzing, and the buzz spread throughout SUUSI during the day. Community conversations with Loehr were heavily attended, and printed copies of his talk, selling for $1 each in the Bookstore, promptly sold out and had to be reprinted. He was invited back the next year for a command performance.

In what was an unusual coup, each theme speaker and worship leader stayed at SUUSI for the entire week in 2003, giving participants an opportunity to interact with them in a variety of informal as well as formal settings. This had long been a goal of Denominational Coordinator Mina Greenfield.

The Young Adult Program explored Unitarian Universalism as well, and offered a UU Trivia Contest for the entire community at Common Ground. Participants led discussions about what being a UU means and what it calls us to do in the world. They took a survey of the SUUSI community and discovered that the 40 YAs in attendance that year had a combined 307 total SUUSIs of

John Buehrens speaking at SUUSI 2003

experience and had volunteered 870 SUUSI work hours that week alone. The survey also revealed 46 tattoos and 114 body piercings.

Nature, under the direction of Jen Lucas and Allie Gooding, put together a new kind of SUUSI Service Project – a river cleanup canoe trip. When participants returned from the New River, their canoes were laden with trash; items ranged from automobile wheel rims to a lounge chair. Other nature trips included a new cave, James Cave, with an entrance just one and a half feet high, and a "Spirit Journey" complete with a hayride to the top of Buckeye Mountain, drumming, and shamanic work. There was even a tour of the Montgomery County Wastewater Treatment Plant titled "Who Gives a Crap?"

A water main break during the week caused the Friday Picnic to be relocated to Lee Quad, a space far less conducive to the kind of close-knit, community feel participants were accustomed to at the Eggleston Quad. There were other incidents that taxed both the Staff and new Risk Manager Eric Kaminetzky. A serious medical

Dancin' at the 'Dip (2004)

situation hospitalized one participant, and widespread underage drinking in the Teen Dorm led to several teens being expelled. There was even a surprise inspection of the Youth Programming space by the fire marshal. Through it all, Kaminetzky provided a helpful, non-anxious, professional presence.

Music was continuing to grow in importance at SUUSI. With the addition of "Showcase of the Stars" in the afternoons, participants enjoyed even more opportunities to see and hear their favorite performers in intimate, informal settings. The ever-evolving SUUSI Chamber Music Ensemble was, by now, a regular feature on Thursdays at Concert Hour. Some Cabaret-based afternoon workshops were offered. Greg Greenway and Stephanie Corby made their first SUUSI appearances, at Concert Hour and Cabaret, respectively.

Teen Way Off Broadway presented "Forest Guump," even singing their way through the Friday afternoon picnic as they went to the theater at Burruss to make their final preparations for the show.

By the end of the week, in fact, the teen community had touched the hearts of many participants. Teens were in charge of Community Time that year, bringing what they called "teen flair" to the laid-back, afternoon gathering time. They helped out on Youth Staff and in other key roles throughout the week. Marybeth Chaconas expressed her appreciation in a testimonial that appeared in the Friday NUUS:

SIMPLE GIFTS THAT MAKE SUUSI POSSIBLE

This is my 5th SUUSI that I have attended with my 4 children, now ages 13, 10, 8 and 4 (my husband doesn't join us). I am often asked, "How in the world do you manage?" I am able to [come to SUUSI] because of the loving support I've received from the SUUSI community – mostly from the pre-teens and teens... [and] I'd like to share some specific memories.

Paul Nevin, at age 12, walking patiently behind my daughter Kinny, then 4, as she drew one chalk line all the way down the sidewalk at Radford. It took an hour!... Meredith Nevin ... noticing me in the cafeteria, frazzled and close to meltdown, would take kids and trays and help get us calmed down and settled before rejoining her friends. Stacy Hines and Emily Madara would appear and take the kids during almost every spare moment in their SUUSI-filled days. Now they have moved on to Teenland, and the torch has been passed. Stephanie Madara and Emily Gonzalez find us whenever they are free, and take over skillfully and cheerfully.

I probably couldn't attend SUUSI without [this kind of] support... I certainly couldn't be on Teen Staff. I love them all dearly, and I am eternally and profoundly grateful. The future of SUUSI and our denomination is in capable, caring hands.

There was a dramatic increase in Median participation in 2003 as well. While 35 spaces had been set aside for Median housing, a total of 70 people signed up for the option. SUUSI was, indeed, becoming a much younger community. Reflecting this fact, more and more programming was happening late at night, and at all hours. SUUSI was becoming a 24/7 happening.

At the end of the week, dates were announced for the next two SUUSIs. Because of changes in startup dates for many public schools in the South, those with children – and in particular those educators in the SUUSI community – had begun to advocate for moving to an earlier week. In response to those requests, SUUSI 2004 and 2005 would shift to the third week in July.

The two-year commitment was seen as a vote of confidence for SUUSI's place at Virginia Tech, although the Board now had an active Site Selection Committee, and the minutes of its meeting in November 2003 indicate a belief that "VT is becoming less friendly and more costly." SUUSI 2003 barely broke even, despite a significant rise in attendance.

There were other issues as well. In the past couple of years, tensions had developed between the Board and Staff. What some on the Core Staff had experienced as micromanagement, Board members had believed to be simply the kind of policy decisions required of the Trustees of a large and complex all-volunteer institution in the litigious culture of the 21st century. Meanwhile, the relationship between The Mountain and SUUSI had changed, and for some time the two institutions had been offering similar programming for certain age groups on the same week each summer.

To further complicate things, in 2003 the Florida District informed SUUSI that it would no longer be appointing representatives to the SUUSI Board. A new era of at-large Board representation was coming, one more reflective of the reality that SUUSI was now a national, rather than a regional, Summer Institute.

Karyn Machler's theme for 2004 was "Reunions," and an intentional effort was made to invite past participants who had not attended recently to come to Blacksburg for a family reunion, SUUSI style. There were literal family reunions, in which members who had not seen one another in some time gathered to reconnect at SUUSI – and there were group reunions, from TWOB alumni to Nature Staffers to the La Leche League.

Whitewater rafting in West Virginia, which had not been offered in many years, returned to the Nature Program, this time with "breakfast on our luxury coach, lunch on the river and dinner at the outfitters" all included in the full day that began with departure on Wednesday morning at 5:15 a.m., and return to campus around midnight. Many other brand new Nature trips provided variety. There was an outing to Floyd, Va., to "Shop and Dine." Cavers could stand in Virginia's second largest underground "room" at Giant Caverns Vertical Cave, or explore the Greenville Saltpeter Cave, with remnants of mining activity dating back to the Revolutionary War. A "Fire and the Forest" trip offered participants the opportunity to visit the site of a recent forest fire to learn how forests recover from these natural events, and what humans can do to help.

Workshop choices were quite eclectic in 2004. Participants could work on "Psychic Skills Development" or "Humor as a Survival Technique," learn the ins and outs of "Ecstatic Worship," or even get certified in CPR. There was a "Lego Geometry" workshop, and two different sessions of a "Book and Beverage" book discussion group. Fran Lynch convened the "Socrates Café," a daily philosophy discussion group perhaps reminiscent, at least in subject matter, of the Wisdom Tree.

For the first time, workshops specifically by and for Medians were available, as denoted by small yin-yang symbols in the catalog. Offerings included "Mini-Me Chalice Making," "Alternative Beer Tasting," "SUUSI Music Swap" and "Ancient Prophecy and Modern Conspiracy." Medians were once again housed together, this time in air conditioned space.

SUUSI's different age groupings had become so numerous, and so confusing, that Sunday's Arrival NUUS provided some guidance: "SUUSI Terminology Note – At SUUSI, the Youth are infants to [age] 13; the Teens are 14-17; and the Young Adults are 18-25. People over 25 are either Medians, Boomers, Seniors, or otherwise self-defined!"

Teens were reminded in the same newsletter to be sure to get their "Four a Day" during the week – "sleep some amount, drink water til you pee clear, eat something green and touch your parent or guardian" each and every day. New Teen Directors Marybeth Chaconas and Tom Macon put into place some changes in the Teen Dorm, where there were now more housing options – separate boys' and girls' floors, as well as the usual coed floors – and more nighttime adult supervision. A peer Spirit Committee was formed to help monitor behavior, intervene when deemed necessary, and mediate between teens and adults should concerns arise.

In addition, the Board had revised the rules for SUUSI Teens, for the first time passing a policy explicitly banning sexual activity and clearly stating what offenses would lead to the removal of a teen participant from SUUSI:

2004 RULES FOR TEENS

1. No weapons, violence or destructive behavior.
2. No use or possession or alcohol or illegal drugs.
3. There will be no leaving the teen dorm between 1 a.m. and 6 a.m. unless accompanied by your parent or guardian, or for a pre-approved, scheduled activity. A pre-approved, scheduled activity is one that appears in the SUUSI brochure and/or confirmation newsletter and/or Sunday newsletter.

Violation of rules 1, 2 or 3 will result in expulsion from SUUSI.

4. No abuse of legal drugs.
5. No smoking in the teen dorm.
6. Parent/guardian will be responsible for damages done to an individual teen's room.

7. Parents/guardians will establish their own expectations for their teen, and will maintain daily communication. Also, they will inform Teen Staff prior to removal of their teen from the campus.

8. In keeping with UUA guidelines, Article 4, Section 1.6a, sexual intercourse and patently sexual behavior between participants under 18 is prohibited at SUUSI. The SUUSI Director shall provide information to encourage and empower teens to decline sexual intimacy of any kind, and further, that education shall be provided about sexual identity, violence, and safe sex.

9. The Board recommends that parents/guardians of SUUSI teens discuss sexuality with their teen prior to SUUSI.

A letter was sent from the Board and the Risk Manager to all teens and parents prior to SUUSI, reminding them that several teens had been expelled the previous year for drinking alcohol, and explaining the new rules.

In 2004 Dietrick was undergoing a major renovation, so meals were taken in Owens Food Court. Though vegetarians were generally pleased with the move (tofu scramble became a breakfast favorite), the space was cramped, and frustrations – and trays – sometimes overflowed. Other renovations relegated many workshops to the distant Litton-Reeves, prompting this notice in the Tuesday NUUS:

> Our apologies for the treks to Litton-Reeves... These are the best available spaces based on our needs, and we appreciate your understanding and cooperation. Want to know the best path to your workshop? Check out the Workshops bulletin board in the Info Office.
>
> As always, please check with the Info Office for up-to-date information. Please do not assume that your workshop will be in the same location tomorrow, or even

this afternoon! And remember to grab a schedule each morning at breakfast.

The newsletter also offered helpful tips on how to use an ethernet cable to access the high speed internet now available in all rooms. Participants were urged to take their own trash to the dumpsters (otherwise, Tech had threatened to charge SUUSI for trash pickup at the end of the week); despite these in-week reminders, most waited until Saturday morning to "take out the trash," resulting in overflowing dumpsters all over campus.

Wednesday night at dusk, Nightlife Director Devin Gordon arranged for SUUSI's first outdoor movie night, approximating the experience of a classic drive-in movie. The idea was a hit, as families and kids of all ages brought their beach towels, folding chairs and popcorn to enjoy a showing of *E.T.* under the stars.

The last two morning theme talks in 2004 brought home the "Reunions" theme with particular poignancy. On Thursday, Barbara Wells ten Hove, co-minister in Adelphi, Md., spoke powerfully about her experience as a lifelong Unitarian Universalist, in a talk titled "A Stranger in My Own Home Town." Then on Friday morning, five long-time SUUSI attendees held a fictional "reunion at The Mountain" to reminisce about SUUSI's history. Roger Comstock, Nancy Heath, Bob Irwin, Alexis Jones and Kathee Williams shared an oral history of the Summer Institute, informing a new generation of participants about the legend and lore of SUUSI. The service culminated with Jones' traditional singing of Ric Masten's "Let It Be a Dance."

The worship services that week were also memorable, beginning with a "Revival" on Monday night led by Alane Cameron Miles (who also served as Youth Minister for the week). The Revival experience "re-ignited, re-invigorated, re-emboldened and re-united" those in attendance "with the joy of our UU beliefs and practice." The week's worship concluded on Friday night in Owens Ballroom with a unique "Ekstasis" experience led by Thomas Anastasi and the members of his week-long "Ecstatic Worship" workshop. The charismatic, piano-pounding minister from Shoreline, Wash., brought an energy to SUUSI worship seldom seen, before or since. Here is how it was billed in the newsletter:

> Ekstasis is an exciting and innovative worship service which celebrates being fully human, welcoming and taking pleasure in the whole body's amazing ability to sense and feel and think within the realm of worship.
>
> Ekstasis invites participants into a physical and cerebral worship, encouraging everyone to enjoy their body's wondrous, natural responses and sensations, in primal yearnings to engage ecstasy, as well as their rational sensibilities.
>
> Ekstasis promotes the "hallowed use" of modern technology: computer-generated art, visual slide shows, live video feeds, dynamic sound systems and techno dance music.
>
> Ekstasis offers worshippers a time of reunion with their ancient human impulses to sing and dance and move into the flow of sacred time.

Teen Way Off Broadway provided powerful memories of its own later that night, with the production of "Batman UUnmasked." Though they were not yet a couple, Alan Jackoway (who played Batman) and Sarah Gonzalez (who played Catwoman) were destined to be married in real life, come 2012. "Batman UUnmasked" also holds the distinction of being the first time TWOB required (free) tickets for admittance, and the only time it was held in the Haymarket Theatre of the Squires Student Center. For the first time since SUUSI's return to Virginia Tech, there were two performances.

Serendipity: Let it be a dance!

New TWOB Director Jennifer Sanders, who had appeared in "Tommy" 16 years earlier, told the cast and crew:

> SUUSI loves you. That's why Teen Way Off Broadway is a safe place to try things outside of your comfort zone. What do you mean you can't sing? Try it and SUUSI will love you, just for trying. What do you mean you're scared to walk out on stage because you might forget your lines? It doesn't even matter if you forget your lines. SUUSI will still love you – for trying, for reaching, for growing, and yes, for giving the community such an amazing gift.

TWOB is just one of the many amazing experiences participants try, each year, to squeeze into the last few hours of SUUSI. There was so much going on in 2004, in fact, that the Friday NUUS published a tongue-in-cheek schedule:

FRIDAY NIGHT TO-DO LIST
4:30 – Picnic in Eggleston Quad
7:00 – Ekstasis Worship at Owens
8:15 – Teen Way Off Broadway at Squires
9:30 – Nap
9:37 – Pack
9:45 – Nightlife!

The next morning, of course – whether one had slept or not – Closing Circle brought another year of memories to a tearful conclusion. Soon after, an appreciative parent wrote to Teen Directors Marybeth Chaconas and Tom Macon:

Dear Marybeth and Tom,

What in the world did you do with my teen?...My surly mumbly grumpy guy went to SUUSI and didn't come back. There's a fellow here that looks like him, but is a talkative, engaged and relatively cheerful young man who suddenly hugs and kisses his Moms several times a day, unprompted. He's talking and talking and talking of art and politics and movies and books and how beautiful the sky is at night, and then inviting – INVITING – his little brother into his room to read together when they can't fall asleep. So whatever it is you did, may I please have the recipe to keep it going until next SUUSI?

More seriously, our most heartfelt thanks for your work as Teen Directors for SUUSI 2004. Once Alex woke up after SUUSI, he said the Teen Dorm was "different" this year – "still intense, but in a different way. The best it's been for me." And then (gasp) he shared his SUUSI photos!

Thank you for fielding our concerns over the last year, and working toward a healthier system for the Teen Dorm. You've created a safer space for the teens to learn who they are, grow together, and emerge into the world prepared for the hard work at hand – exactly what we hoped for. May you be as blessed as we are by your work for the SUUSI teens.

We salute you!
Many thanks,
Amy Carol Webb and Brooke Bell

Though good feelings abounded after SUUSI, the financial news was not as upbeat. When the books were closed on the year, it was learned that SUUSI had operated in the red in 2004, despite fact that total adult fees were at an all-time high of $430 (the number of registration forms, too, was at an all-time high; along with seven total pages of registration instructions in the catalog, there were another six pages of registration forms and two pages of release and liability waivers.) It was calculated that given the attendance in 2004, adult fees would have had to be $495 just to break even, and pressure began to mount to find a less expensive location for SUUSI.

The Institute was booked through 2005 at Virginia Tech, however, and those universities that had been contacted previously by the Site Selection Committee either did not allow alcohol, or were in the process of major building projects that would make them unable to accommodate SUUSI for a few more years. Meanwhile, the Core Staff was saddened to see the departure of Julie Kamienski from her invaluable role as SUUSI's liaison with Tech's Conference Services Department. She was replaced by Joey Wilkerson for the 2005 year.

Director Jen Lucas chose "Time to Fly" as the theme in 2005, and right from the start, the theme pervaded every aspect of SUUSI. Those who pre-registered received a "Boarding Pass" with their confirmation: "Welcome aboard SUUSI flight 2005. We expect an outstanding week!" Included on the Boarding Pass was a "Flight Plan" with instructions for ticketing (Sunday check-in), baggage check (moving into your room), long-term parking, and encouragement to "fly standby" if one's workshop or nature trip choices were full.

The 2005 catalog had been significantly revamped, with more (and clearer) pictures, better graphics, short SUUSI testimonials sprinkled throughout and, for the first time, a helpful two-page planning grid. One grid included the schedule of major community-wide events like Ingathering, theme talks, and Teen Way Off Broadway; the other was broken down into blank programming blocks, and could be personalized by the participant.

The front page of the catalog included a guide for how to "Create Your Own SUUSI":

- Are you an early bird? Get up at sunrise and do an early morning nature trip, or greet newcomers and chat at length with friends over breakfast in the dining hall.
- Are you a night owl? There are plenty of nightlife activities that happen until the wee hours of the morning. Or you can find some folks to chat with long into the night.
- Do you like to plan your day? There are activities, services and workshops every day to keep you busy.
- Do you have a more laid-back approach? Wake up late and see where the day takes you!
- Need some intellectual stimulation? There are daily theme talks and great workshops to satisfy your appetite.
- Want adventurous or strenuous activities? Rappel cliff sides, go caving, or learn Eskimo rolls in a kayak in various nature trips.
- Want family trips? Hike and canoe with other families on special nature trips.
- More on the quiet side? Enjoy community time in a chair with your book, taking in sight and sound, quiet conversations with friends, Cabaret in the evenings, bird watching.

> We cannot even begin to describe the almost 40,000 different SUUSI weeks designed by enrollees through the history of SUUSI. Just come ... [and] design your own!

Come they did – 973 in all, more than 700 of whom were either youth, teens, or parents and guardians of youth and teens. There were 261 first-timers. To the dismay of some veteran participants, Sunday check-in was once again back at Shultz Hall off North Main Street, which had last been the scene of check-in way back in 1992. But the mood this particular afternoon was kept festive, with helium-filled balloons decorating the check-in area and friendly faces welcoming newcomers and returnees alike. Even a late afternoon thunderstorm could not dampen the spirits of those who were arriving.

Waiver forms had now been greatly simplified, with one single release form covering all SUUSI activities. Each participant (or parent or guardian, if a minor) was required to sign an "umbrella waiver" releasing SUUSI from liability before they could complete their registration and receive a nametag. Registrants were given a four-page, green SUUSI Safety Information Sheet that detailed accessibility, transportation and parking, hydration and other self-care for the week, as well as nature trip information and requirements. There was also a broadside titled "First Timers' Guide to (Gasp!) Bathroom Sharing." Everything was covered in one of the most well-organized check-in procedures to date.

Balloons once more greeted those taking part in the banner parade, marking a "flight path" across the Drill Field from Payne to Burruss. The motif continued during Ingathering, with a "flight attendant" and other aeronautical references. Pete Leary sang a song he had written especially for the occasion, "Time to Fly," which included the lines "Let's celebrate our freedom, and all humanity – Our family of families, one big community – We make it safe outside the nest..." The singer-songwriter duo Emma's Revolution closed the Ingathering celebration and sent participants back out onto the Drill Field for the giant Opening Circle – this year, complete with balloons.

The new D2 Cafeteria at Virginia Tech

Emma's Revolution also performed at Tuesday's Concert Hour. It was a great year for new musicians at SUUSI in 2005; Miriam Davidson and Kiya Heartwood (Wishing Chair) were the Concert Hour performers on Wednesday, and Joe Jencks appeared at the "Showcase of the Stars." All three would become SUUSI regulars for years to come. The week's music offerings concluded with a Friday night Jamboree – one song per artist – featuring all of SUUSI's favorites on one stage.

Paper airplanes – a natural outgrowth of the theme – popped up all around campus during the week. Youth programming, of course, turned paper airplane making into an official workshop, but then again, so did the Medians. Other Median workshops included Texas Hold'Em, a triple slog hike, two beer tastings and two "Moving Picture Potlucks." The Board held a forum with the Medians on Friday afternoon to hear their concerns and desires for even more programming that would be targeted to their needs.

Participants were happy to be back in the dining hall formerly known as Dietrick (now renamed "D2," prompting many a joke asking "So what happened to R2?"). Dietrick had undergone a complete makeover that turned it from an old-style cafeteria into a very modern, very large series of food courts. Options for vegetarians and others with special dietary needs were plentiful at D2, but so was the crowd; SUUSI folks were encouraged to eat dinner early in the evening to avoid the crush of students and parents from VT freshman orientation. Meal cards doubled as building access cards.

By now, space changes and their attendant disruptions had come to be expected at Tech. Besides having to hold check-in at Shultz, it turned out that Slusher was not available, forcing hundreds of participants (and some programs) to move into Lee Hall. And in an unusually hot year, the swimming pool in War Memorial Gym was also unavailable.

Theme speakers in 2005 were Melanie Morel-Ensminger, Maj-Britt Johnson, Suzanne Meyer, Steve Crump and Alex Richardson. Worship services were led by Keith Kron, Mary Grigolia, Mary Ann Somervill, Michael Tino and Bill Neely. Though there was no longer a "theme book" being produced, printed copies of individual theme talks were once again available at the Bookstore for $2 each.

For some, "Time to Fly" meant scaling a giant, inflatable climbing wall in Lee Quad during Community Time. For others, it was an opportunity to engage in deeper self-reflection. Workshops focusing on personality styles, such as "Having the Type of Your Life," "The Enneagram: Path to Your Secret Self," and "Quadrants and Stages" were popular offerings. Other titles included "Spiritual Growth" and "Working Spiritually."

Camp Roanoke, an outdoor adventure center and recreation area, became part of the SUUSI Nature experience in 2005. Two different all-day ropes courses and two similar half-day outings gave participants the opportunity to challenge themselves in difficult physical and emotional circumstances high above the ground, deep in the woods. A new combination canoe/caving trip, to Cracker Neck Cave, appealed to other adventure enthusiasts.

The teens got in on the action at Camp Roanoke with their own ropes/initiative challenge – nor were they to be left out of the paper airplane craze. And on Friday evening – after what would be the very last SUUSI Picnic – participants trooped by the hundreds to "downtown" Blacksburg, where Teen Way Off Broadway put on two shows of "The Hitchhiker's Guide to SUUSI" in the historic Lyric Theatre. Amy Carol Webb, who was on TWOB staff as vocal coach in the mid-2000s, recalls that show:

> The joy and beauty of TWOB for me is witnessing young people step up, step out, and find their voices – in dance and dialogue as well as song – all in a loving environment. A favorite moment?... When Brian [Daniel, who was singing a Switchfoot song] hit a note he, and just about everybody else, didn't think he could – and blew the lid off the place! And off our hearts...

It was another Friday night to remember at SUUSI.

The combination of increased participant fees and increased attendance created a banner year for SUUSI financially; whereas the Institute in 2004 had lost $19,000, in 2005 there was a surplus of $26,000 – more than offsetting the previous year's deficit. As the Board met the following spring, it weighed the relative costs of Virginia Tech and Radford (the Site Selection Committee had received quotes from Radford over the winter). To the Board's surprise, initial cost estimates from Radford showed Virginia Tech as the less-expensive alternative. A decision was made to enter into a contract with Tech through 2007, while continuing to negotiate with Radford for the future.

During the off-season, Michael Ivey and Devin Gordon retooled the website, and for the first time staff applications and electronic staff credit vouchers could all be handled online. Most participants, however, still chose to do their registering on paper, and in the spring, when the catalogs arrived in the mail for SUUSI 2006, everyone was glad to see that – given the previous year's budget windfall – fees had not increased. However, many found the sheer number of registration forms and the complexity of the process to be bewildering. Though the intent had been to make the forms easier to read and follow, the visual redesign resulted in many a wise crack comparing registering for SUUSI with filling out a federal tax return. There were now sections and forms lettered A through Q. Each individual registrant, regardless of age, was required to have completed sections A-G; Form H was for each family or group to be housed together, while forms I-Q contained various releases, waivers, and other information.

The changes made a positive difference, however, when participants arrived at SUUSI. Those who had already pre-paid their balance (and key deposits) in full, had completed and mailed in the various requisite forms, and did not need to make changes to workshops or nature trips, could enjoy "Express Check-In." Core Staff members Marianne Vakiener (Registrar) and Hanna Bosman (Assistant to the Director, a crucial organizational role she has quietly but capably filled ever since) coordinated a new team of "ambassadors" to welcome and greet arrivals at the door, directing them to the appropriate line, including "Express." There were many more tellers in place to receive payments, and the process flowed very smoothly.

Virginia Tech was now distributing linens in one large bag per bed, with the clear admonition that unless each piece included was returned, in the same bag, at the end of the week, the participant would be charged for every missing item – up to a total of $50 if the entire bag went missing. Teens, however, were required to provide their own linens.

As the 2006 banner parade began, there was a new twist – a Grand Marshal. "Uncle Flip" Lower led the way to Burruss, where SUUSI officially began for 924 registrants (the lowest total in five years).

With portions of Owens unavailable for SUUSI's use, several

location changes involving major events created confusion early in the week. Monday morning in the Hokie Grill, Rosemary Bray McNatt kicked off the week's theme talks by sharing "some thoughts on finding room in our lives for the sacred, from a minister/writer/mother/wife/woman in process." Common Ground was hard to find in Deet's Place, and Serendipity was moved to an even more distant location – the "West End" at Cochrane. Nightlife, with new coordinator Elizabeth Thompson, even offered a late-night experiment that began after Serendipity – the so-called "After Hours CACHE," which ran from 1-4 a.m. in the West End and featured current dance music for all participants age 18 and up in an alcohol-free environment.

The 2006 catalog, T-shirts and logo depicted joyous, jumping and leaping stylized stick figures, harkening back to the hand-holding "people logo" of the early 1980s at Radford. In keeping with the theme of "Rejoice and Renew," Community Time got a makeover; each afternoon there was a "Community Sun Dance" offering "a time dedicated to renewal, sharing, rejuvenation and play as a community." There was a welcoming carnival on Monday, which included a drawing for free SUUSI 2007 registration. In order to be part of the drawing, one had to meet, befriend, and then receive a validation sticker from any newcomer (first-timers were identified that year with a "Carpe Diem" sticker on their nametag). The winner of the free SUUSI was Sandy Macon from Charlottesville.

Among the first-time attendees was 4-year-old Lesley Akers, who quickly became one of the SUUSI community's most adored children. Her mother, Daria Akers, tells the story of her family's 2006 SUUSI experience:

> [My husband] Todd and I had both attended SUUSI while in college. However, once we left the Blacksburg area, we didn't even think of going. When Lesley was 4, we decided to look into SUUSI again, but we were hesitant since she still had problems walking. I wrote Dianna

[MacPherson], who was Youth Staff leader at that time, about having a special needs child, and asking did they think they could accommodate her? Her response was something along the lines of "SUUSI is a time when kids barely sleep and are hopped up on sugar; by Wednesday, they're all special needs! Bring her and we will make it work."

So I signed up, and we hoofed it down to Blacksburg for our first SUUSI as a family. Lesley had gotten new leg braces the week before, and I forgot to put her on a wearing schedule to break them in. By Tuesday, she had huge blisters on her feet and could barely walk. We went to the store to buy "regular" shoes, and she just couldn't walk in them. I was in tears, thinking that we would have to leave SUUSI.

I went to Dianna again, and she said "You're not going home. We will make this work." We decided that Lesley would be barefoot all the time, and Youth Staff would make sure to cover her blisters with band-aids. They must have gone through a dozen a day. Lesley was carried around the cafeteria, so she wouldn't get in trouble for not having shoes on. It was amazing, the lengths Dianna and her staff went to make sure we enjoyed SUUSI.

I don't know that we would have come back if we had left that year, but because of the outpouring of love from everyone who helped us, we have been to every SUUSI since. It is the one place where Lesley is accepted for who she is, and loved unconditionally.

Another young SUUSI star that year was 9-year-old Elijah Long, a budding entrepreneur and social activist. At the "treasure swap" during Community Sun Dance on Tuesday, Elijah sold handmade penguin earrings, raising more than $150 to give to Water Partners International, a non-profit organization seeking to bring safe drinking water to impoverished third-world communities.

Toenail painting at Community Sun Dance

The next day, "gruuvy tunes" filled the air at the Sun Dance, with live music from many of SUUSI's favorite, and lesser-known, performers. Thursday's gathering featured games for all ages (athletics included dodgeball, soccer and kickball), a beautiful ceremony led by Alane Cameron Miles in which committed couples renewed their vows, and an auction. The earth ball, long a SUUSI mainstay – and the source of more than one serious SUUSI injury – was now tattered, torn and in disrepair, so it was auctioned off to raise money for SUUSIships. The week of Sun Dance concluded with a "spa day" on Friday, where participants could receive a massage, do yoga or tai chi, or even get makeovers provided by the teens.

Friday's Teen Way Off Broadway, once again with two shows at the Lyric Theatre, played off the popular Broadway musical "Wicked", and its tie-in with "The Wizard of Oz." Director Jennifer Sanders put TWOB 2006 in historical context within the mythology of Teen Way Off Broadway, and explained the storyline of her play "Totally Wicked" in the playbill:

> Once upon a time (1987 to be exact), a green witch named Elphaba first attended SUUSI. Her roommate, Glinda, was very popular and a little too fond of the color pink. Her boyfriend, Fiyero, was a little too fond of Glinda.
>
> In 1990, the TWOB Director created a performance that showed Elphaba in a negative light ("The Wizard of Blacksburg"). This hurt her feelings, and she left SUUSI, vowing never to return. Glinda, of course, never missed a SUUSI, where she continued her mission of perkiness, pink dresses and fairy hats for all.
>
> Flash forward to 2006. Phoebe (Elphaba and Fiyero's daughter) decides to attend SUUSI. Find out what happens when she meets Lisa (Glinda's daughter), Dave (a TWOB history buff) and a host of memorable characters.
>
> (Please note that flashback scenes are in black and white.)

Social action was returning to the SUUSI community in 2006. In addition to Elijah Long's inspiring "Penguins for the Planet" project at Tuesday's Community Sun Dance, a "meditation for peace" was held on Thursday and Friday afternoons. Another participant shared a photo documentary, with commentary, on the aftermath of hurricanes Katrina and Rita. Participants organized to petition,

Joe Jencks

protest and work against the "Virginia Marriage Amendment," which defined marriage as "only a union between one man and one woman" and was to be on the ballot in November. Sadly, the bill passed with 57 percent of the vote statewide.

The Thursday night Transitions Service was a moving musical celebration of life and death. Joe Jencks wrote a song, titled "We Will Hold You," specifically for the occasion, and its chorus provided the refrain that wove together each celebrated transition, from baby dedications through memorials. Amy Carol Webb's "On Holy Ground" opened the service and set the mood, helping to turn the Hokie Grill into a sacred space for ceremony and ritual.

What has since become a SUUSI late-night tradition got off to a somewhat controversial start in 2006. The first BBQUUsi, a wee-hours, middle-of-the-night barbecue and grill party, took place outside Cochrane, and Virginia Tech was none too pleased. The minutes from the Board meeting at the end of the week indicate that the event "was not cleared with VT hierarchy – only with the VT managers – and [it] happened three nights instead of one, as [had been] understood by the Director. The event was not good for VT-SUUSI relations [because] barbecues with open flames are not allowed" on the Virginia Tech campus.

Meanwhile, Tanya Ridpath – the new Director of Conference Services at Radford – was actively pursuing SUUSI in hopes of facilitating its return to RU. And though Tech also indicated a desire to keep SUUSI in Blacksburg, Director Jen Lucas was told that VT could no longer accomodate both SUUSI and their Orientation for incoming freshman students during the same week. Incoming classes at Tech were now so large that Orientation spanned the last three weeks of July. SUUSI was welcome to stay at Virginia Tech for as long as it liked – but not during those three weeks.

A Difficult Decision to Move On

By Wednesday afternoon of SUUSI 2006, it was apparent that SUUSI faced two choices – either change *when* it was meeting, or *where*. The Board called a town hall meeting to inform participants of the situation and get their feedback. An overflow crowd jammed into the Hokie Grill for the meeting. The anxiety created by the situation was palpable as Board members shared with participants the status of SUUSI beyond the next year (2007 was already contracted with Virginia Tech). Old feelings and emotions about the respective pros and cons of Radford and Virginia Tech surfaced. Some participants expressed concern about what seemed like a perpetual "bouncing back and forth" between the two universities. Others advocated for finding a completely new location.

The Board distributed a questionnaire, which was completed and returned by 264 people. It provided insights into the community's preferences regarding SUUSI's date, location and even programming. The most significant piece of data gleaned from the survey was the fact that one-fourth of the participants indicated they would not come to SUUSI if it were held the first week in July. Meanwhile, fully 89% of respondents said they would still attend SUUSI if it were not at Tech – while another 9.8% indicated they actually "would be happier" if it were not held in Blacksburg. Ninety percent preferred that SUUSI be held in either Virginia or West Virginia, while 75% said they would still come if it were in the Carolinas and 70% said they would come if it were in Tennessee or Kentucky. Any potential site's policy about alcohol was important to most respondents, but 84.5% said they could live with alcohol being "limited to certain public spaces" (5.7% said they would, in fact, "be happier" if it were limited).

In considering future sites, respondents were asked to indicate how important various programming spaces would be to them. Appropriate space for youth programming, theme talks and worship services, workshops and the teens topped the list. Perhaps the most intriguing concept that was floated in the survey – how participants might react "if there were two smaller SUUSIs held on consecutive weeks" – drew the strongest reaction. Half indicated they would still come to one of the weeks, 14% said they would "try to come to both," and a third said they would quit coming altogether. Many participants added written comments that indicated the idea was not a popular one.

Armed with this data, the Board and Core Staff held a joint meeting in Decatur, Ga., on the morning of Sept. 23, 2006, in which, according to the minutes, both groups "shared from the heart personal memories about SUUSI sites." The options were thoroughly discussed. Following lunch, the Board met separately and received the following recommendation from the Site Selection Committee (Valerie Fleming, Devin Gordon, Bill Gupton, Jerry King, Jen Lucas, Karyn Machler, Dianna MacPherson and Alex Winner):

> "We have reviewed the options available…and given that the first week of July (the date suggested to us by Virginia Tech) ranked fifth out of seven possible choices [of possible weeks for SUUSI in the survey of participants] … the Site Selection Committee unanimously recommends that the Board approve a move to Radford University beginning in July 2008, pending successful negotiations with Radford."

After some discussion, the Board voted to accept the recommendation, and formal negotiations with Radford began. In December, following another on-site visit to Radford to discuss a contract for 2008, Director Devin Gordon and Board President Bill Gupton reported to the Board in a conference call that there had been "very positive interactions with Radford so far. SUUSI requests are greeted positively. Radford is eager to have us, and the bottom line [cost] seems to be dropping. We are likely to sign contracts with Radford" in the next few weeks.

However, when the proposed contract from Radford finally arrived in February, the negotiating team was dismayed to learn that many things they had been verbally promised were not included in the document. In addition to the perhaps inevitable financial dance, it was revealed in the contract that what Gordon called "the hub of SUUSI" at Radford – Heth Hall – would be unavailable. A lively debate took place at the Board meeting in April, where the minutes of the Director's report indicated that "Devin has significant concerns, and believes that we should reconsider going to Radford... This is a difficult situation from a programmatic standpoint. Many of our large gatherings will have to be held in less desirable locations. Every large space will be used [with] no backups" available.

"After substantial discussion," the Board chose to continue talks with Radford. Three more months of contract negotiation ensued; the contract with Radford was not signed until the day that SUUSI 2007 began in Blacksburg.

Meanwhile, tragedy had struck. The April meeting of the Board of Trustees, held at the UU Fellowship of Raleigh, was convened just four days after a shooting rampage at Virginia Tech left 33 people, including the gunman, dead. Like the nation, the SUUSI community was stunned and heartbroken by the events of April 16, 2007. Within hours of the shootings, both the Board President and the Director reached out to their contacts at Tech to express SUUSI's sympathy and solidarity. Bill Gupton posted a pastoral letter to the suusi-friends listserv, declaring that "as an extended part of [the] Virginia Tech community, we too feel the pain and loss they are suffering." Others soon began communicating their sorrow on the list, and sending their love and support to those SUUSI community members who lived in and around Blacksburg.

Local residents described their experience in the aftermath of the massacre later that week on suusi-friends. Amy Lythgoe wrote:

Everyone's words of solace, support and peace have meant so much the last few days. The world still feels quite separate from us in many ways, and I think a sense of maintaining our space has helped as we still work to move through the shock and anger and toward grief. Mike [Lythgoe] has worked tirelessly as the local Red Cross disaster response chair, spending countless hours on campus coordinating respite services for emergency personnel, and helping in whatever ways are most wanted and needed.

All the emergency services and relief personnel, the VT professors and administrators, the campus ministries and social clubs, the town agencies and groups – students, neighbors, friends and strangers alike – are helping in tangible and meaningful ways. I am humbled and overwhelmed by their gifts of time and talent, compassion and care. Our community will be here working and coping together for a long, long time.

In the three months between the shooting and SUUSI 2007, the Blacksburg community grappled not only with almost unbearable grief and pain, but also with incessant media attention and intrusion. An unprecedented outpouring of condolence and support flowed into Blacksburg literally from all around the world. The Drill Field itself became a vast memorial garden, where flowers, candles, notes, children's drawings and every kind of commemorative object imaginable were interspersed with impromptu arrangements of Hokie Stones.

By the time SUUSI arrived in mid-July, the tens of thousands of objects had been moved indoors to Shultz, which was turned into a massive viewing area and memorial exhibition. Meanwhile, a temporary memorial to the shooting victims had been created at the base of the reviewing stand on the Drill Field, and a permanent one was well on its way to completion. Many SUUSI participants wore maroon-and-orange T-shirts and bore heavy hearts on the first day of the last SUUSI at Virginia Tech.

"We Are Virginia Tech":
An Emotional Farewell (2007)

Sunday, July 15, 2007, was like no other opening day in the history of SUUSI. While those who had come were of course happy to be with one another again at SUUSI, the shadow of the April shootings hung over the community, and tinged the air with a bittersweet taste. The banner parade that evening was a silent procession across the Drill Field. Many lingered at the top of the hill to pay their respects at the temporary memorial, where candles were lit and prayers were offered. As people filed, still silently, into the huge auditorium in Burruss, the drummers took their accustomed positions up front in the orchestra pit but stood at attention in silence.

The 2007 banner parade was a solemn, silent procession across the Drill Field

Bill Gupton, who earlier that day had signed the contract that would take SUUSI to Radford in 2008, took the stage and said to a hushed crowd:

> We gather tonight, on holy ground. We gather tonight, in respectful silence – and joyful anticipation. We have come, from near and from far – some of us for the very first time, in a leap of faith; others on an annual pilgrimage, a ritual as cherished as any in our lives.
>
> We have come with one shared purpose, one sacred intention: To create, if only for one week, the kind of human community we would have, for our world, 52

weeks a year...

We cannot gather here on this beautiful campus – this home to so many memories, for so many of us – without acknowledging the terrible events of April 16. Just beyond these walls, on a perfectly ordinary spring day, the unthinkable occurred. Just outside these doors, for months now, mourners have gathered, and memorials have been placed. This university, our home away from home for so many years, our sacred ground, has been forever changed – and so have we.

Those of us who love SUUSI, love Virginia Tech. Tonight, we feel the echoes of how our hearts broke, and our spirits ached, that awful day in April. At the Memorial Convocation soon after, Nikki Giovanni addressed those who were grieving, and said to them, "We are sad today, and we will be sad for quite a while. We are Virginia Tech. We are embracing our mourning. We are Virginia Tech. We are strong enough to stand tall, tearlessly. We are brave enough to bend and cry... We are sad enough to know that [one day], we must laugh again."

SUUSI – let us embrace our own sadness, just as we embrace one another. Let us be strong and brave. Let us cry and laugh. Life is a precious gift – beautiful, and terribly, terribly fragile. Therefore, let us live this evening – let us live this week – fully.

We, too, are Virginia Tech. We are SUUSI...

He lit the SUUSI chalice, Joe Jencks sang his now poignantly apropos song from the previous summer, "We Will Hold You" – and then the drummers slowly began to drum. After a moment, those in the auditorium caught the beat, and a new energy started building as tension was released. Participants began to clap, and then yell, as they would at a normal Ingathering, and then the banners entered the hall. Though things would not be completely the same that week – many in the SUUSI community would

Participants pause to pay their respects at the temporary memorial on the way into Ingathering 2007

walk to Shultz, to silently visit the memorials displayed there, while others gravitated toward the Drill Field to remember those who died on April 16 – once the banners had paraded into the auditorium, and the clapping and singing had begun, participants were ready, in the words of the 2007 theme, "To Live Fully."

Devin Gordon had used those words to describe the SUUSI experience in his Director's letter in the 2007 catalog. "I know of nowhere else," he wrote, "where the morning can be spent hiking, the afternoon spent learning how to make a drum, the evening spent in the company of happy children as they play, carefree – and the night spent sharing music with friends. To me, that is living fully."

For SUUSI youth, living fully in 2007 meant enjoying a wide variety of workshops ranging from learning sign language to playing "wink" (yes, wink was an official youth workshop that year, thanks to Youth Director Dianna MacPherson). The kids could write songs with Joe Jencks, build forts with friends, or make everything from wallets to shoes out of duct tape. Youth-friendly nature trips numbered more than 30, thanks to Nature Co-Directors Valerie Fleming and Ralph Phipps, including SUUSI's first geocaching outing, family canoe and Cascades trips, age-specific youth tubing and caving, and a trip to the Mountain Lake Biological Station.

Adult nature trips included two new caves (Picket's Cave and Giant Caverns), as well as a day at Mountain Lake and a 35-mile course for road bikes billed as the "Tour De SUUSI." Unfortunately, the SUUSI Service Project, which had been a tradition now for many years, fell through the cracks and did not happen.

One project that did launch successfully was SOLIS (pronounced "solace") – the SUUSI Online Information System. Designed and put in place by Michael Ivey, SOLIS allowed 2007 participants to register online for the first time. The result was that some programs filled up very early; for example, the Child Care Co-Op, which housed 197 of the 970 total SUUSI registrants, was full a month before SUUSI.

The Director's Report for 2007 mentioned two major medical incidents. One participant fell onto the pavement between D2 and Peddrew-Yates, suffered a badly cut head, and had to be taken to the emergency room. There was also a significant caving accident on Monday. Andy Crum had fallen off a slippery wall inside Picket's Cave, landing on his back directly on a boulder. "I was stunned and had trouble breathing, but nothing seemed broken," he recalls. "I was able to drag myself the rest of the way out of the cave, up and down some more walls, and through long crawls in tight spots, around corkscrews, and finally into the fresh air of a cow pasture."

From there, he was taken to the hospital, where X-rays revealed a collapsed lung. Crum, who was on TWOB staff, had to remain in the hospital until Friday; he was released just in time to make it to the first performance of the show that night.

Teens were able to enjoy a new workshop titled "Rock and Roll Band" – which the following year morphed into School of Rock. For those 18 and older, After-Hours CACHE returned. Meanwhile, Pritchard Hall, which had housed the Youth Program for several years, was under renovation, so the Youth Staff made do in Slusher Wing. Those who had been at SUUSI in Blacksburg in the 1990s found it nice to play outdoor games once again in the Slusher Quad. Common Ground was back in Slusher Lounge. And for SUUSI's final year at Tech, Owens was again fully available for theme talks and worship services.

Dream expert Jeremy Taylor returned to SUUSI to begin the week's theme talks with a program titled "A Mid-Summer Night's Dream." Friday's theme talk was by UUA Moderator Gini Courter. Evening worship leaders in 2007 included Edward Scott Michael, Tracy Sprowls-Jenks, Bill Neely and Chip Roush.

On Monday afternoon, there was a traditional Community Time (with a "street fair"), but for the remainder of the week, the late-afternoon time period was reframed. Tuesday, a town hall meeting was followed by a Community Concert by Kym Tuvim. Wednesday brought a "play day," while on Thursday, Beaucoup Blue performed another Community Concert. There was no all-community gathering on Friday afternoon. (Participant feedback led to the return of Community Time for the entire week in 2008).

All meals were again in D2, which was open for extended hours to accommodate SUUSI participants. The UUs were asked to eat dinner only between 6:30 and 8:00 p.m., so as not to overlap with the hundreds of incoming freshmen students on campus for their Orientation. Unfortunately, on Wednesday more than 400 SUUSI diners apparently tried to eat before 6:30, creating an impossible bottleneck in D2's stairwell and serving lines. The situation prompted a stern reprimand in the Thursday NUUS, and a complete change in dinnertime on Friday.

It was Friday night that brought what, for many, will long be remembered as the highlight of SUUSI 2007. The final book in the Harry Potter series, "Harry Potter and the Deathly Hallows", was to be released at midnight on Friday – witching hour on SUUSI's very last night at Virginia Tech. Jackie Winner, who had begun volunteering in the Bookstore as a SUUSI first-timer in 1991, and had been in charge of the store since 1993,

took advantage of the rare opportunity to have an actual book release party at SUUSI. All week long, anticipation was building for the denouement of the best-selling book series of all time. Harry Potter fans were dressing in costume, speculating

about possible endings, and staging Quidditch matches on the Quad. During the week the SUUSI NUUS ran several contests, including one for the most creative final sentence for the book (author J.K. Rowling had revealed that the last word was "scar"). Clare Donohue won first prize, a large chocolate frog.

Adding to the excitement was the fact that Friday night's Teen Way Off Broadway, written by TWOB Director Jennifer Sanders, was the perfectly timed "Harriet Potter and the Flaming Chalice." The title role that evening was played by Emily Gonzalez, whose solo was "This Is My Now," by Jordin Sparks. When the unusually late second performance (9:30 curtain) ended and the stage at the Lyric Theatre was struck for the last time, midnight – and the worldwide release of the final Harry Potter book – was fast approaching.

Jackie Winner describes that day:

> Friday afternoon, the shipment of books arrived, and was quickly stashed under a Cloak of Invisibility (OK, so it was really a big black sheet of plastic, but we pretended it was invisible!). The Bookstore closed early for its "transformation." The TWOB performance that year was "Harriet Potter and the Flaming Chalice," which utilized

several witch capes and hats. Janice DeLoach, one of our staff and mother to a cast member, got permission to borrow the costumes after the final performance for the Bookstore staff to wear.

At 11:30 p.m., the Bookstore reopened. There was magic-wand making, and a special reading by Rev. Tom Rhodes of part of one of his sermons [on Harry Potter]. At the stroke of midnight, the Cloak of Invisibility was lifted off the huge pile of "Harry Potter and the Deathly Hallows" books!

Pre-orders were distributed, the few remaining copies sold, and the once-in-a-lifetime magical experience came to a close.

The magical Friday night / Saturday morning of July 20-21, 2007, was a fitting conclusion for SUUSI's second tenure at Virginia Tech. Through 14 different summers, SUUSI had indeed "lived fully" on the large, stately campus in Blacksburg. There had been logistical highs (including two of the largest SUUSIs ever, in the early 1990s) and emotional lows (the tragic shootings of April 16, 2007). SUUSI had experienced many changes – in organizational structure, in the use of technology, in camper expectations about creature comforts (air conditioning and the like), in round-the-clock programming. New traditions had been added. A new generation of SUUSI leaders had experienced the SUUSI magic for the first time at Blacksburg, and were now familiar faces.

But as the Closing Circle concluded on Saturday morning, few were looking back. There was excitement and hope in the air, as participants bid goodbye for another 12 months, and told one another, "I'll see you in Radford." Business-card size refrigerator magnets were distributed to everyone, which listed the date, location, theme, website and email contact information for the next SUUSI. The theme for 2008, appropriately enough, would be "Pilgrimage."

A Pilgrimage Back to Radford (2008)

Though SUUSI was quite familiar with Radford, many things felt fresh and new the next summer when the community made its pilgrimage to the smaller campus just 15 miles southwest of Blacksburg. As folks arrived on July 20, 2008, they found that Adams Street, which had once run outside the Governors Quad, was no more. They were directed to check-in at the Bonnie Hurlburt Student Center, a new state-of-the-art facility that had opened three years earlier. "The Bonnie," as it was called, replaced Heth as the center of SUUSI activity. In addition to Sunday's check-in, the Info Office, the Registration Office, the Artisan's Bazaar and the SUUSI Bookstore – as well as evening musical performances and CACHE – took place at The Bonnie.

The beloved Governors Quad itself had been landscaped, much of its grass replaced with sidewalks and a central, brick meeting area with metal benches. The dorms themselves were now air conditioned and renovated. WiFi was available all over campus. Peters Gym had undergone a complete makeover, and there was now a soon-to-be-very-popular indoor climbing wall. Teens loved their space in Bolling, especially the remodeled, air conditioned basement lounge.

Dalton Food Court had also been upgraded. Though vegetarians were delighted at the quality and variety of their choices, thanks in part to the presence of a nationally recognized vegetarian chef on staff, parents of smaller children, as well as the elderly, were less than pleased with one particular change at Dalton. Trays were no longer provided. And everyone was dismayed when the soft serve ice cream machine went out on Monday – a problem that would continue to plague Dalton for years to come.

Fees for SUUSI 2008 had actually been reduced (by $15 for adults, to $450 with air conditioning and $410 without). There was a $50 discount for people who registered by May 17 – and online registration was once again fully available. Demand for air conditioned rooms was so high that late in the spring, those rooms were sold out. Come SUUSI, there were 257 non-A/C rooms in use by participants. Overall attendance was up by nearly a hundred from 2007, as the final number of "pilgrims" for SUUSI's return to Radford reached 1,064.

In his Director's letter inviting participants to SUUSI 2008, Devin Gordon wrote, "SUUSI is a holy place for me – one to which I journey each year. It's also like a home, with each successive year reminiscent of a homecoming. I've long considered my trips to SUUSI every July as a pilgrimage. Yes, SUUSI is a place of great fun for me ... but it's also a sacred, spiritual place."

For the first time, participants could sign up to be part of a covenant group, a smaller group of 6-8 people who would meet once a day to share their experiences with one another, explore spirituality and life questions, and create the kind of deeper connections that can often be lost in a community of a thousand members. Through the work of Morris Hudgins, SUUSI had received a grant from the UUA to offer a two-year pilot program for covenant groups in a UU camp and conference setting. In 2007 at Blacksburg, Hudgins had helped train group facilitators, and at Radford the next year those facilitators, under the direction of Rev. Marti Keller from the UU Congregation of Atlanta, led six SUUSI Covenant Groups.

The groups met from 6-7 p.m. Monday through Friday, while each group's co-facilitators met with Keller earlier in the day. The intention was not only to provide a meaningful experience for members of the SUUSI community who had signed up, but also – in the spirit of the original Summer Institutes' leadership training programs – to send back to local UU congregations skilled, experienced covenant group facilitators. It seemed to work; facilitators and participants alike raved about the process.

The "Pilgrimage" theme provided a spiritual focus to many other aspects of SUUSI community life. Some began the week with a Monday morning silent walk at nearby Wildwood Park. Back on campus, Jan Taddeo, a fifth-generation Unitarian Universalist and seminary student at Meadville-Lombard Theological School, arranged for a room on the first floor of Floyd to be open, 24/7, for silent meditation and contemplation. Dim lighting, soothing music, comfortable seating, finger labyrinths and other tools made the meditation room an ideal place to spend a few quiet, centering moments, night or day, amid the hustle and bustle of SUUSI.

Taddeo had been coming to SUUSI for more than a decade, and shared what the experience meant to her in a Monday night worship service titled "Sacred Places":

> SUUSI is a sacred place for me. When my husband, Russ, and I were finally persuaded by our good friend Sharon Harrell to take our family vacation to a UU summer camp, we were dubious that it would ever live up to the sky-high expectations she offered in her enthusiastic descriptions. How could any place, event or community be that great?
>
> But it didn't take long for us to be convinced. Russ says he thinks one of the startling things about this place is that as soon as people arrive here, especially for the first time, they find that their normal outer layers of protection – the way we guard ourselves when we are among strangers in a new community – have dissipated, without effort and [even] without awareness of the transition as it happens.
>
> This is one of the effects of what is affectionately referred to as "SUUSI magic."

Similar testimonials were offered by other clergy and lay leaders throughout the week. On Thursday morning Chip Roush, a minister from Michigan – who also offered a workshop that week on "The Spirituality of the Grateful Dead" – gave a theme talk titled "What a Long Strange Trip It's Been," in which he shared about his own experience as a SUUSI newcomer the previous summer.

The other theme speakers in 2008 were Rebecca Parker, President of the Starr King School for the Ministry in Berkeley, Calif., Alison Miller, minister in Morristown, N.J.; Gail

Geisenheimer, minister in Vero Beach, Fla.; and Anthony David, minister at UUCA in Atlanta. For the first time, all the theme talks were later made available by podcast.

Peter Morales, a minister from Golden, Colo., who was then a candidate for President of the UUA, visited SUUSI on Thursday, meeting participants that afternoon at Community Time in the Governors Quad.

It was also a strong year for music. Amy Carol Webb wedded music and ministry at the Thursday night transitions worship service. Concert Hour

Candidate Peter Morales speaks to an afternoon crowd in the Governors Quad

performers included Tret Fure, Greg Greenway and Alastair Moock. Thursday night brought the School of Rock to the Porterfield stage for the first time, starting a brand new, high-energy SUUSI musical tradition.

Nature presented a number of popular tours, including trips to the Blacksnake Meadery, the Foggy Ridge Cidery, Chateau Morrisette Winery, the "Art Galleries of Floyd, Virginia," and a "Historic Churches Tour." Those seeking a more adventurous day trip could, on Monday, travel to Bozoo, W.Va., for an "Introduction to Rock Climbing, Rappelling and Ascending Extravaganza." For families, Nature Staff arranged a Monday afternoon "Family Friendly Flotilla," which was described in the catalog as "a creative ad-lib trip [in which] we could squirt/splash each other, or maybe toss a frisbee or some other plaything while we meander down the river... There will be a staffer in a kayak riding along as a retriever/herdsman/referee-type person. The required stuff to bring: big smiles, funny hats and water-squirting devices..."

The Youth and Nature staffs coordinated their services, with Youth Staff providing morning child care for parent participants who were going on adult-only nature trips. This service was only available to those who had pre-registered for it online. The Youth Program was housed in Moffett, at the far corner of the campus, and was once again led by Youth Director Dianna MacPherson. The 11-12s enjoyed a special trip to Claytor Lake on Friday morning, before everyone gathered on Moffett Quad for Friday afternoon's Closing Circle, which featured age-group goodbyes and big-group sharing and songs, as well as the now-traditional "Cups" demonstration by the 13-year-olds and skits and performances by popular SUUSI and youth musicians.

Medians in 2008 had the choice of such workshops as a "High-Tech Scavenger Hunt," "Geekercize," "Brews for UUs" and the ever-popular Median Meet-and-Greet. A tango workshop on Thursday night (9:30 p.m. to 1:00 a.m.) had the following description in that day's NUUS: "It Takes Two. Trinkle Basement. Hardwood floors. Leather bottom shoes, or socks. Hot music. Dramatic flair. Rose between teeth. Let it be."

Workshop Coordinator Torie Camp included several food-related workshops in that year's very diverse program. There were Truffles. There was Garnish 101, Chocolate 101, Chocolate and Sugar Eggs, and Cake Decorating. And BBQUUsi found a happy home in Radford, where the wee-hours cookout took up residence next to the fountain between Heth and Muse. The fountain itself quickly became a popular meeting spot for younger participants.

The lawn behind Heth was also the location for the fifth-annual Family Movie Night, though the showing of that year's selection, *Charlotte's Web*, had to be postponed until Thursday due to a powerful rain and hail storm that swept through Radford late Wednesday.

A number of logistical issues made for some headaches the first year back at Radford. As is often the case, many spaces that had been expected were unavailable. Even more frustrating, early in the week some workshop leaders arrived at their workshop locations only to discover the doors were locked. Campus security scrambled to unlock first one door, then another – sometimes not arriving until up to an hour after the scheduled starting time of the workshop. The elevator in Madison was out of service on Sunday, making move-in – not to mention reaching the Madison Penthouse, where Common Ground was being held – problematic for all, and impossible for those with accessibility needs. The elevator was not fixed until Wednesday night.

However, thanks to the diligent and dedicated efforts of two particular Radford University Conference Services employees, Bobby Harris and Alicia Morris, "a majority of the problems were resolved by the end of the week," said Director Devin Gordon. The pair made themselves available round the clock, providing their home and cell phone numbers to SUUSI Staff and remaining on call throughout the week, earning SUUSI's undying gratitude and affection.

Lindsay Bennett-Jacobs, Teen Director at the time, recalls the pair's impact on the SUUSI community, particularly those in the Teen Program. "Bobby and Alicia were amazing resources to us in our first two years back at Radford. They constantly went above and beyond the call of duty to make sure we had what we needed, and they integrated themselves into the community like they had been coming to SUUSI all their lives," she says. "Some of my favorite memories include them performing participatory songs at the first Teen Coffeehouse, held at about 2 a.m. in 2008, and then Bobby's goofy getup during Drag Night in 2009. Bobby was even immortalized in TWOB... The teens and staff all loved them, and they made my job easier every day. They [became] some of the dearest friends I could have asked for."

One seemingly irreconcilable issue at Radford in 2008 concerned Serendipity. SUUSI's nightly adult dance party had been placed in Cook Hall, a somewhat remote space at the edge of campus that was not at all conducive to the kind of energy Serendipity generates. To make matters worse, police officers were stationed just outside the doors each night, giving some participants the feeling that they were running a gauntlet just to enter the building. Certain outlandish costumes, long a SUUSI Serendipity tradition, resulted in less-than-positive interactions between individual police officers and SUUSI revelers. Many participants felt harassed by some of the security guards – and as the week wore on, the tone of their exchanges deteriorated. Eventually, according to the year-end report, "at least one participant was arrested who should not have been."

Perhaps some of the difficulties of 2008 were inevitable. For one thing, SUUSI had not been at Radford in nine years. Facilities had changed, and there had been personnel turnover in both the administrative and service staffs. It is likely that local security officers were already on edge, given the size of SUUSI's crowd, and its reputation for excessive exuberance.

Ultimately, though, most participants were either unaffected or unfazed by the challenges the SUUSI Staff experienced that year, and in the end, the week was deemed a huge success. Though there was some talk about continuing to look for a new SUUSI location, when they were polled, the Core Staff was nearly unanimous in their praise for the new facilities at Radford, for the cooperation of RU personnel in working out logistical problems, and for the comfort they, and participants, largely felt on the Radford campus. The 2009 dates, theme and location – Radford – were announced on Friday, and at Saturday's Closing Circle, Director-Elect Jerry King invited participants to return the following year and "Rekindle the Flame Within."

Back home the next day – Sunday, July 27, 2008 – SUUSI participants were stunned to learn of the tragic shooting, that morning, in the sanctuary at the Tennessee Valley UU Church in Knoxville. The SUUSI community joined Unitarian Universalists across the nation in mourning and shock, reaching out to those in Knoxville (some of whom had been at SUUSI just one day earlier) and sharing their grief with one another on Facebook and the suusi-friends listserv. The gunman, James David Adkisson, had attended SUUSI briefly, in the mid-1990s, along with his then-wife, Liza Alexander, who was a former member of the Knoxville church. In a manifesto found by police, Adkisson cited a hatred for liberals as motivation for the shooting.

The attack – which happened shortly before the Sunday service while several children were on the stage rehearsing a scene from the musical "Annie," which they were about to perform for the congregation – left two people dead and eight injured. For Unitarian Universalists everywhere, including long-time SUUSI participants, the pain, fear and soul-searching would last until the next summer, and well beyond.

At Home Again (2009-2012)

Chris Buice, the minister in Knoxville, gave the first theme talk on Monday morning that next July. Speaking to an emotional, standing-room only audience in Porterfield, he told of the suffering – and the healing – his congregation had experienced in the previous 12 months. His talk, titled "Lift Every Voice and Sing: Seeking a Spirituality of Transformation," began with Buice's declaration, "Rain falls on both the just and the unjust. Spirituality is our attitude toward the weather."

Buice went on to tell the stories of various people in the Knoxville congregation whose faithful and heroic actions in the seconds after the first shot was fired saved many lives, and transformed countless others. He told of John Bohstedt, a Vietnam War era conscientious objector, who wrestled the shooter to the ground. He told of religious education volunteer Ann Snyder, who was holding a copy of the "Annie" script at the time of the shooting. The pages, Buice said, were riddled with bullets, but Snyder was thankfully unharmed, and acted quickly to shield and usher all the children to safety.

Buice also shared about the past 12 months of transformation, in his own life and in that of his congregation. He told of "Tammy Sommers, a mother of two small kids, [who] was injured badly that day. She was in a coma, and I did not even recognize her when I saw her in the hospital," he said. "It was six months before she could go back to work. I remember the day she walked back into that sanctuary for the first time... A miracle in the New Testament is Jesus walking on water; a miracle in my lifetime has been watching Tammy Sommers and others walk into that sanctuary without bitterness or resentment or anger, but overflowing with gratitude for life..."

There were few dry eyes in the Porterfield Auditorium by the time Buice had finished. That theme talk set the tone for the SUUSI week – one of reverence and deep appreciation for the blessings of life, and of SUUSI. The week concluded, on a similar note, with Teen Way Off Broadway's production of "Andy," a TWOB takeoff on "Annie." Aware of the symbolic significance of the selection of that particular show, co-writers Michael and Emily Ivey said in the SUUSI NUUS on Wednesday morning:

> We had selected "Annie" as our source for the show more than a year ago, and even dropped a hint at the very end of last year's TWOB. As we were driving home from SUUSI, Emily hard at work on the first draft on the laptop, we heard the horrible news of the shooting at the Knoxville church, during [their] children's performance of "Annie."
>
> Our immediate thought was to choose something else for TWOB. [But] as we heard of the response from the Knoxville community, and the wider network of UU friends and family, we realized that the message of this show was important. When we heard about the church coming together to finish the show, and joining in singing [the theme song] "Tomorrow" together, we knew we'd stick to the plan and bring "Annie" to the SUUSI stage.
>
> This is a show about hope. This is a show about finding your home, and where you belong. This is a show about the endless possibilities that the future holds. In many

ways, this is a show about SUUSI, and we're delighted to have adapted it for this audience.

Heeding Chris Buice's charge, given just four days earlier from the same stage, another packed house in Porterfield lifted every voice and sang along with the TWOB cast during the "Tomorrow" finale Friday night. Once again, tears flowed freely. The show proved to be the perfect bookend, complementing Buice's start-of-the-week theme talk.

The week also included a powerful mid-week worship experience led by charismatic Maryland minister John Crestwell on Wednesday. Peter Morales, now UUA President, returned to SUUSI to offer Friday morning's theme talk, and Alison Miller of New Jersey led a moving Thursday night Transitions Service. Director Jerry King, in his post-SUUSI report to the Board, declared that the year's "theme talk and worship leaders were super."

Covenant groups and a meditation room were once again offered in 2009, giving participants a space in which to process both joys and sorrows. A labyrinth was available for the first time in several years, located just outside of Jefferson. There were eight different yoga workshops to choose from; one even encouraged parents and children to come dressed in their pajamas for a gentle 8 p.m. "bedtime" practice.

Other workshops ranged from bookbinding to couponing to Kabbalah. There were seven different workshops focused on singing or songwriting, while folks were able to explore their interest in fabrics and creativity with programs on crocheting (both introductory and advanced), knitting, spindle-spinning yarn and dyeing yarn.

Despite such homespun offerings, SUUSI was becoming a brave new world. During the year, the Winter NUUS had touted the many different online ways to "stay in touch with the SUUSI community year-round." There were email groups like the suusi-friends listserv, and two groups dedicated, respectively, to teens and

Bubble fun in the Governors Quad

young adults. By now, Facebook was perhaps the primary means of social networking for SUUSI-goers of all ages, and multiple SUUSI Facebook groups had been created. One could choose to follow SUUSI on Twitter and Flickr. It should be noted that 2009 also marked the first time Skype was used during TWOB; Michael and Emily Ivey were able to view the show they had written, live, from their home in south Alabama.

The offerings in 2009 reflected these transformations in the way human beings were now interacting. One workshop highlighted "Second Life," which is described on its website as a "3D virtual world where users can socialize, connect and create." Participants learned that there is actually a Unitarian Universalist Congregation of the Second Life. Teenagers through the middle-aged brought their latest video-game obsession, Guitar Hero, with them to SUUSI; there were multiple Guitar Hero tournaments, including an official one coordinated as a workshop. The YA lounge was alive every night with players strumming their plastic guitars.

Youth Program closing circle

For those who liked their music more raw and real, School of Rock made a triumphant return to the Porterfield stage on Thursday night, solidifying that week-long workshop's place as a SUUSI institution. "Bring your friends, cameras and earplugs – and get there early, 'cause last year it was standing room only," touted the SUUSI NUUS. On the quieter front, Monday night's "Acoustic Late-Night Revival" featured a stellar lineup, with Greg Greenway, Pat Wictor, Ellen Buckstel, Mindy Simmons and more. Wishing Chair performed at Concert Hour on Monday.

Serendipity experienced a resurgence in popularity as participants found their way to a new location – the lower level of Muse Hall – to dance to tunes spun primarily by an array of guest DJs. Thursday night's theme, "Prom Gone Wrong," was shared by both Serendipity and CACHE, resulting in a great display of costumes in the basement lobby that connected the two dance venues.

Nature had to adjust to the cancellation of all its caving trips due to an outbreak of White-Nose Syndrome, a disease that over the course of the next couple of years would kill roughly 6 million American bats. Nature Co-Directors Stephanie Lowenhaupt and Randy Walther explained the situation in the SUUSI NUUS and in a Thursday night information session in the Peery basement. Additional hikes and several new trips were offered to help fill out the Nature Program. By now, many participants had discovered the indoor climbing wall in Peters Gym. The well-appointed workout room across the hall was also made available to SUUSI registrants.

The SUUSI NUUS offered a daily dose of regional trivia in 2009, with questions related to soft drinks (they're all called "Coke" in the Southeast) and the correct pronunciation of "Appalachian." There were also humorous articles seeking to help participants find various events and locations. In addition to the change in venue for Serendipity, many other major SUUSI events were not in the same place they had been the previous summer. Hurlburt was only available for check-in. Cabaret had been moved to Porterfield, and the Bookstore, which originally had been slated for Peters, eventually ended up in an obscure location, Room 223 of McGuffey. Regardless, the store managed to sell out of 2009 logo T-shirts, and offered to take orders and ship shirts to participants later in the summer.

The NUUS reported on how to "Break the Code" of signage around campus: Signs that were colored "electric pollen yellow" directed participants to morning events, while "Tibetan monk-meets-dayglo-disco orange" signified afternoon events. "Rekindling the Red" signs (a play on the year's theme "Rekindling the Flame Within") meant evening events. Signs colored "Florida key lime green" were reserved for those "wacky events that refuse to be stuck with a single time period."

The NUUS also brought this testimonial from Bonnie Gramlich, on Tuesday morning:

Have you ever had the experience of finally being at your beach vacation and stepping with bare feet onto the soft, warm sand? Or maybe putting your feet into the water of a beautiful swimming pool and finding the feel and the temperature just right, and so inviting [that] you plunge on in with a big, luxuriant body sigh? Ahhhh....

That's how it feels, along with some bit of surreal feeling, for me to be back at SUUSI after an unwanted 11-year absence. Just wonderful!

A heartfelt thank you to SUUSI, and all who are and have been working hard to make this week possible... I'm so ready, and so grateful.

Among those who deserved thanks for working hard, behind the scenes, to make SUUSI 2009 happen was the Board of Trustees. A drastic economic downturn the previous fall had shattered the economy, sending America and global markets into a major recession – and prompting Radford to issue what the March 2009 Board minutes called a "bombshell." The university not only proposed to raise fees by 15 percent, but it wanted SUUSI to pay its full costs, up front, within 90 days – even before SUUSI 2009 had taken place. The Board noted that although "this seems reasonable, with the economy," paying in full, up front, would leave SUUSI itself in a precarious financial position. Negotiations resulted in Radford lowering its demand to a $50,000 deposit (non-refundable, should SUUSI not take place that year).

But despite the financial crisis that had affected the lives of each and every American, there was never any question that SUUSI would continue. When July rolled around, attendance fell by less than three dozen compared to the prior year. Thanks to small operating surpluses from the previous two SUUSIs, the Board even was able to keep registration fees unchanged from the year before. Though the same cannot be said for many families, SUUSI itself survived the Great Recession relatively unscathed, and the 2009 edition of the community exuded a remarkable sense of strength and resilience – in the face of not only the Knoxville tragedy, but also the economic crisis.

By 2010, attendance was even up slightly, to 1,046. Among those present was an unusually large number of new participants, some of whom may have been attracted to SUUSI via YouTube, where a SUUSI promotional video had been uploaded during the year. Past attendees were encouraged, when the Winter NUUS arrived in their mailboxes, to be patient: "If you're longing for that third week of July, when the world feels at peace and time seems to stand still, hang in there! SUUSI is just around the corner." When registration at last opened in April, knowing veterans were delighted to discover that many of the required permission and release forms (which it had previously been necessary to print out, sign and mail in) could now be "signed" electronically. Check-in, on July 20 at Cook Hall, was streamlined accordingly.

The theme in 2010, "Beyond Tomorrow," had a dual purpose – functioning during the year to help SUUSI regulars look forward to the annual reunion in Radford, while also creating, during SUUSI week itself, an awareness of the history and traditions of the now 60-year-old Summer Institute. Theme talk topics such as "Developing the Faith of Tomorrow," "New Stories for Times Beyond Tomorrow," "Stewards of a Sacred Place" and "Great Expectations" were reminiscent of some of those in the 1950s and 1960s, as first Unitarians and later Unitarian Universalists struggled to find their place in a complex and changing world. Workshops, too, had titles like "Embracing Your Next Chapter," in which participants explored both life after retirement and alternatives to retirement.

At Ingathering 2010, "Beyond Tomorrow," Michael Tino greets a visitor from the future.

Nearly a dozen workshops

focused on spirituality. Sarah Lammert facilitated "Exploring Spiritual Practice" and Bill Neely led "Sacred Reading." Shelley Graf gathered "Women Singing in Sacred Circle." On Thursday afternoon, a "Conscious Convergence" invited SUUSI-goers to participate in an ongoing "worldwide meditation" for peace, goodwill and global unity.

As always, many found their spiritual path outdoors, some watching birds as either a "Morning Bird" or "Not an Early Bird." Nature offered nine different canoe trips, four kayaking trips, four biking excursions and both 5K and 10K "River Runs" overlooking Claytor Lake (the runs were in addition to the annual Fun Run near campus). There was a new hike, to Chamberlain Trail, and an all-day "Two Cliffs Endurance Hike" with a stop at beautiful Warspur Overlook and, later in the day, a picnic dinner around a campfire at Wind Rock.

A generous spirit of giving back pervaded the week, as participants took part in a Red Cross blood drive. SUUSIships, which each year provide scholarship-type financial assistance for individual attendees and families who might otherwise not be able to afford SUUSI, benefitted from auctions and raffles that included prizes like a hand-woven SUUSI afghan and a set of SUUSI "Home Brews." A donation designed to jump-start a SUUSI Endowment Fund was presented to the Board at the beginning of the week.

High temperatures regularly hit in the 90s in 2010 – much to the chagrin of almost half the SUUSI population, which found itself without air conditioning. The traditional quadrangle of Peery, Floyd, Stuart and Trinkle – 600 beds in all – was the only living space with A/C available to SUUSI in 2010. Jefferson and Madison were being remodeled, and all the other air conditioned dorms were allotted to the Governor's School for the Arts. Thus families and the Youth Program were back in Moffett. Dianna MacPherson was wrapping up a five-year stint as Youth Director, while Torie Camp helped coordinate an unusually large Child Care Co-Op.

During their workshop time, SUUSI youngsters could make "SUUSI wreaths" or "UU prayer beads," friendship bracelets or marble speedways. Outdoors, they could tie-dye, play croquet, throw frisbee or geocache. A special workshop co-sponsored with Nature called "Messing with Boats" promised, "This will be a really fun trip with super-cool and really fantastic instructors. Learn safety, the buddy system, and the paddling basics of tandem canoeing." Friday's Youth Closing Circle was a sweet celebration not only of the week, but of MacPherson's long and much-appreciated service as Youth Director.

Teen Director Lindsay Bennett-Jacobs and her staff empowered more than a hundred teens to create a safe, meaningful and memorable week. On Monday in the Teen Dorm there was a "mandatory intimacy chat – an informative and entertaining presentation about life in the teen community ... including a conversation about what intimate behaviors are appropriate at SUUSI, how to handle life in intensive community, and who teens can talk to if they have any questions or concerns during the week." Touch groups, a teen version of covenant groups, met twice each day to give the teens an opportunity for sharing and activities in a peer-led small group of roughly a dozen participants. Teen touch groups, with creative names like the Flaming Mohawks, Dumbledore's Militia and Operation Reptar-Lazer even had their group pictures appear in the mugbook.

Ballroom dancing, which for many years had been a mainstay of the SUUSI program, made its return, kicking off Serendipity for an hour each night from 9-10 p.m. Dancers enjoyed honing their skills at the foxtrot, waltz, rumba and more. Hooping made a splash at SUUSI in 2010. At night, hoops could be found on the dance floor, while in the daytime, participants were able to select workshops such as "Hooping for Health" and "Fundamentals of Hoop Dance."

Workshop Coordinator Jenian Gebeaux, however, was left juggling an inordinate number of space changes. The Monday NUUS reported that "Many, many workshop locations have had to change at the last minute – so many that we couldn't print them all in the NUUS... Pick up a new workshop schedule in the cafeteria or the Info Office. SUUSI Staff apologizes for the inconvenience." A new family friendly Casino Night had been slated for a larger space, but had to be held in a small room in the basement of Heth, with the crowd sometimes spilling out into the hallway. While no money changed hands, players of all ages enjoyed blackjack, Texas Hold 'Em, bingo and more.

Sophia Taylor sings a solo during TWOB 2010, "SUUSI the 13th."

With both a large group from the Governor's School and all of SUUSI attempting to eat at Dalton at the same time, mealtime crowds taxed the patience of participants. The food, on the other hand, received rave reviews. The Dalton staff was exemplary. Dalton Dining Hall Director and Head Chef Brian Mann, in particular, made a name for himself among SUUSI diners for his calm and creativity as he skillfully balanced the special requests of those who needed low fat, vegan or gluten-free meals, while providing a variety of entrees that went well above and beyond the typical college cafeteria fare. At the same time, RU reported that studies had shown "a drastic decrease in electric and water usage and significant decrease in the amount of customer-produced waste" since it had eliminated the use of trays in Dalton.

Concert Hour featured spirited and joyful singer and storyteller Reggie Harris. On Tuesday night, the headliners were an eclectic group of young SUUSI musicians who gave their own meaning to the theme "Beyond Tomorrow." The New SUUSI Revue: The Next Generation of SUUSI Stars included talented young performers like Ned Durrett, Emily Gonzalez, Sarah Gonzalez, Angel Wall and Jennifer Teeter, who proved that the musical future of SUUSI was not only "beyond tomorrow," but right now as well.

Ask anyone who attended SUUSI the following year what they remember most about SUUSI 2011, and the answer is invariably a single word: "Fireworks!" Jake Walther, a long-time SUUSI participant and professional pyrotechnician, designed and coordinated a Wednesday night fireworks display that left all of SUUSI – as well as the surrounding Radford community – buzzing for days. Thanks to the fact that Moffett was closed for major building construction on that end of the Radford campus, Walther was able to arrange for SUUSI's first-ever fireworks show – and to give participants an unusually close front-row seat for the action.

The mid-week gala was one of the most highly anticipated SUUSI events in memory. Publicity, word of mouth – and strategically placed collection jars (to help defray the cost of the pyrotechnics) – served to build excitement, and on Wednesday evening, the SUUSI community began gathering early in the north end of Moffett Quad, between Ingles

SUUSI's first fireworks display

and Pocahontas, rolling out beach blankets and lawn chairs and creating a festive, family friendly, holiday atmosphere. Shortly after dark, the first fireworks began to shoot skyward as cheers and squeals of delight erupted from young and old alike. As with any good fireworks show, the display gradually grew in size, intensity and color, even including special SUUSI touches like what appeared to be a large chalice and a "UU."

As one young person squealed, "It felt like the fireworks were right in my lap!" Indeed, few had ever been as close to a large fireworks display. Another person who was there said, "The fireworks were the perfect expression of SUUSI 'Joy'!"

"Joy!" was Director Wendell Putney theme for SUUSI 2011. In his Director's letter in the catalog, Putney spoke for many who have lived a significant portion of their lives as part of the SUUSI community:

> I'd like to share with you how SUUSI has meant Joy in our family's life for over 30 years... My wife and I were introduced to SUUSI by a fellow church member in 1980, and we have been coming almost every year since then.
>
> Right away, we saw this as a place where we could each explore and expand our individual interests in ways we couldn't at home. At SUUSI I learned to slog through caves, rappel down rock outcroppings, and handle myself in tubes, canoes, kayaks and rafts in rushing mountain waters. Phoenix spent her days hiking, attending various workshops, and playing tennis. Together, we enjoyed the rich nightlife experience at Serendipity and Cabaret. We made lots of friends, many of whom we still see every year at SUUSI.
>
> When our son Bing was born, our SUUSI experience entered a new phase: minivan, nursery care, childcare cooperative, air mattress on the floor, and on through Youth, Teen, and Young Adult Programs. We shared his joy as the community helped to nurture his growing humanity and spirituality, and before we knew it he was an independent adult, out in the world trying to earn a living. He longs to return to SUUSI, as I'm sure he will when his circumstances allow.
>
> We are now a part of the "mature adult" contingent at SUUSI. My joy now is in being able to give back to the community...

More than 1,100 people accepted Putney's invitation to experience the joy of SUUSI 2011. Back at "The Bonnie" after a year at Cook Hall, the Sunday arrival and check-in process flowed more smoothly than ever. Registration and Housing Coordinator Gary Gonzalez oversaw a large, helpful staff that efficiently guided participants through the arrival process. Participants were even provided with biodegradable nametag holders, and encouraged to "put them in your compost" after returning home.

Once again, SUUSI was sharing the Radford campus with the Governor's School, and there were just 405 air conditioned beds available. By the end of the week, temperatures were in the mid to upper 90s, but the community made the best of it, expanding what had originally been "Water Day" at Community Time on Monday to multiple long afternoons and evenings of water play.

The closure of Moffett put the Youth Program, led by new Youth Director Jane Peavy (formerly Sanders), back in Washington. Workshops for the children included "Myth Busters," miming, pretzel-making and finger labyrinths. Kids were even able to design and dye their own tapestries. Adult workshops, meanwhile, were particularly eclectic in 2011. There was an "Introduction to Blogging" and a "Guided Reading of Homer's 'The Odyssey'." One could play either "Killer Sudoku" or Scrabble; learn about "Hip-Hop History" or spend "An Afternoon with Woody Guthrie;" express joy through "Ecstatic Dance" or meditate through "Dances of Universal Peace." "Gender Crosstalk" sessions allowed participants to learn more about how the opposite sex thinks through a "fishbowl" process that encouraged honest discussion within a safe environment.

Though caving was still off the program, Nature Staff Co-Directors Randy Walther and Amy Davis provided an equally eclectic array of offerings. A hands-on day of service helping the Nature Conservancy of Virginia at the Falls Creek Preserve, and an educational workshop on the Conservancy's Headwaters of the Roanoke Project appealed to SUUSI environmentalists. Adventure trips ranged from the easygoing "Cascades for Slowpokes" to the excitement of bouldering. Participants could tour a local water processing plant ("From the River to the Tap") or do gravestone rubbings at a nearby cemetery.

By popular demand, an extra "Silent Cascades" trip was added for those of a more meditative bent. The traditional naked-eye night of stargazing was augmented by views from a large telescope during a tour of the Selu Observatory, just four miles from campus, led by RU physics professor and observatory director Jack Brockway. Meanwhile, baseball enthusiasts and fans of Americana could spend an evening at the local minor league baseball park, taking in a Pulaski Mariners game after enjoying a pre-game cookout.

For dancers, Serendipity 2011 added a new program called "Serendipity Special," from 9:00-10:30 p.m., with a different flavor each night. Tuesday was "Smooth" (foxtrot, waltz), Wednesday was "Swing" (East and West Coast, jive), and Thursday was "Latin" (rumba, cha-cha and salsa). Friday was set aside solely for the highly popular tango. Later each night, Serendipity had a theme hour from 11:00 to midnight, with 80s music highlighting Sunday night, and country on Monday. Motown, hip-hop and other genres filled out the remainder of the week. Throughout the week, the Serendipity and CACHE themes were coordinated, so that participants over the age of 21 could move back and forth across the lower level of Muse "in costume." Current events served as the basis for most themes. Monday night was "Glee," Tuesday night was "Royal Wedding" (Britain's Prince William and Kate Middleton had been married that April), and on Friday "Twilight" brought more than one vampire or victim out into the night.

Late Night at Common Ground was divided into two spaces in 2011 – the Common Ground Listening Room, for singers, songwriters, instrumentalists and jamming, and the Common Ground Sing-Along Room, for group singing and poetry readings. Concert Hour featured Gary Gonzalez, Don White and David Roth. Then on Thursday night, right after Tracy Sprowls-Jenks' moving transitions worship service, it was "The Next Generation of SUUSI Stars Meets School of Rock."

A pick-up choir was formed by Miriam Davidson, which

sang at worship services late in the week. "Creating a New Earth," organized by Phoenix Harmony Putney, gave the entire community an opportunity for mid-day meditation. Participants could drop in to the outdoor gathering between lunchtime and afternoon workshops as SUUSI ministers and leaders offered centering practices designed both to ground and refresh the individual, and to "heal and transform the planet."

A SUUSI Singles Group formed following an initial meeting at Common Ground Cafe on Monday evening. Later in the week, participants met for dinner together at Dalton, held a discussion group, and then on Friday night danced together at Serendipity. As for couples at SUUSI 2011, Phil and Linda Sterner invited participants to celebrate their "25 years of joy and marriage" in a reception at Muse following Wednesday night's fireworks.

The NUUS began publishing daily haikus, including this one from SUUSI "nUUbi" Linda Shuee of Greensboro:

> I'm feeling welcome
> A part of the joy and fun
> Our hearts beat as one

Meanwhile, SUUSI was continuing to mature technologically. Director Wendell Putney had created a new Core Staff position, "Technology Services," which was ably handled by Wilson Farrell. "You cannot underestimate or understate the effect of technology on the SUUSI experience over the years," Putney says. "Phone calls and snail mail were quite time consuming. Computers and cell phones changed everything, and now – with SOLIS and online registration – institutionally, we are so much more efficient. Wilson, Devin [Gordon], Gary [Jackoway] – we owe a lot to those guys."

The Monday edition of the SUUSI NUUS – though it was still being distributed the old-fashioned way, on paper – included a front-page article about the first SUUSI "app," complete with QR code:

Now you can download an electronic version of the 2011 SUUSI catalog (complete with event descriptions, meeting locations and maps) to your Android Smartphone. Share workshops, nature trips and other event info with friends  via Facebook, Twitter or email. You can even export your entire schedule or look up the latest listings for age-related programming: youth, YA or medians. The app is available on Android Market Place, and all donations support SUUSIships. Just use your Android to scan the QR code above.

Jake Walther and Jackson

Tuesday morning's worship service, led by Erika Hewitt, provided participants with a multi-media experience. Author of the UU worship collection "Story, Song and Spirit," Hewitt wove together storytelling, imagination and striking visual images of the Earth and outer space that were projected on a large screen above the stage. Other worship leaders in 2011 (both the morning and evening community gatherings in Porterfield were now being called "worship") included David Carl Olson, Amy Carol Webb and Michael Tino.

On Friday, SUUSI's creativity was on display on the au bon

pain side of Dalton Dining Hall, where an art exhibit consisting of paintings, drawings and craft projects from a variety of SUUSI workshops was arranged for diners to enjoy. Also by week's end, contributions to the "Fireworks Fund" had more than exceeded Jake Walther's costs, and there was talk of having another fireworks show the next year.

Teen Way Off Broadway celebrated its 25th performance with a TWOB Reunion on Thursday night in the Norwood Lounge. Dozens of Teen Way Off Broadway alumni gathered to reminisce while looking through old photographs, playbills and a complete collection of the previous 24 TWOB T-shirts. The teens' production on Friday night was called "SUUSI Street," based on the popular children's television show "Sesame Street." Charles Sterner and Keenan Gladd-Brown starred as Bert and Ernie, respectively.

Earlier that day, the NUUS reported that the SUUSI Board had created an Endowment Fund – an action 20 years in the making:

> Was this a meaningful, transformative week for you? Do you want to assure that future generations will be able to have the same experience?
>
> This week, the Board established the SUUSI Endowment Fund, "to provide for SUUSI in perpetuity." Acting on a recommendation from the 1991 SUUSI Vision Committee, a fund has been established to guarantee there will always be a SUUSI, while allowing for the stable generation of income to help future SUUSI-ites with unforeseen capital needs, leadership development and educational outreach. Gifts of stock, cash, bequests, life insurance policies, etc., are fully tax deductible.
>
> The Endowment Fund already has nearly $2,000 in it! For more information on how you can contribute to our future, email treasurer@suusi.org.

Director Wendell Putney chose as the following year's theme

"Look to This Day," from the Kalidasa poem: "Look to this day, for it is life, the very life of life. In its brief course lie all the verities and realities of your existence. ... Today, well-lived, makes yesterday a dream of happiness, and every tomorrow a vision of hope."

The Arrival NUUS for Sunday, July 15, 2012 proclaimed, "Yes! This is the day! SUUSI welcomes you with open arms and a happy heart. Get your love-tank filled as you prepare for a week of inspiration, relaxation and motivation!"

A total of 1,120 registrants –the largest attendance in 20 years – were pleased to learn that both Jefferson and Madison had been renovated, increasing SUUSI's air conditioned bed space by 40 percent. More than a third of those participants (437 people) had registered for SUUSI by midnight on April 11, the first day of online registration. New Registrar Jennifer Sanders and her staff had entered a new era. Paper forms were no longer included in the ever-shrinking number of mailed, paper catalogs; instead, most people filled out forms online, while those who wanted or needed to print out paper forms could do so on their computers.

The lineup of speakers and worship leaders arranged by Denominational Coordinator Bill Neely explored the theme in various ways. Craig Schwalenberg reflected on the meaning – and mystery – of time itself, while Susan Rak urged attendees to "Seize the Day." Scott McNeill focused on "Every Tomorrow [As] a Vision of Hope." The two candidates for Moderator of the Unitarian Universalist Association, Tamara Payne-Alex and Jim Key, also spoke, on Monday and Thursday morning, respectively.

Jan Taddeo's Thursday night Transitions Service reminded young and old alike to "Savor This Day." Following the service, the pathway outside Porterfield was transformed into a "Remembrance Walk" honoring those who were struggling with, or had succumbed to, cancer or other serious illness or life obstacles. Paper bags had been provided at mealtimes during the week for participants to decorate in honor of a loved one, and then placed on the ground on Thursday evening to create a path of luminaries adorned with names and celebrations of friends and family members

The next morning, after he sang his traditional rendition of "Let It Be a Dance," Alexis Jones was surprised by long-time SUUSI-goer Marc Nevin, who came onto the stage and presented him with an autographed Ric Masten "Let It Be a Dance" sweatshirt. Nevin had gotten the shirt when Masten visited SUUSI in 1993 – the year Masten "gifted" his signature song to Jones for SUUSI.

Nature fans were thrilled that, after a two-year absence, there were once again caving trips. Tawney's Cave was the destination on Tuesday, Wednesday and Thursday afternoons. As explained in the 2012 catalog:

> Caving is back!! New information and research on White-Nose Syndrome (WNS) and documents from U.S. Fish and Wildlife Service and the National Speleological Society outline responsible caving procedures that can prevent human spread of the fungus [to bat populations]. Nature Staff is excited to be able to reintroduce this amazing trip.
>
> According to research, WNS is primarily transmitted bat-to-bat; human-to-bat transmission has not been proven. It has been thought that any human transmission is due to caving in multiple caves and carrying the fungus on gear, thus spreading it through various caves and states. For this reason, we are limiting our caving to a single site... Recommended decontamination procedures for caving will be strictly followed by all SUUSI participants wishing to enter the cave.

Other new trips included an "Introduction to Stand-Up Paddleboarding" for those who wanted to try something unique on the water, and for those who preferred their thumbs green rather than wet, a "Garden Tour" of five Blacksburg gardens, led by a Master Gardener. Fees received for that trip were donated by SUUSI to the Friends of the Blacksburg Library, which had arranged the tour. Also new in Nature in 2012 were a night geocaching excursion and the "Family Friendly Museum Mixup," a quick tour of three different museums in downtown Roanoke.

The year brought a particularly strong lineup to Concert Hour. Brother Sun, a trio featuring Pat Wictor, Joe Jencks and Greg Greenway, kicked off the week on Monday. Bob Sima followed on Tuesday, and SONiA wowed the crowd on Wednesday. The School of Rock rocked the house as usual on Thursday night, while Friday afternoon introduced a new tradition and another set of musicians into the SUUSI milieu; "Sweet Spot in the Afternoon" featured a jazz ensemble that had been created during the week, a la School of Rock, in a workshop format. That performance took place in the Muse Ballroom, since Teen Way Off Broadway was going through its final dress rehearsal at Porterfield.

TWOB 2012 was an interactive mystery – "Cluue," based on the popular board game and complete with colorful suspects like Colonel Mustard, Rev. Greene and Percival Plum. The audience was led in trying to solve the mystery of who stole the TWOB

The TWOB Cow (held by Haley Noll)

Cow by a slapstick sleuth, Inspector Klugh-Seaux (Patrick Sanders). Another twist was the use of two different endings, in which there was a different culprit in each performance. Miss Scarlett (Shayli Lesser, who sang a solo of Katy Perry's "Firework" in homage to the SUUSI fireworks show) proved to be the guilty party in the early show, and Bobbi White (Rebecca Klopp) stole the TWOB Cow in the second performance.

The actual fireworks display on Wednesday night was bigger and brighter than the previous year, although the location disappointed many participants. Unlike 2011, when participants got an intimate "private show" in the Moffett Quad, this time regulations required that the show take place at quite a distance from its intended audience – on the other side of the railroad tracks beyond the Dedmon Center. No one seemed to know exactly where the best vantage point would be, and participants self-divided into several smaller groups, lining up on the hillsides behind Preston and Porterfield, separated by parking lots, streets and street lights from each other, and from the fireworks.

As folks returned to campus following the pyrotechnics, they discovered that a huge movie screen had been set up behind Heth, where the Governor's School was watching *The Hunger Games*. Large speakers amplified the dialogue and soundtrack, which reverberated throughout campus, much to the dismay of the parents of small children. By contrast, SUUSI's Family Movie Night earlier the same evening had been the sedate *Nanny McPhee*, shown in Cook Hall.

The Youth Program, which for many years had been holding a Sunday night "Open House" for parents, opted in 2012 to follow the lead of the Teen Program and hold a mandatory youth-parent meeting to open the week. Parents and children were made aware of expectations, with a particular emphasis on safety, supervision and the prevention of bullying. During the week, SUUSI Youth enjoyed many new and challenging workshops, including slacklining, in which participants attempt to balance on a flat, tightrope-like line suspended a couple of feet off the ground. Mina

Greenfield introduced slacklining to all ages at SUUSI in 2012. The transitioning 13-year-olds had a new after-dark program that featured worship and leadership training, as well as the return of the popular "13's Triple Slog."

For teens, there was a Tuesday night Teen Coffeehouse and Poetry Slam, and the now-traditional midweek "Drag Races." Each night at 1 a.m. in Madison, the Young Adults and Medians put on a "Gen-X Concert and Variety Hour," which was advertised as a "hilarious hour of sketches, songs, stories, poems and more to keep you giggling well into the night."

Common Ground provided standup comedy as well as karaoke throughout the week. Community Time took advantage of beautiful afternoon weather to keep the water fun going ("Neptune would be proud of what we are doing," the NUUS opined). The aquatic highlight of the week may have been the full-size, rented dunking booth set up behind Heth – the first time there had been a dunking booth at SUUSI in decades. Adults lined up for a chance to dunk various SUUSI celebrities in the large pool of water, while children of all ages delighted in both dunking and being dunked. There were also water balloon fights, "soggy relay races" and the ever popular slip-n-slide.

Workshops appealed to the inner child as perhaps never before, with a wide variety of adult arts and crafts offerings. Game workshops ranged from bridge to Mahjong, while dance workshops ran the gamut from Zumba to hoop dancing to ecstatic dance to both belly and ballroom dance. In addition to the usual array of beer-tasting workshops, there were "Wines of South America" and tequila tasting and even a "Hot Sauce Tasting."

A raffle benefitted SUUSIships, this time with three prizes – one afghan bearing the previous year's "Joy!" logo and another adorned with the 2012 theme "Look to This Day," as well as a basket of CDs by SUUSI musicians.

Social media played an increasingly prominent role in participants' SUUSI experience during the week. Facebook status updates were seemingly ubiquitous. Friends kept up in real time with activities both on and off campus in a variety of ways, including a new feature on the SUUSI website, where live postings were available.

Others chose to express themselves in more time-honored ways. The NUUS' daily haikus were particularly memorable in 2012. Here is a taste of what participants were able to say in just a few well-chosen words:

We've waited all year
SUUSI in all its glory
Is finally here
(Mary Henderson)

The Ingathering.
Storms make us wet.
We march anyway.
(Jim Blowers)

Boss phones. Not now.
No! My SUUSI vacation!
Learning, music, friends.
(Patricia Huff)

S-U-U-S-I
All day fun for you and me
Let's go tubing – NOW!
(Rosie Calnek, age 8)

Here I find comfort:
Love, joy, learning all day long. SUUSI feeds my soul.
(Emily Mellgren)

And then there was this one, which appeared on the home page of the SUUSI website:

Community time
Ocean of tie-dyed children
Youth forever friends
(Gladys D. Smith-Mangan)

Perhaps the most fascinating expression of the SUUSI experience in 2012, however, evolved all week, right before participants' eyes, in the grassy area behind Madison. As hundreds of SUUSI-goers passed by each day, a new, brightly painted plywood panel appeared, slowly telling the story in sequence painting of a pirate, a cat, an octopus and a robot who found a special place that had a strange, seafaring similarity to SUUSI. Jason Thomas, an artist from Atlanta who was attending SUUSI for only the second time,

captured the essence of the now 63-year-old Summer Institute, while capturing the hearts and imaginations of every SUUSI participant in 2012:

The sea is vast, and has many wonders, but is not always kind. The sea can bring great sadness, and make you feel alone. Sometimes, the sea takes more from you than it gives back.

But there is a place...

Once a year, there is a place where the sea is calm.
One by one, so many lives come together there.
The familiar faces and voices bring the feelings back.

It is a time of peace, compassion, and incredible closeness.
A wonderful time of jokes, stories and strength.
Reuniting with old friends, and making new ones.
There is nothing like it.
These are days of grace.

But nothing lasts forever, and too soon it is gone.
The love, laughter, holding, trust and joy have made them stronger.
They will try to take it with them as best they can.
But their sea family would be missed beyond words.

Looking Back –
And Beyond Tomorrow

When Alfred Hobart and Richard Henry invited a few dozen Unitarians to a leadership retreat in the summer of 1950, they could not in their wildest dreams have imagined what would be the result. As I look back at that pioneering meeting, held at a small hotel in a remote corner of eastern North Carolina, I am amazed at the challenges our forebears faced. They communicated by mail and telegraph and telephone. In order to be together, they traveled long distances over two-lane back roads in a time well before the interstate highway system. Each was, in his or her own way and in very widespread locales, trying to plant the seeds of liberal religion in very conservative Southern soil. Many were engaged in the difficult work of starting brand new congregations – some of which survived and some of which did not – in places that were less than welcoming of their efforts.

Decades later, more than a thousand of us come together each summer, meeting on modern college campuses in air conditioned rooms and playing in the waters and woods of the southwest Virginia mountains. We remain connected throughout the year by Facebook and Twitter, email and Skype. Though some of us still feel religiously isolated back home, the entire world is at our fingertips on the internet – and we feel as well that all of life is in the palm of our hands when we are together for that one magical week in July.

Memories, says Roger Comstock, are sketchy. This book has been a combination of memories and research, anecdotes and analysis. It is only as historically accurate as those fickle human qualities can be. I know that for myself, when I think back on my first SUUSIs in the 1980s, I remember certain things like hayrides and hanging out in the Quad, whitewater rafting and falling asleep under the stars, far better than I remember specifics. I remember hugs and tears and people – oh so many beautiful, vibrant, fully alive and deeply loving people. Some of these memories, like the ones from my very first hours at SUUSI in 1982, are crystal clear, but most are somewhat hazy, like recalling a dream. What lingers most powerfully – what I remember and hold onto and treasure – is the *feeling*. In this, I suspect, I am not alone.

And when I envision SUUSIs of the future, SUUSIs beyond tomorrow, I think back to Hobart and Henry and realize that the community created by our successors, whatever form it will take a couple of generations hence, will surely be something beyond my imagining. Those who inherit SUUSI from us will live in a world I cannot hope to know. My prayer for them is that they, too, will know and treasure the special feeling that has always been at the heart of this beloved community.

In the meantime, I can only agree with Karen Gonzalez, who said in a sermon about SUUSI at her church in Florida, "As I watch the new babies arrive each summer, I can't help but look forward to my grandchildren running barefoot through the soft green grass of a SUUSI summer evening with their tie-dye T-shirts, sparkly fairy crowns, and messy, hand-painted tattoos. SUUSI will forever give our family a place to reunite each year, regardless of where life takes us between Julys."

May it be so.

Remember the Feeling!

Chapter 6:
Photographs and
Memories

379

Morris Hudgins:

"One of the most spiritual experiences of my life occurred at SUUSI – walking in the early morning, toward Muse. It was so foggy I could hardly see 10 feet in front of me, but I could make out a faint sound in the distance. As I got closer, I began to recognize the sound – bagpipes! – and the tune: "Amazing Grace."
Just thinking about it still brings tears to my eyes."

Karen Gonzalez:

"It was not our intention when we first brought our 2- and 4-year-old daughters to SUUSI, to find them husbands. But both Sarah and Emily met their soul mates at SUUSI, and we are now blessed with two sons who were also brought up in our faith."

Nancy Kellman:

"A couple of years ago, my son [David Grimm], who had grown up going each summer to Blue Ridge, said to me out of thin air, "Mom, I want to thank you for that Blue Ridge experience. It meant more to me than just about anything I can remember from my childhood." How rewarding it was, to hear those words from your child!"

Marc Nevin:

"If someone asks where I'm from, I will say Roanoke. But that's wrong. I'm from SUUSI, and I just park my stuff 40 miles up the road all year, waiting for SUUSI to come back home."

Jim Deaton:

"I was returning to my Radford dorm late Wednesday afternoon of my first SUUSI, in 1981, when I had this thought: "I can see myself coming here the rest of my life." Those were the exact words that occurred to me near the Wisdom Tree and – lo and behold – I've now been a part of 32 consecutive SUUSIs.

While our special community still inspires, educates and delights me, one compelling purpose keeps drawing me back – the chance to again enjoy and affirm those meaningful friendships that have blessed and enriched my years. I cannot think of SUUSI without moist eyes."

Melanie Walsh:

"I am 14 years old and have been going to SUUSI for 6 years… The memories, connections and friends I've made at SUUSI mean so much to me. The atmosphere of love, understanding and community is like nowhere else I've been. After getting to know people at SUUSI, I feel like I've known them for years. SUUSI is a place where I can sing, dance, laugh, hug, cry – and always be myself!"

Judy Newell:

"There was such a tremendous esprit de corps on the staff. SUUSI has a soul, and we were dedicated to that soul. I've only known two groups in my life that I would say that about: that the group had a soul. It doesn't matter that the people change over time. They naturally will. But the spirit of the group does not change. It is so much larger than the individuals."

Janette Muir:

"The year my son was 11, he cried for hours in the car on the way home from SUUSI, and kept sobbing all that night. The next morning, he got up, very serious, and announced, "I think I know what love is like.""

"Uncle Flip" Lower:

"One of the biggest things that happened to me at SUUSI was on the first full day of my first SUUSI (1997). It was something that quite literally changed my life.

First thing Monday morning, a vanload of us set out on the Nature Photography trip led by Bob Lynch. Somewhere along the trip, Bob (71 at the time, if my memory serves properly) mentioned that he had just returned from his seventh continent, where he had broken his toe climbing Kilimanjaro. In that moment, I decided that if he could set foot on all seven continents in his 71 years, I would do it by the time I turned 35. The quest to reach my goal took me on some amazing adventures…

In 2005, I think I nearly brought Bob to tears of joy when I told him the influence he'd had on me in giving me that goal and then told him I had reached the goal that January."

Joe Jencks:

"I had no idea how deep the waters of Unitarian Universalism were until I came to SUUSI."

Manish Mishra:

"I was talking to my partner on the phone [while I was attending my first SUUSI in 2009], explaining how much fun I was having. I said, "I've gone rock climbing and rappelling; at one point I was even dangling upside down over the side of a cliff." I came back from that trip with a broken finger. I told him the finger was broken in two places, swollen and painful. I then said, "This place is great! You've got to come next year.""

Jean McCarty:

"In the summer of 2012, there was a chance we might not be going to SUUSI. My granddaughter Alayna was absolutely insistent. She told me, "We're never going to miss SUUSI, ever again! And I'm bringing my children and grandchildren every year forever.""

Carol Hull:

"I have been to SUUSIs as far back as Brevard, but one of my most powerful memories was the year of the shootings at Virginia Tech. The silent walk across that Drill Field was an unforgettable moment. That's the thing about SUUSI – it gives you times to dance, times to have goosebumps, and times for family. Now my child and grandchildren are here. The circle is complete."

Blair Benson:

"I remember the year my grandfather [long-time SUUSI attendee Dean Shelton] had died. I came to SUUSI that year specifically to honor him. That was part of what I needed to do to say goodbye to him. There were so many people who came up to me, whom I didn't even know, and told me how much he had meant to them. The Greensboro group all wore deely-boppers that year [Shelton was known for wearing colorful, deely-bopper-adorned hats].

Alexis [Jones] took me aside and shared with me how special it had been to him that Dean had loved his song "Let It Be a Dance." I still can't hear that song without crying."

Millicent Simmons:

"We brought our daughter to SUUSI one year. She was a very sassy, stubborn teenager, and to say she did not want to go to SUUSI would be an understatement. We took her very much against her will – but we brought her home against her will, too! We had hardly seen her all week, since she was in the Teen Dorm, but then when it came time to leave on Saturday morning, we found her on the roof of the dorm with the kids, where they had slept out under the stars. She absolutely did not want to leave her new friends. The first words out of her mouth were, "Can we come back next year?""

Ann Blowers:

One of the most special moments of SUUSI for me, each year, is that moment in Ingathering when they ask how long you have been coming to SUUSI. I love knowing there are so many people who love this place so much that they keep coming back for 20, 30 years and more. It's truly inspiring."

Mike Plummer:

"My son Bob wrote about SUUSI for his college entrance essay. Need I say more?"

Melissa Matthews:

"I still have little handprints that my kids made at SUUSI, and pieces of string that they cut that are as long as they were tall that particular year. They are cherished keepsakes. I have been so blessed to have this community as part of my life."

Dick Weston-Jones:

"It is very meaningful to me that I was both one of the [teen] LRY'ers at Summer Institute, and then later served as an LRY advisor at Summer Institute. I only did that [work with the teenagers] for one year, but it was that experience which led me to believe this was something I could commit my life to. I can say without hesitation that Summer Institute was the stimulus for my decision to enter the Unitarian ministry."

Priscilla Phillips:

"The thing that amazes me most about SUUSI – it did the very first year I came, and it still does – is that all this can happen with just volunteers. No one gets paid to do this. There must be something very special about this place, to make so many people so committed to it."

Sonya Prestridge:

"The thing that I loved the most about SUUSI was the feeling of family. I don't think, in all my years, I've ever felt as close to a group of people as that staff who worked and played together with me that year [1982, when she was Director]."

Randy Walther:

"Our son Jake tried to get us to come to SUUSI for years. We never followed through until he moved out... [Then, when] we finally started going, he was working for Ringling Bros. / Barnum & Bailey Circus, so he couldn't join us.

Within two years, he had a motorcycle wreck and his injury left him [in a wheelchair]. We missed SUUSI '05, but brought him with us in '06. The acceptance by his peer group and all of SUUSI was such an affirming action. He has since produced two fireworks shows for SUUSI; he says this is his way of giving back for all that he has received here.

We will always do our best to remain a part of this community."

Terry Sweetser:

"SUUSI represents a unique community that for many people is their only long-term, ongoing connection to Unitarian Universalism. There is a primal sense of connection that carries on though the years, through all the changes of our lives. It is a very powerful thing. SUUSI has this incredible, almost tribal feeling to it. It's one of the great gems of our movement."

Marti Toms:

"The way SUUSI spans the generations is one of its great strengths. I brought my children here as tiny children, and they grew up here. Now one of them is the Youth Director, and brings her baby to SUUSI, while another is the Registrar and brings her teenager here. That connection across the generations is what is most meaningful to me."

Kay Montgomery:

"Much more than going to church, SUUSI is how my kids really became Unitarian Universalists."

Wendell Putney:

"I learned to kayak, canoe, and cave at SUUSI. I remember a two-day whitewater canoeing course with Neal Sanders – going over McCoy Falls first forward, then backward. We learned lots of maneuvers. Rappelling at Castle Rock was a great experience. We were 150 feet up, over the Norfolk & Western railroad. You can do anything at SUUSI. I also sang in Way Off Broadway – "Tonight," from "West Side Story."

A peak experience, though, was helping a man who was in trouble on a kayak trip. It was solo kayaking. We got out on the river one morning, very early, and all of a sudden one guy veered off to the side of the river, and was unable to continue. We tied his kayak to mine, and I towed him the rest of the way home. When we got back, they gave me a Nature shirt (and I wasn't even on staff!). It is still one of my most prized possessions."

Louisa Wimberger:

"So SUUSI – It's this thing where people go and live all together on a campus and eat meals, including ice cream and still-warm cookies. And they worship and bang on drums and play music. And talk a lot and dance and yell things from down the sidewalk. And tie-dye and nap and hardly sleep and take classes and workshops and go on nature trips and taste wines and beers and whiskeys and pray and meditate and play a lot of music at all hours and do yoga and dance and dance and dance and eat and laugh and smile and restore and renew and look ahead and reflect and dance, and also there are really good cookies and tater tots, and people connect and hug a lot. Like, a lot!"

Trudy Atkin:

"I will never forget that fateful August day when I passed Lynn Wheal, each of us pushing our daughters in strollers. I was new to the neighborhood, but we soon became good and fast friends, as would our children. After a year of Lynn insisting I attend this "family camp," I relented and found myself in the middle of what I had looked for my whole life.

...SUUSI is a feeling in your soul. The compassion and love that emanated from those great people I came to call friends and staff will never leave my heart. Those years together linked us in ways that cannot be undone. Years and decades have passed – without contact, in some cases – but when thinking about those days, there is a familiar warmth that surrounds me. I can't help but smile. What a gift we have given to each other: The gift of loving memories."

Appendix

Year	Theme	Dates	Attendance	Location
2012	Look to This Day	July 15-21	1120	Radford
2011	Joy!	July 17-23	1107	Radford
2010	Beyond Tomorrow	July 18-24	1046	Radford
2009	Rekindle the Flame Within	July 19-25	1035	Radford
2008	Pilgrimage	July 20-26	1064	Radford
2007	To Live Fully	July 15-21	970	Virginia Tech
2006	Rejoice & Renew	July 16-22	924	Virginia Tech
2005	Time to Fly	July 17-23	973	Virginia Tech
2004	Reunions	July 18-24	937	Virginia Tech
2003	Simple Gifts	July 20-26	987	Virginia Tech
2002	Blessings	July 21-27	886	Virginia Tech
2001	The Interdependent Web	July 22-28	1038	Virginia Tech
2000	Neighbors: Ancient Civilizations	July 23-29	977	Virginia Tech
1999	Reach Out	July 25-31	839	Radford
1998	Circles	July 26-Aug 1	930	Radford
1997	Celebrate Diversity	July 27-Aug 2	897	Radford
1996	Imagine	July 14-20	950	Radford
1995	Creating Community	July 23-29	991	Virginia Tech
1994	World Healing	July 24-30	1050	Virginia Tech
1993	Maintain the Vision	July 25-31	1095	Virginia Tech
1992	Renew the Spirit	July 26-Aug 1	1255	Virginia Tech
1991	We Believe	July 21-27	1360	Virginia Tech
1990	Roots & Wings	July 22-28	1425	Virginia Tech
1989	Share Your Light	July 23-29	1425	Radford
1988	Live Your Dream	July 24-30	1318	Radford
1987	Horizons	July 26-Aug 1	1230	Radford
1986	Community	July 27-Aug 2	1208	Radford
1985	Directions	July 21-27	1017	Radford
1984	Connections	July 22-28	1188	Radford
1983	Celebrate	July 24-30	1121	Radford
1982	Humanness: Rights, Dignity, Fullfillment	July 25-31	1019	Radford
1981	Who Am I ... And Why?	July 26-Aug 1	1020	Radford
1980	Belonging, Breaking Away and Returning	July 27-Aug 2	1071	Radford
1979	CHANGing	July 22-28	951	Radford
1978	Today's Tomorrows	July 23-29	850	Radford

Year	Theme	Dates	Count	Location
1977	Family	July 24-30	763	Radford
1976	The Price of Liberty	July 25-31	695	Radford
1975		July 20-26	640	Radford
1974	Other Rushes and Other Highs	July 21-27		Fontana Village
1973		Aug. 12-18		Appalachian State
1972		Aug. 13-19	375	Appalachian State
1971		Aug. 23-28		Appalachian State
1970				
1969	Tetrology of the Disaffected	June 15-21		Univ. of the South
1968	(there were two themes this year)	June 23-29		Brevard
1967	The Individual on Trial	June 25-July 2	266	Brevard
1966	Morality for a Secular Culture	July 3-10	486	Blue Ridge
1965	The Contemporary Revolution	July 4-11	541	Blue Ridge
1964	Science and Human Purpose	July 5-12	450	Blue Ridge
1963	The Forward Edge of Concern	July 7-14	698	Blue Ridge
1962	Bridges of Understanding	July 8-15	628	Blue Ridge
1961	Religion in the Modern World	July 10-16	542	Blue Ridge
1960	A Look at Ourselves	July 4-10	468	Blue Ridge
1959	The Anatomy of Prejudice	July 6-12	584	Blue Ridge
1958		July 7-13	418	Blue Ridge
1957	Person to Person: Workshop for Life	July 8-14		Blue Ridge
1956	Toward Creative Religion	July 13-17	337	Blue Ridge
1955	Religion in Action	Aug. 23-28	282	Blue Ridge
1954		Aug 24-29	144	Blue Ridge
1953	Morality in an Age of Science	Aug 25-30	139	Blue Ridge
1952	The Family and Democracy	Aug 27-Sep 1	136	Blue Ridge
1951		Aug 23-27	110	Blue Ridge
1950		Aug 30-Sep 4	47	Lake Waccamaw

Directors ("Chairmen" prior to 1976)

2011-2012 – Wendell Putney
2009-2010 – Jerry King
2007-2008 – Devin Gordon
2005-2006 – Jen Lucas
2003-2004 – Karyn Machler
2002 – Nancy Massel
2000-2001 – Dee Medley
1997-1999 – Nancy Massel
1996 – Sharon Mayes
1994-1995 – Maureen McAndrews
1992-1993 – Dawn Kenny
1990-1991 – Reid Swanson
1988-1989 – Louis Bregger
1986-1987 – Phil Sterner
1984-1985 – Karen Chandler
1983 – Florence Cohan
1982 – Sonya Prestridge
1980-1981 – Jake Haun
1979 – Kay Montgomery
1977-1978 – Larry and Mo Wheeler
1976 – Sue Leonard
1975 – Brad Brown
1974 – William and Jean Benedict
1973 – David and Margaret Link
1972 – Alan Downing
1971 – Mildred and Dave Rosenbaum
1970
1969 – Mrs. Lee B. Spaulding
1968 – Manuel Holland
1967 – Luke and Ellen Dohner
1966 – John and Reina Cleland
1965 – Gordon and Nancy Grimm
1964 – Mr. and Mrs. Walter Carter

1963 – Robert Conklin
1962 – Robert and Pat Sonen
1961 – Dale Blosser and Henry Teeter
1960 – Henry McKown
1959 – Dr. and Mrs. Francis Binkley
1958 – Mary C. Lane
1957 – John C. Fuller
1956 – Owen D. Lewis
1955 – Thomas L. Carroll
1954 – Ray Rutledge
1953 – Richard Henry
1952 – Malcolm Sutherland
1951 – Alfred Hobart
1950 – Ray Shute

Teen Way Off Broadway

1987 – Hair
1988 – Tommy
1989 – Alice in SUUSI Land
1990 – The Wizard of Blacksburg
1991 – Hair 1991
1992 – The SUUSI Brothers
1993 – Let There Be SUUSI
1994 –The Miracle of Summer
1995 – Jesus Christ SUUSIstar
1996 – Searching for SUUSI
1997 – How the Grinch Stole SUUSI
1998 – The UU Files
1999 – Return of the UUs
2000 – The SUUSI Bunch
2001 – Scooby-DUU
2002 – A Mid-SUUSI Night's Dream
2003 – Forrest Guump
2004 – Batman UUnmasked
2005 – The Hitchhiker's Guide to SUUSI
2006 – Totally Wicked!
2007 – Harriet Potter and the Flaming Chalice
2008 – Once Upon a SUUSI
2009 – Andy
2010 – SUUSI the 13th
2011 – SUUSI Street
2012 – Cluue

Way Off Broadway

1979 – Oliver, a medley
1980 – Godspell
1981 – Hair
1982 – Fiddler on the Roof
1983 – Oklahoma
1984 – Big Brother's Watching UU
1985 – The Music Man
1986 – West Side Story
1987 – South Pacific
1988 – Oliver
1989 – Way Off Broadway Revisited
1991 – Oklahoma

Concert Hour Performers

(Monday night returning favorites in parentheses)

1991 – Last Rights / Carole and Bren / Will Tuttle / SUUSI Chamber Music Ensemble

1992 – Jim Scott / Will Tuttle / SUUSI Chamber Music Ensemble / (Bill and Lorraine Harouff)

1993 – Carole Eagleheart / Bill and Lorraine Harouff / Aztec Two Step / (Chuck Larkin)

1994 – Fred Small / Rayne / Joyce Poley / (Relative Viewpoint)

1995 – Tom Prasada Rao / Barb Martin & Rare Bird / Velma Frye

1996 – Steve Gillette & Cindy Mangsen / Elaine Silver / New Hope Harmony

1997 – The Nudes / Lui Collins / David LaMotte

1998 – David Roth / Arianne Lydon / (Pete Leary)

1999 – Amy Carol Webb / Dana Robinson / (Sharon Robles)

2000 – Dave Nachmanoff / Peggy Bertsch / (Bill & Lorraine Harouff)

2001 – Kim & Reggie Harris / Carla Ulbrich / (Bonnie Whitehurst)

2002 – Kat Eggleston / Peter Mayer / (New Last Rights)

2003 – Greg Greenway / Amy Carol Webb / Meg Barnhouse / (Mindy Simmons)

2004 –Stephanie Corby / Johnsmith / (Meg Barnhouse)

2005 – Emma's Revolution / Wishing Chair / (Alexis Jones)

2006 – Rod MacDonald / Joe Jencks / (Amy Carol Webb)

2007 – Beaucoup Blue / Kym Tuvim / (no Monday concert)

2008 – Tret Fure / Alastair Mook / (Greg Greenway)

2009 – Ellen Bukstel / Pat Wictor / (Wishing Chair)

2010 – Reggie Harris / The New SUUSI Revue / The Music of Phil Ochs, emceed by Sonny Ochs

2011 - Don White / David Roth / (Gary Gonzalez)

2012 – Bob Sima / SONiA / (Brother Sun)

<u>Contributors</u>

The following persons graciously granted interviews, provided written records, photographs and archival material, attended "SUUSI Memories" workshops or otherwise shared their SUUSI stories and histories during the production of this book. Together, their memories have made it possible for future generations to "remember the feeling."

Daria Akers
Steve Anderson
Annsley Atkin
Trudy Atkin (Moneyhan)
Audrey Barcelo
Charley Barcelo
Kip Barkley
Margaret Baucus
Sharon Beecher
Jimmie Benedict
William Benedict
Lindsay Bennett-Jacobs
Blair Benson
Allen Bergal
Ann Blowers
Jim Blowers
Judy Bonner
Carl Bretz
Herb Bryant
John Buehrens
John Burciaga
John Burns
Karen Chandler
Mary Clark
Phoenix Cockerham
Sarah Cole

Roger Comstock
Bonnie Crouse
Andy Crum
Amy Davis
Jim Deaton
Phelps Dillon
Bonnie Dixon
Gertrude Edge
Ron Edge
Sue Folk
Gordon Gibson
Jeff Glover
Karen Gonzalez
Sarah Gonzalez
John Goodhart
Devin Gordon
Robby Greenberg
Steve Greenberg
Mina Greenfield
Nancy Grimm (Kellman)
Ames Guyton
Lorien Haavik
Marge Hallmark
Rick Hallmark
Chuck Harty
Nancy Heath

Poncho Heavener

Richard Henry

Vonnie Hicks

Barbara Hobart (Mathews)

James Hobart

Manuel Holland

Olive Holland

Leon Hopper

Morris Hudgins

Carol Hull

Bob Irwin

Glenn Johnson

Alexis (John) Jones

Peggy Joseph

Sheila Kaminsky

Tom Kersen

Jerry King

Lee Knight

Jim Landis

Paul Langrock

Pete Leary

Patric Leedom

Marge Link

Nilsa Lobdell

David Long

Elle Long

Thomas "Uncle Flip" Lower

Jen Lucas

Jan Machler

Karyn Machler

Ted Machler

Dianna MacPherson

Sue Male

Oreon Mann

Nancy Massel (Farese)

Melissa Matthews

David Maynard

Susan McAlpin

Nancy McDermott

Mary Nell McLauchlin

Boomslang Meade

Dee Medley

Jill Menadier

Manish Mishra

Kay Montgomery

Samuel Moore

Mark Nevin

J.P. Newell

Judy Newell

Phil Nungesser

Stephan Papa

Karla Peterson

Priscilla Phillips

Eugene Pickett

Walt Pirie

Mike Plummer

Sonya Prestridge

Wendell Putney

Eleanor Sableski

Jennifer Sanders

Patrick Sanders

Dante Santacroce

Heather Schulz

Dick Scobie

Bonnie Sheppard

Millicent Simmons

Marcia Slosser

Myles Smith

Quentin Smith

Mary Ann Somervill

Linda Sterner
Phil Sterner
Terry Sweetser
Carol Taylor
Dana Taylor
Jason Thomas
Elizabeth Thompson
Doug Throp
Pete Tolleson
Marti Toms
Noralee Traylor
Dane Victorine

George Vockroth
Robbie Walsh
Randy Walther
Frony Ward
Andy Wasilewski
Amy Carol Webb
Dick Weston-Jones
Lynn Wheal (Halsey)
Larry Wheeler
Ortrude White
Louisa Wimberger
Jackie Winner

Photo Credits

p. 225: Photo by and courtesy Doug Throp.

p. 229: Courtesy Trudy Moneyhan (Atkin).

p. 230: Photo by and courtesy Doug Throp.

p. 244: Courtesy Alexis Jones.

p. 249: Photo by and courtesy Alex Winner.

p. 250: Photo by and courtesy Doug Throp.

p. 261: Courtesy Jen Lucas.

p. 270: Relative Viewpoint photo courtesy Jen Lucas. Nature tent photo courtesy Jen Lucas.

p. 277: Courtesy Jen Lucas.

p. 282: Courtesy Jen Lucas.

p. 287: Courtesy Jim Blowers.

p. 293: Photo by and courtesy Doug Throp.

p. 294: Photo by and courtesy Devin Gordon.

p. 305: Photo by and courtesy Doug Throp.

p. 306: Photo by and courtesy Devin Gordon.

p. 314: Photo by and courtesy Doug Throp.

p. 319: Courtesy Jim Blowers.

p. 325: Photo by and courtesy Devin Gordon.

p. 326: Photo by and courtesy Devin Gordon.

p. 332: Photo by and courtesy Thomas "Uncle Flip" Lower.

p. 334: Photo by and courtesy Rick Hallmark.

p. 337: Photo by and courtesy Devin Gordon.

p. 342: Photo by and courtesy Devin Gordon.

p. 349: Photo by and courtesy Devin Gordon.

p. 350: Photo by and courtesy Devin Gordon.

p. 353: Photo by and courtesy Thomas "Uncle Flip" Lower.

p. 356: Photo by and courtesy Thomas "Uncle Flip" Lower.

p. 357: Photo by and courtesy Jennifer Sanders.

p. 362: Courtesy Jim Blowers.

p. 366: Photo by and courtesy Thomas "Uncle Flip" Lower.

p. 370: Artwork by Jason Thomas. © 2012 Red Rocket Farm, used by permission. Courtesy Jason Thomas.

p. 375: Three girls photo courtesy Sue Male. My first SUUSI photo of Brayden Gordon by and courtesy Devin Gordon. Wendell and Bing Putney photo by and courtesy Doug Throp.

p. 376: Jen and Becker Lucas photo by and courtesy Devin Gordon. Four girls photo source unknown. Drumming photo courtesy Jen Lucas.

p. 377: Three friends photo by and courtesy Doug Throp. Belly dance photo courtesy Trudy Moneyhan (Atkin). Two friends photo by and courtesy Devin Gordon.

p. 378: Deely-bopper photo courtesy Jen Lucas. Debbie and Paul Langrock

photo courtesy Jen Lucas. Clown photo by and courtesy Doug Throp. Lady with hat photo by and courtesy Doug Throp.
p. 379: Gupton-Sanders family at Cascades photo courtesy Jennifer Sanders. Three Sanders girls photo courtesy Jennifer Sanders. SUUSI hug photo courtesy Peggy Joseph.
p. 380: Matthews sisters photo courtesy Melissa Matthews. Elsa Lafferty and Bob Sax photo courtesy Phil Sterner. Dear friends photo courtesy Jen Lucas.
p. 381: Photo of car source unknown. Guitar goddesses photo courtesy Louisa Wimberger. Painted face photo by and courtesy Doug Throp.
p. 382: Banner parade photo source unknown. Girls dancing in the grass photo courtesy Trudy Moneyhan (Atkin).

Index

J

K

L

M

T

V

W